PERGAMON INTERNATIONAL LIBRARY
of Science, Technology, Engineering and Social Studies
The 1000-volume original paperback library in aid of education, industrial training and the enjoyment of leisure
Publisher: Robert Maxwell, M.C.

Machina Ex Dea

THE ATHENE SERIES
An International Collection of Feminist Books
General Editors: Gloria Bowles and Renate Duelli-Klein
Consulting Editor: Dale Spender

The ATHENE SERIES assumes that all those who are concerned with formulating explanations of the way the world works need to know and appreciate the significance of basic feminist principles.

The growth of feminist research has challenged almost all aspects of social organization in our culture. The ATHENE SERIES focuses on the construction of knowledge and the exclusion of women from the process—both as theorists and subjects of study—and offers innovative studies that challenge established theories and research.

Volumes in the Series

MEN'S STUDIES MODIFIED
The Impact of Feminism on the Academic Disciplines
edited by Dale Spender

WOMAN'S NATURE
Rationalizations of Inequality
edited by Marian Lowe and Ruth Hubbard

NOTICE TO READERS

May we suggest that your library places a standing/continuation order to receive all future volumes in the Athene Series immediately on publication? Your order can be cancelled at any time.

Also of interest

WOMEN, POWER AND POLICY
edited by Ellen Boneparth

WOMEN'S STUDIES INTERNATIONAL FORUM*
A Multidisciplinary Journal for the Rapid Publication of Research Communications & Review Articles in Women's Studies
Editor: Dale Spender

Special Issues of Women's Studies International Forum available in hardcover:

WOMEN AND MEN'S WARS/Judith Stiehm

WOMEN AND ISLAM/Azizah al-Hibri

THE WOMEN'S LIBERATION MOVEMENT—EUROPE AND NORTH AMERICA/J. Bradshaw

**Free sample copy available on request*

Machina Ex Dea

Feminist Perspectives on Technology

Joan Rothschild
University of Lowell

Pergamon Press

New York • Oxford • Toronto • Sydney • Paris • Frankfurt

Pergamon Press Offices:

U.S.A.	Pergamon Press Inc., Maxwell House, Fairview Park, Elmsford, New York 10523, U.S.A.
U.K.	Pergamon Press Ltd., Headington Hill Hall, Oxford OX3 0BW, England
CANADA	Pergamon Press Canada Ltd., Suite 104, 150 Consumers Road, Willowdale, Ontario M2J 1P9, Canada
AUSTRALIA	Pergamon Press (Aust.) Pty. Ltd., P.O. Box 544, Potts Point, NSW 2011, Australia
FRANCE	Pergamon Press SARL, 24 rue des Ecoles, 75240 Paris, Cedex 05, France
FEDERAL REPUBLIC OF GERMANY	Pergamon Press GmbH, Hammerweg 6, D-6242 Kronberg-Taunus, Federal Republic of Germany

Library of Congress Cataloging in Publication Data
Main entry under title:

Machina ex dea.

(Athene series)
Bibliography: p.
Includes index.
1. Technology--Social Aspects. 2. Feminism
I. Rothschild, Joan. II. Series.
T14.5.M3 1983 303.4'83 83-8353
ISBN 0-08-029404-9
ISBN 0-08-029403-0 (soft)

Printed in the United States of America

Contents

Foreword

Technology is part of our culture; and, of course, our culture, which is male dominated, has developed technologies that reinforce male supremacy. Can this be changed by women becoming more involved with technology—not only as its users, but as its inventors, makers, and repairers? Only to the extent that women become genuinely equal partners in the economy and body politic. Only to the extent that we gain control of the design and fruits of our labor. But that is a revolutionary agenda, for today very few people—women *or* men—control our tools and our work. Yet, even within the limited control that most people have, there is no denying that women tend to be users of machines and men their inventors, makers, and repairers.

This collection explores the historical, social, and psychological reasons for this anomaly. There is nothing intrinsically "unfeminine" about machines, as those of us who like to tinker with them will readily testify. To those of us who feel comfortable with machines—whether we be girls or boys, women or men—machines are interesting, fun. Why do they frighten some people?

As a scholar, asked to write a foreword to a scholarly book about women and technology, I want to take the liberty to be unscholarly, introspective, autobiographical, and to explore the roots of my own feelings of comradeliness toward machines—or at least toward the machines that I regard as my friends and helpers and that don't threaten and dominate me. I do this not merely out of middle-aged self-indulgence. I think that we must individually and as social groups sort out our relationships to technologies so that we can insist on having them as tools when they can improve our lives, and reject them unequivocally in areas where they come to dominate or threaten us.

At a recent conference in Vancouver, sponsored by the Society for Canadian Women in Science and Technology, Margaret Benston, Professor of Computer Science and Coordinator of Women's Studies at Simon Fraser University, mused that though as a girl and adult she had never been afraid of mathematics, she had always felt uneasy about machines. This led me to ask myself why I wasn't uneasy about them—not as a class of objects, just about individual kinds that I thought were inappropriate or dangerous. I have come to believe that the reason is that I was raised in a Central European, Jewish, professional household. My parents were Jewish intellectuals. When a light bulb burned out, one called the electrician; when a faucet leaked, the plumber; when there was dust on the window sill, the maid; when one was hungry, the cook. And this was not because my parents were wealthy. They were first-generation university graduates of humble, east-European descent. Initially they scraped by, later they were comfortable, but never rich. But they lived their lives within a strict division between mental and manual labor. They did their own mental work and paid others to do the manual work.

So, for me as I grew up, machines were not something I associated with my father or brother, with men. Machines were class-different. After I came to the United States and that particular class difference disappeared, I initially failed to notice that my sex was supposed to disqualify me from feeling comfortable with machines (or with mathematics and science, for that matter). And in fact, so did my mother. It was she who bought the first set of tools and started repairing the simpler household equipment, and I followed suit.

An individual story, yes, but one with a moral. Different social formations have integrated technology differently. Machines as male territory—irrespective of class—are not universal. Social attitudes toward manual labor matter. So do attitudes toward who may get dirty. Another scientist at the Vancouver conference remarked that she had steered clear of machines because of an inbred horror of getting her hands dirty and covered with grease. She spoke of a college friend whose hands and nails were unwashably "dirty" because he earned his pocket-money repairing bicycles—something clearly not for her. (Not for me, either, as a way to earn money, but I did learn how to repair my bike.) Yes, feminine clothing and decorum are not conducive to friendliness toward machines. Nor is being afraid of breaking or damaging machines or tools. If a malfunctioning machine inspires fear—Clumsy! Now you've wrecked it!—we'll never learn to fix it! And we are unlikely to be comfortable with machines we are afraid to tinker with and try to fix, because machines do break down—and unlike people, they don't heal.

I realize that I am mixing up systemic societal issues with personal ones, but this is because I think they are as intertwined in this realm as in all aspects of people's lives. Machines become our tools, friends, and/or oppressors for political and personal reasons that become interwoven and hard to sort out. It is the merit of this collection to describe and sort some of the ways they fit into women's lives, to analyze historical, economic, and social roots of our relationships with machines, and so, hopefully, to help us devise strategies to increase our control over our work and our lives.

RUTH HUBBARD
Woods Hole, MA
June, 1983

Introduction: Why Machina Ex Dea?

Joan Rothschild

This book is for more than one audience. It is for those familiar with feminist scholarship in other fields who wish to see this approach extended to the area of technology. But it is also for those unfamiliar with, indifferent to, skeptical of, or even affronted by a feminist approach to knowledge, particularly its application to the field of technology studies. Therefore, one purpose of this introductory essay will be to explain the meaning of "feminist perspectives on technology" and thus outline the contents of the book. But the main emphasis will be to show why such perspectives are necessary, and the impact they can have for the field.

In Greek drama, and later in Roman and Renaissance theater, *deus ex machina* described a stage convention in which a god or goddess in the person of an actor was literally produced on stage by a machine. In its simplest and earliest form, a crane and pulley arrangement suspended the actor in the air or deposited the actor on the roof of the scene building at the close of the play, there to deliver the epilogue (Bieber 1961, Flickinger 1960 and 1961). Although it was sometimes criticized as a dramatic device—lesser dramatists used it to untangle confused strands of plot into a tidy denouement—literary critics have not seen *deus ex machina* as metaphor for the relationship between god/human and machine.

Lynn White, however, in choosing *Machina ex Deo* as the title for his collection of essays published in 1968, goes beyond mere reversal of the classic phrase. Concerned with exploring the forces affecting the relationship of man and nature* and the interplay of technology, society, and values, White uses "machine from the god" metaphorically to express the dualism between god/mind or spirit on the one hand, and matter or machine on the other. Thus the title became a point of departure for his critical appraisal of the relationship between soul or spirit and technology in our technological age. The retitling of the collection as *Dynamo and Virgin Reconsidered*

* In this book, words such as *man*, *mankind*, and masculine pronouns will not be used in their so-called generic sense, except when they accurately represent usage by an author, as here with White. For a critique of such usage, see Miller and Swift (1980), Hofstadter (1982), Sperder (1980), and below.

when published in paperback three years later in 1971 provided a more explicit metaphor for his theme.

My own choice of *Machine Ex Dea* for this volume thus owes an obvious debt to Professor White.[1] My title, too, is metaphorical, *machina* representing *technology*, *dea* standing for *female*, and the entire phrase signifying the relationship between the two. But *dea* as *female* is also used consciously and literally, in sharp contrast to the uncritical, unconscious, and yet often literal use of masculine forms when the subject is technology. And thereby hangs my tale.

White's use of *deo* is not just a matter of bowing to a linguistic convention which holds that the masculine form encompasses the female. White himself saw a problem here. Writing about the power and significance of symbols which challenge the canon of logic and language, White finds the use of language related to continued sex inequality. "The reasons for this widespread and unwarranted feminine sense of being secondary are many, but at least one of them is linguistic." He explains, the

> grammar of English dictates that when a referent is either of indeterminate sex or of both sexes, it shall be considered masculine. The penetration of this habit of language into the minds of little girls as they grow up to be women is more profound than most people, including most women, have recognized; for it implies that personality is really a male attribute and that women are a human subspecies. . . . It would be a miracle if a girl baby, learning to use the symbols of our tongue, could escape some unverbalized wound to her self-respect, whereas a boy baby's ego is bolstered by the pattern of our language (1968, p. 19).

These are surprising and prescient words for *anyone* to have written in the year 1968! But once written, they are ignored. Throughout *Machina ex Deo*, White continues to use *man*, *mankind*, and male pronouns, presumably when he means all of humanity. Or does he? White's failure to transfer his example of the symbolic use of language to his own writing reveals the paradox that underlies the use of masculine forms:[2] *Deo* does not include, but excludes, *dea*—or at most relegates her to appendage status in the history and philosophy of technology. Several examples will illustrate.

Writing from the perspective of the 1960s, White joined in questioning the hallowed canons of Western culture, which he defined as parochialism, linguistic logic, rationalism, and the Western hierarchy of values. He perceptively invokes the values of globalism, symbols, the unconscious, and a spectrum of values to challenge these canons (1968, ch. 2). The framework of "ancient Platonic-Cartesian dualism," in which these canons existed, "polarized experience between mind and body, spirit and substance, time and eternity, man and nature, natural and supernatural" (p. 14). One aspect of this dualism—perhaps the oldest of all—is not mentioned, however: that of male and female. As described by Simone de Beauvoir (1953), the intellectual foremother of modern feminist scholarship, women as reproducers are identified with nature, viewed as body and not mind, unable to gain transcendence and thus full humanity. Throughout Western cultural history, women have been seen as Other, existing as reflected selves of the men who create and keep culture and achieve through it their human transcendence.

Exploration of female-male dualism and of the woman-nature theme is also absent from White's well-known essay on ecology, reprinted in *Machina ex Deo*, in which he traces the "historical roots of our ecologic crisis" to the "Judeo-Christian teleology" (1968, p. 85). In Genesis, God created the world and its creatures, and man in His image to rule over them. With this impetus to dominate and exploit nature deep in the Western religious belief systems, the power generated since the mid-nineteenth century by the wedding of science and technology has brought us to the brink of ecological destruction. Invoking St. Francis as patron saint of a new environmental religious awareness, White declares, "What we do about ecology depends on our ideas of the man-nature relationship" (1968, p. 91). But what of the man-woman-nature relationship? Here, White is silent.

White's suppression of the female element is perhaps most glaring in his response to the dynamo and virgin metaphor in Henry Adams' autobiography (1918). In what was to become White's title essay in the 1971 edition of his book, *Dynamo and Virgin Reconsidered*, White counters Adams' contention that by the beginning of the twentieth century the dynamo or powerhouse had become the new symbol of energy and infinity. As such, it drove out the Church, symbolized by the Virgin, which had reached its height of symbolic power in the cathedral building of the twelfth and thirteenth centuries. White argues that the Virgin and dynamo are not "opposing principles," but "allies" (p. 72), machine power freeing us from human toil, thus freeing the human spirit. White carefully points out that Adams, writing at the turn of the twentieth century, did not use the symbol of the Virgin as medieval Catholics used it. Rather, Adams saw the Virgin as "the life force, the wellspring of fecundity, 'reproduction—the greatest and most mysterious of all energies' " (in White, p. 58). The Virgin symbolized sexual energy as well, Adams contending that American art, language, and education were "as far as possible sexless" (in White, p. 58). How odd, then, as White adapts Adams' metaphor, he drops its female import entirely (and inadvertently illustrates Adams' point!) Gone is the reproductive and sexual power so central to Adams' concept of the Virgin's spiritual power as it confronts the power of the dynamo. Seeking to reconcile opposites into a positive and mutually beneficial synthesis, White reduces Adams' duality to spirit and matter, religion and technology. In so distorting Adams' metaphor, White not only fails to make his own case. He fails to deal with

Adams' deep pessimism that the new technological age, symbolized by the powerhouse, would not only snuff out the spirit, but the life force itself.[3]

Obviously, we are dealing here with something more profound than mere linguistic omission. Women are outside, invisible, in White and in most of technological scholarship. Despite his insights about the effects of language, White did not, perhaps could not, change his language because his thinking did not change. He remains part of a Western cultural tradition that has been overwhelmingly male. I have singled out White, not to label him unfairly as patriarchal and sexist, but to suggest two points. First, little has changed in the literature in the decade and a half between the publication of our two similarly titled books. And second, even among the most perceptive and humanistic works on the relationship of technology, culture, and values, the omission of the female leaves a crucial intellectual gap in the analysis, and makes all analysis suspect.

What does omission of the female mean in more explicit terms? First, women's contributions have by and large been left out of technological history. Second, what women do as producers and reproducers—described by Ruth Cowan (1979) as bearers and rearers of children, workers, and homemakers—and the relationship of "women's work" to technological developments and change have been given short shrift in the standard technological literature. And third, the omission of the female affects how we know and what we know, and our very deepest beliefs and concerns about technology, a relationship explored especially by Gearhart, Bush, and King in this volume.

After a brief discussion of the "discipline" of technology studies, the following section will look at the record, documenting these omissions in the technology literature and discussing reasons why they occur. Many of the examples are drawn from *Technology and Culture*, for most of the last two-and-a-half decades the leading journal in the field.[4] The concluding section of this essay will show the impact that feminist perspectives can have on the study of technology.

A LOOK AT THE RECORD

The study of technology has been self-defined as a historical discipline. Although emerging from a group within engineering (the American Society for Engineering Education), the Society for the History of Technology (SHOT) was founded in 1958 mainly by historians. Yet, in establishing their journal one year later, members chose the title *Technology and Culture** rather

---

* Referred to hereafter as "T&C" or "the journal."

than, for example, Journal of the History of Technology. Writing in the initial issue, editor Melvin Kranzberg explained and supported this choice with a commitment to publishing "general articles dealing with the relations of technology with society and culture as well as more specialized articles on the history of technological processes and devices" (1959, p. 9). According to John Staudenmaier's (1980) analysis of the intellectual content of the journal since its inception through 1977, an interdisciplinary character prevailed in its early years, with half the authors drawn from disciplines other than history. But starting in the mid-1960s, journal articles grew less interdisciplinary and more historical so that, by 1977, 85 percent of the authors were historians (Staudenmaier 1980). Yet, in reports of conferences, the numerous book reviews, and its extensive bibliographies, the journal has remained hospitable to members and works from other disciplines, especially those in philosophy and social sciences. And although disciplinary debates and thematic discussions follow the approach and methodology of the historian, the journal continues to reflect a concern with technology and culture, often emerging as a tension which was defined by Staudenmaier as one of "design-ambience."

Thus, the field known as the history of technology, represented by the journal *Technology and Culture*, is in one sense firmly linked to history. But, in another sense, it casts its net wide enough to include the rest of us from other disciplines who engage in technology studies. Because the historiographic debates indicate an openness to critical analysis from new quarters, feminist analysis, with its interdisciplinary perspective, can speak constructively to the technology-culture tensions expressed.

In my brief review of T&C, I shall first document the omission of the female by counting, and then move on to an analysis of content. However, I shall not focus on women authors, but on the subject of women as it appears or does not appear in T&C's pages. Although a positive correlation exists between numbers of women in a given publication or discipline and research on women, the presence of women authors is no guarantee that the subject matter will be women. Further, men have written and do write about women and technology as in other fields. In the following, "women or subjects pertaining to women" will include those activities ascribed to women, through biology or socioeconomic practice, and theoretical or philosophical analyses that embody a feminist approach.

Appearing quarterly each year—with the exception of 1959 and 1960—T&C has published 23 volumes, or a total of 93 issues, from 1959 through 1982. An issue is usually comprised of from two to four articles (more for symposia and special issues), and various other cover design, research, communication, and organizational notes, with the bulk of each issue devoted to book reviews. A bibliography on the history of technology has been published annually since 1964 in the Spring or April issue.

In 24 years of publishing, four articles on women's subjects have appeared in T&C. The first, in January 1976, was Ruth Schwartz Cowan's "The 'Industrial Revolution' in the Home," which exploded some cherished myths about the impact of household technology on American society. This was followed in July 1978 by Joann Vanek's article on the changed relationship between household technology and social status, the former no longer an indicator of the latter. Another article by Cowan appeared in January 1979, "From Virginia Dare to Virginia Slims," adapted from her invited presentation at the SHOT bicentennial meeting (October 1975) in which she outlined areas for research on the interplay of women and technology. And in April 1982, T&C published Charles Thrall's "The Conservative Use of Household Technology," indicating ways in which such technology reinforced old sex role patterns.

In addition to the four articles above, the first mention of a women's subject in T&C was Alison Ravetz' "Communication," "Modern Technology and an Ancient Occupation: Housework in Present-Day Society," in Spring 1965. Replying to Peter Drucker (Summer 1963) on how social factors contribute to selective "technological lag" in developing nations, Ravetz noted that today the "ancient occupation" of housework also suffers such a lag due to social factors: the English experience of the last 50 years shows that women's roles and living patterns have not changed, despite new technology. In July 1981, Carroll Pursell explained the issue's cover design on "Women Inventors in America," one of the isolated T&C covers devoted to a woman's theme. In the July 1976 issue, a short exchange of letters complimented and criticized T&C on Cowan's first article (Fitzsimons/Cowan, July 1976). And in October 1969, a "Research Note" appeared on "The Male Weavers of Pompeii," in which Walter Moeller, drawing his evidence mainly from graffiti, discovered the presence of male weavers in what was traditionally a female occupation. He concluded that they did not organize as did other wool processors because of "their completely servile condition and the feminine nature of their tasks" (p. 566). There was no follow-up of Moeller's findings in T&C, especially concerning the more numerous women weavers of Pompeii, their work and its technology.

In the same 24-year period, 23 book reviews on women's subjects have appeared in T&C. If the category extends to works on family history, office automation, the Shakers, and housewares history that have not dealt with women explicitly, the total rises to 27. This is less than the number of reviews that generally appear in a single issue. Seventy-two of the T&C issues contained no book reviews on women's subjects at all. Counting by volume, rather than by issue, produces the following: five book reviews on women's subjects in 1982, two each in 1981, 1980, and 1979, three in 1978, but none in 1977. While these figures represent a marginal increase, we must set them against the recent average of 30 reviews in a single issue or a 120 total for a year.

The annual bibliographies, published since 1964 and now covering 16 categories, have extensive listings, often briefly annotated. For most of the years of publication, each has run between 50 and 100 pages, with well over 1,000 entries in the heavier years. All bibliographies in this 19-year period have produced 44 entries on women's subjects. Only eight of these were also reviewed in T&C. Three of the 44 were works published in Swedish and French. And eight entries were marginal for inclusion under the women's subjects category. With no entries or one or two in the early years, the number increased starting in the mid-1970s: three each in the 1974 and 1975 bibliographies, eight in 1976, and five each in 1977 through 1980, the last surveyed for this article. Because of a two-year time-lag in publishing these bibliographies—e.g., the 1980 Bibliography appeared in the April 1982 issue of T&C—and books cited may go back even one or two years earlier, the most recent work on women and technology, which has markedly increased, is understandably not included. The same point must be made for book reviews which work on one-, two-, and three-year time-lags. Five book reviews out of 130 in 1982, and five bibliographic entries out of over 800 for the 1980 Bibliography published in 1982, however, do not necessarily indicate a trend.

In the 1970s, the first papers and panels on women and technology began to appear at the Society for the History of Technology (SHOT) annual meetings. But numbers remained relatively scant, and few papers found their way into T&C's pages.[5] In 1976, Women in Technological History (WITH) was formed as a subgroup of SHOT, with a major purpose to promote "scholarly research, publication, and teaching about women in the history of technology" (Women in Technological History, July 1977, p. 497). Evidently in response to pressure,[6] the first woman was appointed to the SHOT Advisory Council in 1975; in 1978, the first woman was named to SHOT's Executive Council, and the first woman joined T&C's advisory editors. By 1982, there were three women among the 17 T&C advisory editors, three women on the 8-member SHOT Executive Council (usually a 9-member body), and three women among 32 members of the SHOT Advisory Council—down from a high of four in a once 35-member body. Most, although not all, of these women appointees have distinguished themselves in the field at least partly through their work on women and technology.

Looking at the record so far we find that, although some individual women have gained professional recognition for their feminist contributions to the field, this has yet to translate itself into any serious recognition that women and technology and feminist perspectives on technology are legitimate concerns in T&C's pages. The coverage has been quite narrow. Three of the four articles devoted to women's subjects were on technology and household labor. The 27 book reviews and 44 bibliographic entries broadened to cover various aspects of women's work and economic roles, often from historical perspectives. But this nowhere nearly represents one of the most prolific areas of feminist scholarship, as McGaw (1982) has amply demonstrated for the history of American technology alone. The anthropological literature dealing with many facets of women's labor and economic roles, often at least indirectly relating to technology, is unrepresented. And with the exception of the October 1982 issue's review of Carolyn Merchant's book (1980), the journal has paid no attention to the philosophic literature that raises feminist issues about the ideology, epistemology, and values of both our science and technology. While most of this material is quite new, much of it dates from at least the mid-1970s and has been readily accessible.

The record, however, is not uniformly bleak. Particularly in the historiographic and disciplinary discussions, certain members in the field recognize *dea* and the need to include factors about women in technological scholarship. The problem is that these suggestions do not really carry through into the discipline. The following examples show three reasons why such promise is not fulfilled.

Discussing the "big questions" in the history of American technology, George Daniels (January 1970) describes technology as a social phenomenon, stating that "the direction in which the society is going determines the nature of its technological innovations" (p. 3). Illustrating his point, he questions the conventional wisdom as to whether the typewriter "liberated" women and, indeed, whether it brought women into offices in the first place (pp. 4–5), questions which feminist scholars have since revealingly explored (see below). He further notes that among the socioeconomic changes upon which "the pattern of invention . . . depends in large measure" (and not the other way around) are "declining family size" and the "changing status of women" (p. 8). Five years later, Ruth Schwartz Cowan gave an invited presentation on the "state of the art" regarding women and technology at the Bicentennial Meeting of SHOT (October 1975). Her remarks were subsequently published, along with others on the status and development of American technology from that conference, in the January 1979 issue of T&C. Yet in an article the following October that discussed emerging themes of American technology studies since the Industrial Revolution, Thomas Hughes does not mention women at all!

This is the phenomenon of "ghettoization" or "tokenism," and the first reason why such omissions as Hughes' occur. The article by Cowan duly appeared. The issue of "women" is now taken care of, and the discipline goes its own way. Having paid lip-service, it can ignore the import of Cowan's article, and the issues and themes about women that she raises do not become integrated into the body of the discipline or field of inquiry.

Another example of this occurred in the special issue on "The Mechanization of Work" published by *Scientific American* in September 1982 to which historian Joan Scott contributed a comprehensive article on "The Mechanization of Women's Work." While it may appear as a breakthrough that *Scientific American* devoted specific attention to a women's subject, closer examination of the entire issue suggests tokenism and ghettoism here as well. With the exception of the introductory overview article by Eli Ginzburg which does weave in issues of women and work, and a passing reference to the issue of family income in the final piece, Scott's is the only article that discusses women in relation to the overall theme, even though women are actively engaged in certain fields of work surveyed in other articles. For example, in "The Mechanization of Office Work," Vincent Giuliano mentions women only once, and then to state, erroneously, that "Large numbers of women were employed in offices as a direct result of the introduction of the typewriter" (p. 149). A reference, presumably by the editors, to the Scott article follows, even though Scott hardly makes such an error! Scott's article is also the only one to discuss technology and household labor, even though the impact of such mechanization reaches far beyond "women's work" (see Rothschild this volume).

A lone article or chapter inserted to somehow represent "women" occurs increasingly in technology collections. Cowan's "The 'Industrial Revolution' in the Home" (January 1976) is chosen most often. As we ask why, a second reason for such treatment emerges. In a 1974 article in T&C, Robert Multhauf criticizes four standard histories of technology from four countries: Singer et al. (1954–58), Great Britain; Daumas (1969), France; Zworykin et al. (1964), USSR; and Kranzberg and Pursell (1967), U.S., on the grounds that their organization offers nothing new. Based on earlier traditions of Poppe and Toynbee, such works, being organized by subject matter or chronologically, either lose important technologies or do not give us a good sense of history. Multhauf shows that key technologies have "simply fallen through the cracks" of the organizational scheme, technologies which, if included, would "lead to a significantly different picture" of the historical phenomenon (p. 11). Applying Multhauf's analysis, materials on women and technology can similarly "fall through the cracks," because the organizational schemes for studying technological development and change do not lend themselves to inclusion of such materials, much less integration into a cohesive whole. Isolated inclusion may be the best that can be done under the present scheme of things. I suggest, therefore, that a second reason for the omission of women is that the historiography of technology has a built-in resistance to the subject of women and technology. The very approaches to technology studies will have to undergo serious rethinking if work on women and technology is to be fully included and its impact felt in the entire field of study.

Commenting on Daniels' work on the causes of technological innovation (January 1970) and seeking to show motives in addition to economics to explain such innovation, John Burke (January 1970) writes, "It is hard for me . . . to conceive of any situation other than that some man or men gathered wild wheat and cooked and ate it because of hunger or inquisitiveness, found it satisfying, and commenced to grow it and employ it as a dietary staple" (p. 25). I have no quarrel (and neither does Daniels) with Burke's point that chance and inquisitiveness can play an important role in technological invention and innovation. I do question his ascribing the cultivation and preparation of wheat to the male of the species. By 1970, when this article was published, the anthropological literature had demonstrated that women were and are the chief foragers as well as early plant cultivators in many cultures; in fact, women can be said to have invented agriculture (Ortega 1961, p. 143; Boulding 1976). Burke cannot take refuge in generic conventions; he has denied the generic in using "some man or men." His error points to a third reason for the lack of treatment of women's subjects in the technology literature. As was the case with White and language, the reason is the literal identification of the male with technology.

This male identification appears particularly in the discussions of contextual and philosophical questions, especially those on the "man-machine" relationship. In a typology that analyzed "four angles of vision" of "man and his machines" (p. 531), Donald Shriver (October 1972) shows that only the political and evolutionary views—as opposed to the instrumental and deterministic—can deal with the multiplicity of values that exist in the complex interaction of technology, society, and values. Perceptive and humanistic as his analysis is, as he tries to deal with and clarify these complexities, something is missing. The same is true for "The Fourth Discontinuity" in which Bruce Mazlish (January 1967) optimistically suggests that we are on the threshhold of breaking through man's present discontinuity with the machine, having successfully broken through the discontinuities set up by the Copernican Revolution, Darwin, and Freud. With Theodore Wertime's (April 1968) commentary on Mazlish, as well as on volume 1 of Mumford's *The Myth of the Machine* (1966), the issue is clarified. Wertime traces the discontinuity between man and machine to an earlier one between man and nature. While for Mumford language, not tools, made us human, for Wertime language "marks the crucial breach in the symbiosis of primate and nature, the onset of contrivance and 'sin,' the beginning of that catalogue of human offenses against the natural order that some of us blame wrongly on the Christian ethic or the naked sexual drive" (p. 210). For Wertime, "man [is] . . . obviously at odds with the rhythms of mother earth" (p. 204); "men have ever lamented . . . their sense of alienation from nature" (p. 208); "The lesson of contemporary research into human behavior and cognition is that we must doubt that man has had a naïve and direct rapport with nature since he became man" (p. 211). A woman could never have written these words; conversely, only a man could have. If there is doubt, Wertime again,

> In a yet-unpublished essay, I cite the penis as a primeval concept-forming tool of the primates, and I do so with evidence taken from recent neural inquiries into sex, exploration, and aggressiveness. Man modified primate uses of this instrument as a social weapon by putting a fig leaf over it, but it remains nonetheless a prototype of a whole family of compressing, fire-making, and crepitating devices (p. 211).

In still another example, in a review of the collection *Philosophy and Cybernetics* (Crosson & Sayre 1967), Dale Riepe (October 1968) criticizes one author, Lee Hart, for carrying the man-machine analogy too far. Personifying the computer, Hart suggests "that machines may well have erotic fantasies when the machine 'perceives' the rising nipple of a well-turned dial" (Riepe, p. 627)! Those with psychoanalytic expertise can make their own interpretations of Hart's and Wertime's remarks. For our purposes here, it is clear that for Wertime, Hart, as well as for Burke, the human species, presumably including man-created androids, is literally male.[7] As suggested earlier, this is true even for those who do not go this far or express themselves as literally, and thus helps to explain the inadequacies of Shriver's, Mazlish's, and White's analyses. For most scholars and writers in the technology field, the prototype—the inventor, the user, the thinker about and reactor to technology—is male.

I say for "most." Lewis Mumford, despite his use of male linguistic conventions, is an important exception. Basing the following mainly on his major work, *The Myth of the Machine* (1966, 1970), I find much in Mumford that is feminist (whether or not he would entirely welcome the label). First, Mumford recognized the central role that women played in early domestication, and associated technologies. Second, he argues that so-called female qualities which are undervalued had an important role in technological development. And third, he assigns equal weight to subjective impulses and fantasies as formative influences in creating and transforming culture.

In chapter 7 of *Technics and Human Development* (1966), entitled "Garden, Home, and Mother," Mumford delineates woman's domesticator role:

> Garden culture, different from later field culture, is pre-eminently, almost exclusively, woman's work. Clearly the first steps in domestication were taken by her. If this culture was not politically a matriarchal one, its emphasis was nevertheless maternal: the care and nurture of life. Woman's old role as a discriminating collector of berries, roots, leaves, herbs, 'simples,' has continued among peasants down to our own time, in the old woman (witch doctor) who knows where to find the herbs for medicine and how to apply their 'virtues' in

> curing an ache, lowering a fever, or healing a wound. Neolithic domestication enlarged this role (p. 142).

Mumford thus becomes one of the principal challengers of the persistent notion that man is the central provider and social organizer in early cultures.

As indicated in the passage quoted above, Mumford invokes women's traditional attribute of nurturance as supporting her domesticator role. He more specifically calls on gender dualism when he links women's physiological characteristics to technological development. Chiding scholars who recognize that "tools are mechanical counterfeits of the muscles and limbs of the male body"—the hammer as fist, spear a lengthened arm, pincers human fingers—but who "seem prudishly inhibited against the notion that woman's body is also capable of extrapolation," Mumford describes the womb as "a protective container" and the "breast a pitcher of milk" (p. 140).

> The tool and the utensil, like the sexes themselves, perform complementary functions. One moves, manipulates, assaults; the other remains in place, to hold and protect and preserve.
>
> In general, the mobile, dynamic processes are of male origin: they overcome the resistance of matter, push, pull, tear, penetrate, chip, macerate, move, transport, destroy; while the static processes are female and reflect the predominant anabolism of woman's physiology: for they work from within, as in any chemical transformation, and they remain largely in place, undergoing qualitative changes, from raw meat to boiled meat, from fermenting grain to beer, from planted seed to seeding plant (p. 140).

But let us stop a moment. Aren't these the very stereotypes about male and female that feminists are battling, particularly when linked in this way to nature and not nurture? How can I call Mumford feminist, even in some small degree? Mumford makes two crucial points in connection with this dualism. First, he notes that it is "a modern solecism to regard stable states as inferior to dynamic ones" when they are equally important (p. 140). And second, containers and similar technologies which he associates with women proliferate "precisely at the moment when . . . woman was beginning to play a more distinctive role as food-provider and effective ruler than she had in the earlier foraging and hunting economies" (p. 140). While feminists have warned of real dangers in thus assigning attributes on the basis of gender, many have also pointed out that a science and technology that recognized and valued so-called female attributes would create a healthier and better world in which to live (see, e.g., King, Gearhart, and Schweickart this volume, and Rothschild 1981). Mumford goes on:

> Protection, storage, enclosure, accumulation, continuity—these contributions of neolithic culture largely stem from woman and woman's vocations. In our current preoccupations with speed and motion and spatial extension, we tend

> to devaluate all these stabilizing processes: even our containers, from the drinking cup to the recorder tape, are meant to be as transitory as the materials they contain or the functions they serve. But without this original emphasis on the organs of continuity, first provided by stone itself, then by neolithic domesticity, the higher functions of culture could never have developed (p. 141).

While Mumford may ultimately assign greater value to man as creator of higher culture (although this is debatable), in the technology literature—especially as written mainly by men—Mumford's is an original and perceptive analysis that breaks through the male prototypes described above.

The third count on which Mumford may be viewed as feminist is subtler, but also controversial from feminist perspectives. It speaks more closely to the technology-culture debates among his colleagues and to an important argument of this essay.

In *The Myth of the Machine*, Mumford argues that humans are not essentially tool-makers. Rather, we are distinguished by our mental capacities, the ability to visualize and imagine, to create symbols and thus language. The latter, symbols and language, not tools, separate the human animal from others. Thus, technics from earliest times was used to enhance human expression, to aid human beings in the task of recreating themselves. Technics "was broadly life-centered, not work-centered or power-centered" (1966, v. 1, p. 9). This conception enables Mumford to find in technological and cultural development not only the so-called female qualities described above, but also other "soft" elements such as the subjective and irrational. He maintains that technics has been greatly modified by dreams, wishes, impulses, and religious motives that spring from the unconscious, from our subjective nature (1970, v. 2, p. 415). But with the development of the "megamachine" and the coming of "megatechnics" in our culture, this subjective element has been almost totally submerged. If the trend continues, the human being will become passive and purposeless, a "machine-conditioned animal whose proper functions . . . will either be fed into the machine or strictly limited and controlled for the benefit of de-personalized, collective organizations" (v. 1, p. 3). Any hope or possibility for change lies also in those subjective impulses, producing the "formative idea" that can, through a dialectical process, become incorporated in the present culture and thus help to transform that culture. Like White, writing from the perspective of the sixties, Mumford sees the possibility of such a formative idea in the values, spirit, and lifestyle of the counterculture (v. 2, pp. 413–35).

Although some feminists have cautioned against accepting uncritically the linking of subjectivity, irrationality, or the idea of a life force with the female, there is an element in Mumford's way of thinking with which feminism can agree. Feminist thought has criticized incisively the so-called rational and objective characteristics of our science and technology. Feminist analysis has sought to show how the subjective, intuitive, and irrational can and do play a key role in our science and technology (see, e.g., Keller, Trescott, Hacker, this volume; Fee 1981; Hubbard et al. 1982). Mumford has titled the Epilogue, in which he expresses these ideas of cultural and technological transformation, "The Advancement of Life." In so doing, he suggests his own linking of subjective impulses and life-generating forces or a female principle.

Although one may not always agree fully with Mumford and although he may not satisfy fully a feminist approach, Mumford presents a more holistic view of cultural and technological developments than do most of his colleagues.[8] Recognizing the male-female dualism is an important element in creating that holistic perspective. When other philosophers and critics frame the large issues of technology and culture in a "man-machine" context and thus deny the fundamental gender dualism of Western culture, their analysis is incomplete. Feminist perspectives on technology, by drawing attention to and exploring the dualism, and focusing on the female, can help make our study of technology a much richer, more nearly complete intellectual endeavor.[9]

FEMINIST PERSPECTIVES ON TECHNOLOGY

In the previous section, I argued that the female has been left out of most technological scholarship and that the standard approaches to the study of technology made more than token inclusion difficult. But I also pointed out that the present state of technology studies presented an opportunity for feminist scholarship to make its influence felt in a manner that could both enrich and transform the discipline. In this concluding section, I suggest specific ways that feminist perspectives can speak to the concerns and questions of technology studies and how the articles in this book move in this direction.

One of these concerns has been disciplinary. Discussing the development of a discipline of the history of technology, Eugene Ferguson (January 1974) argues that history is the "primary discipline," but one that broadly encompasses such areas as economic, social, and intellectual history. Describing the task as "an informed, qualitative analysis of the human situation as it affects and is affected by technology," he classes history as one of the humanities and not a social science (p. 30). On the other hand, Reinhard Rürup (April 1974), addressing similar disciplinary issues but from the perspective of European scholarship and a concern particularly with the relationship of technology and production, writes that work in the field of the history of technology "depends on the application of methods in the social sciences" (p. 192), placing the field clearly within social science. How can these positions be reconciled? Rürup finished the above sentence, adding that such work also "requires interdisciplinary cooperation" (p. 192).

As discussed above, the history of technology draws within it the humanities and the social sciences, and the engineering discipline which partly gave it birth. The growing numbers of academic programs in technology are usually interdisciplinary; and public interest in technological issues crosses disciplines as well. Yet, the academic positions of Ferguson and Rürup represent real differences, echoing a much wider difference between those oriented to design questions and those concerned with societal issues. Feminist scholarship can play a role here. By its very nature, it is interdisciplinary. When feminist scholars began to explore women's roles in culture and society, and their shaping ideologies, they were forced to draw on many disciplines—among them, history, psychology, sociology, anthropology, literature—all of which were and are engaged in similar quests about women. Whether the point of departure is a humanities discipline, social science, or more recently the sciences and technical fields, such scholarship follows Ferguson's "informed, qualitative analysis of the human situation." Feminist research can help to create models for interdisciplinary approaches that are academically sound yet cross disciplinary boundaries. The articles by Merchant, Keller, Hacker, and Bush in this volume are among such examples.

A second important theme found in the disciplinary discussion is the one expressed originally by Melvin Kranzberg in the initial issue of T&C, the need to put the study of technology in a social context. Daniels (January 1970) and Rürup (April 1974) have stressed the importance of social factors in shaping technological change, including factors about women's work, lives, and status. As I have argued, such interest in and recognition of the female element is a highly welcome and necessary first step toward inclusion. But it has not been sufficient to take us beyond tokenism to fully integrate such subject matter into the body of the field. The impetus must come from feminist research, which demonstrates that women are more than a mere appendage to or passive recipients of human technological history. The work already done on household technology and on women and technology in paid employment moves clearly in this direction. The articles by Feldberg and Glenn and by Stanley in this volume show in different ways how our perspectives on work and history are changed when we focus on women. We need to integrate these new materials into the mainstream of technological and labor history so that no one can again assert, as Peter Drucker did in Kranzberg and Pursell's history of technology (1967), "In the years before World War I technology, in large measure, brought about the emancipation of women and gave them a new position in society" (v. II, p. 24). Feminist research increasingly questions the role of technology as a "liberating" factor for women in any number of areas (see, for example, Bush 1982, and Rothschild this volume).

Drucker's statement also calls up a third theme found in the technology literature: the determinism debate—or, as Heilbroner has put it, "Do Machines Make History?" (July 1967). I agree with Daniels (January 1970) that it is a mistake to assign causative qualities, especially exclusive ones, to technology, that, indeed, there are no independent variables in history. Yet I also agree with Ferguson (January 1974) that there are strong deterministic elements found in some technologies. For example, as Flink's study of *The Car Culture* (1975) has shown, the development of the internal combustion engine has profoundly shaped the physical and social character of our lives. The same might be said for television, and promises to apply to computers—although none of these examples should be viewed as causative agents in isolation. Feminist scholarship can enrich and clarify here as well. As feminist research begins to be integrated into the mainstream of technology studies, it can contribute the model of technology as an interdependent variable.

The oft-referred to typewriter and its connection with the rise in women's office employment is a good example. Taking neither the deterministic view nor discounting some role for the typewriter in the feminization of office work, feminist research has sought out other variables, such as employment patterns and labor force characteristics, demographics, economic and business conditions, and prevalent ideologies, in order to explain the woman-typewriter connections (see, for example, Davies 1982, Kessler-Harris 1976, Oppenheimer 1970, Rotella 1981). Thus, the presence of a reasonably well-educated female native-born population, the growth and changing practices of business, the shifting of ideologies in the face of market needs, as well as the new technology itself, are among the complex set of forces contributing to the growth of the female clerical labor force in the United States in the late nineteenth and early twentieth centuries. The typewriter or other office technology no more "causes" female employment or "liberates" women than any other single factor could; yet, in combination with other factors, it significantly changed women's lives. Birth control technology provides another example. Its invention alone does not change women's opportunities or status. Its diffusion and use may, but feminist analysis shows that its effects cannot be separated from social and political context (see Gordon 1977; also McGaw 1982, p. 803). Such technology may not "free" women at all if women do not control it or it is harmful to their health. But the existence of safe and effective technologies of birth control can provide women with a tool for control of their own reproduction, which is a necessary condition for liberation. Again, we see technology operating as an interdependent variable.

Turning once again to Eugene Ferguson (January 1974), a fourth concern of technology studies emerges. He writes that, in order for a satisfactory discipline to develop, we must have "studies that look carefully at technology itself and note its nature and influences" (p. 30). Although this concern is related to the determinism debate and the plea for social context, Ferguson is saying something very specific: we must examine the nature of technology, as technology, which in turn will help us to understand its effects. Feminist research provides successful examples of this approach. In focusing on the types, development, and uses of butter churns from 1750–1850 in the mid-Atlantic region, Joan Jensen (1982) not only adds significantly to the design literature, but also illuminates the role of women in the domestic and the emerging industrial economy. She shows that the churn was "an important material link and butter making an important process by which rural women extended the old concept of the productive farm economy into the new industrial era" (p. 93). In this volume, Jalna Hanmer describes current, imminent, and possible human reproductive technologies, in turn situating them in their social context; she thus provides a combined empirical and theoretical basis for assessing the effects of such technologies on women. Feldberg and Glenn use such an approach in part in their article on the impact of office automation. Also in this volume, Bush offers a unique framework for technology assessment that would examine the developmental, user, environmental, and cultural contexts for an "equity analysis" of technology.

In these ways, feminist perspectives speak to concerns of the field of technology studies itself—those of content and methodology, social context, determinism, and the nature of technology. The chapters in this book represent some of these perspectives and contributions. They belong to the body of feminist scholarship in technology that seeks to establish for the female her rightful place in technological history and culture. In so doing, that scholarship brings to technology studies modes of inquiry and categories of analysis from a new and growing scholarly tradition that draws creatively on the total human experience.

Machina Ex Dea is divided into three sections. The first, WOMEN, TECHNOLOGY, AND PRODUCTION, begins to correct the record to show women's positive role in productive technological activity, and to show the differential ways women as producers have been affected by technology. Part II, TECHNOLOGY AND VALUES: DEA AND DEUS RECONSIDERED, discusses the impact of the female-male dualism on science and technology from the differing perspectives of the philosophy and history of science, psychoanalytic theory, and feminist ecology. The third section, FEMINIST PERSPECTIVES FOR A TECHNOLOGICAL AGE, explores and provides new insights on key concerns of technological society: technology assessment, an anti-technology position, developments in human reproductive technology, and alternative technological visions. *Machina Ex Dea* closes with the editor's assessment of where we are and avenues for future research.

NOTES

1. See also Martha Moore Trescott's *Dynamos and Virgins Revisited* (1979) and the Introduction to her volume.
2. In a perceptive article, Hofstadter (1982) argues that such usage rests on "default assumptions" which are implicit assumptions that we make unconsciously and automatically, as those about gender.
3. But see Leo Marx (1964, pp. 345–50) on the female and sexual imagery and Adams' pessimism in Adams' dynamo and Virgin metaphor.
4. Among recent additions to the field are two quarterlies: *Science, Technology, and Human Values* (1978–), co-sponsored by the Massachusetts Institute of Technology and Harvard University, and published by John Wiley (New York); and *Technology in Society* (1979–, published by Pergamon Press (New York and Oxford).
5. These were Cowan's two articles published in the January 1976 and January 1979 issues. Certain papers were reserved for publication in Martha Trescott's anthology (1979).
6. At the Executive Council meeting at the 17th annual meeting of SHOT, Chicago, 1974, "A letter from Carolyn Iltis (University of California, Berkeley), of the Committee on Women in the History of Science, was presented by [Melvin] Kranzberg [editor of T&C]. Dr. Iltis requested that SHOT give serious consideration to the selection of women for its Editorial Board and for other organizational work. The Executive Council approved of Kranzberg's reply, which indicated the desire of SHOT to cooperate in every way but deplored the small number of women active in the history of technology" ("Organizational Notes" July 1975, p. 447). (Ruth Schwartz Cowan became the first woman on the Advisory Council in 1975; Margaret Rossiter was the first woman named to T&C's Advisory Editors in 1978.)
7. Most machines, however, are personified as female, as, for example, cars, ships, or airplanes. The Latin and Romance languages' *machina*, as well as the Greek word for machine from which the others derive, is in every case feminine gender. Whether this has affected English usage or not, it remains that our machines are driven, controlled, and designed to serve.
8. Victor Ferkiss (1969, 1974) has developed an important holistic perspective. See Shriver's perceptive critique (October 1972).
9. Feminist perspectives further this endeavor as well through focusing on race and class issues which are integral to feminist analysis.

REFERENCES

Adams, Henry. 1918. *The education of Henry Adams*. New York: Modern Library.

de Beauvoir, Simone. 1953. *The second sex*. Trans. and ed. H. M. Parshley. New York: Alfred A. Knopf.

Bieber, Margarete. 1961. *The history of Greek and Roman theater*. Princeton, N.J.: Princeton University Press.

Boulding, Elise. 1976. *The underside of history: A view of women through time*. Boulder, Colo.: Westview Press.

Burke, John G. 1970. Comment: The complex nature of explanations in the historiography of technology. *Technology and Culture* 11 (January):22–26.

Bush, Corlann G. 1982. The barn is his, the house is mine: Agricultural technology and sex roles. *Energy and transport*. ed. George Daniels and Mark Rose. Beverly Hills, Calif.: Sage Publications: 235–59.

Cowan, Ruth Schwartz. 1976. The "industrial revolution" in the home: Household technology and social change in the 20th century. *Technology and Culture* 17 (January):1–23.

Cowan, Ruth Schwartz. 1979. From Virginia Dare to Virginia Slims: Women and technology in American life. *Technology and Culture* 20 (January):51–63.

Crosson, Frederick J.; and Sayre, Kenneth M., eds. 1967. *Philosophy and cybernetics*. Notre Dame, Ind.: University of Notre Dame Press.

Daniels, George H. 1970. The big questions in the history of American technology. *Technology and Culture* 11 (January):1–21.

Daumas, Maurice, ed. 1969. *A history of technology & invention: Progress through the ages*. 2 vols. Trans. Eileen B. Hennessy. New York: Crown Publishers.

Davies, Margery W. 1982. *Woman's place is at the typewriter: Office work and office workers, 1870–1930*. Philadelphia: Temple University Press.

Drucker, Peter F. 1963. Modern technology and ancient jobs. *Technology and Culture* 4 (Summer):277–81.

Drucker, Peter F. 1967. Technology and society in the twentieth century. *Technology in Western civilization* v. II. ed. Melvin Kranzberg and Carroll W. Pursell, Jr. New York: Oxford University Press: 22–33.

Fee, Elizabeth. 1981. Is feminism a threat to scientific objectivity? *International Journal of Women's Studies* 4:378–92.

Ferguson, Eugene S. 1974. Toward a discipline of the history of technology. *Technology and Culture* 15 (January):13–30.

Ferkiss, Victor. 1969. *Technological man: The myth and the reality*. New York: George Braziller.

Ferkiss, Victor. 1974. *The future of technological civilization*. New York: George Braziller.

Fitzsimons, Mayvis; Cowan, Ruth Schwartz. 1976. Right on! / Right on—and on! *Technology and Culture* 17 (July):526–7.

Flickinger, Roy C. [1918] 1960 and 1961. *The Greek theater and its drama*. Chicago: University of Chicago Press.

Flink, James J. 1975. *The car culture*. Cambridge, Mass.: MIT Press.

Giuliano, Vincent. 1982. The mechanization of office work. *Scientific American* 247 (September): 148–64.

Gordon, Linda. 1977. *Woman's body, woman's right: A social history of birth control in America*. New York: Penguin Books.

Heilbroner, Robert L. 1967. Do machines make history? *Technology and Culture* 8 (July): 335–45.

Hofstadter, Douglas R. 1982. Metamagical themas: "Default assumptions" and their effects on writing and thinking. *Scientific American* 247 (November):18–36.

Hubbard, Ruth; Henifin, Mary Sue; and Fried, Barbara, eds. 1982. *Biological woman—The convenient myth*. Cambridge, Mass.: Schenkman.

Hughes, Thomas P. 1979. Emerging themes in the history of technology and culture. *Technology and Culture* 20 (October):697–711.

Jensen, Joan M. 1982. Churns and butter making in the mid-Atlantic farm economy, 1750–1850. *Working papers from the Regional Economic History Research Center*. ed. Glenn Porter and William H. Mulligan, Jr., v. 5. Greenville/Wilmington, Del.: Eleutherian Mills-Hagley Foundation: 60–100.

Kessler-Harris, Alice. 1976. Women, work, and the social order. *Liberating women's history*. ed. Berenice Carroll. Urbana: University of Illinois Press: 330–43.

Kranzberg, Melvin. 1959. At the start. *Technology and Culture* 1:1–10.

Kranzberg, Melvin; and Pursell, Carroll, Jr., eds. 1967. *Technology in Western civilization*. 2 vols. New York: Oxford University Press.

Marx, Leo. 1964. *The machine in the garden: Technology and the pastoral ideal in America*. New York: Oxford University Press.

Mazlish, Bruce. 1967. The fourth discontinuity. *Technology and Culture* 8 (January):1–15.

McGaw, Judith A. 1982. Women and the history of American technology. *Signs: Journal of Women in Culture and Society* 7 (Summer):798–828.

The mechanization of work. 1982. *Scientific American* 247 (September).

Merchant, Carolyn. 1980. *The death of nature: Women, ecology, and the Scientific Revolution*. New York: Harper & Row.

Miller, Casey; and Swift, Kate. 1980. *The handbook of nonsexist writing*. New York: Harper & Row.

Moeller, Walter O. 1969. The male weavers of Pompeii. *Technology and Culture* 10 (October): 561–66.

Multhauf, Robert P. 1974. Some observations on the state of the history of technology. *Technology and Culture* 15 (January):1–12.

Mumford, Lewis. 1966, 1970. *The myth of the machine*. 2 vols. v. 1: *Technics and human development*. v. 2: *The pentagon of power*. New York: Harcourt Brace Jovanovich.

Oppenheimer, Valerie Kincade. 1970. *The female labor force in the United States: demographic and economic factors governing its growth and changing composition*. Population Monograph Series, No. 5. Berkeley, Calif.

Organizational notes. 1975. *Technology and Culture* 16 (July):429–53.

Ortega y Gassett, José. 1961. *History as a system and other essays toward a philosophy of history*. Trans. Helene Weyl. New York: W. W. Norton.

Pursell, Carroll. 1981. Women inventors in America. *Technology and Culture* 22 (July): 545–49.

Ravetz, Alison. 1965. Modern technology and an ancient occupation: Housework in present-day society. *Technology and Culture* 6 (Spring):256–60.

Riepe, Dale. 1968. Review of *Philosophy and cybernetics*, ed. Crosson and Sayre. *Technology and Culture* 9 (October):625–27.

Rotella, Elyce J. 1981. *From home to office: U.S. women at work, 1870–1930*. Ann Arbor, Mich.: UMI Research Press.

Rothschild, Joan A. 1981. A feminist perspective on technology and the future. *Women's Studies International Quarterly* 4:65–74.

Rürup, Reinhard. 1974. Historians and modern technology: Reflections on the development and current problems of the history of technology. *Technology and Culture* 15 (April): 161–93.

Scott, Joan Wallach. 1982. The mechanization of women's work. *Scientific American* 247 (September):166–87.

Shriver, Donald W., Jr. 1972. Man and his machines: Four angles of vision. *Technology and Culture* 13 (October):531–55.

Singer, Charles; Holmyard, E. J.; Hall, A. R.; and Williams, Trevor I., eds. 1954–58. *A history of technology*. 5 vols. New York: Oxford University Press.

Sperder, Dale. 1980. *Man made language*. London and Boston: Routledge and Kegan Paul.

Staudenmaier, John Michael, S.J. 1980. Design and ambience: Historians and technology: 1958–1977. Unpublished Ph.D. thesis in American Civilization, University of Pennsylvania.

Thrall, Charles A. 1982. The conservative use of modern household technology. *Technology and Culture* 23 (April):175–94.

Trescott, Martha Moore, ed. 1979. *Dynamos and virgins revisited: Women and technological change in history*. Metuchen, N.J.: Scarecrow Press.

Vanek, Joann. 1978. Household technology and social status: Rising living standards and the status and residence differences in housework. *Technology and Culture* 19 (July): 361–75.

Wertime, Theodore A. 1968. Culture and continuity: A commentary on Mazlish and Mumford. *Technology and Culture* 9 (April):203–12.

White, Lynn, Jr. 1968. *Machina ex deo: Essays in the dynamism of Western culture*. Cambridge, Mass.: MIT Press. Reissued 1971 as *Dynamo and Virgin reconsidered*.

Women in technological history. 1977. *Technology and Culture* 18 (July):496–97.

Zworykin, A. A., et al. 1964. *Geschite der technik*. Trans. from Russian ed., 1962. Leipzig.

Acknowledgments

Every book, even with only one author, is a collective enterprise, drawing on the inspiration, support, and efforts of many persons in seeing the project through from conception to birth. How clearly this is the case with a multi-authored collection of original works in which the authors from a variety of disciplines bring their talents and expertise to bear on a central theme: feminist perspectives on technology. I owe my first and major debt, therefore, to the contributors to *Machina Ex Dea*. There could have been no book without every one of them. I thank my contributors not only for their excellent work, but equally for their forbearance in putting up with my nagging and badgering over everything from commas to language to thrust of their arguments. The authors' intelligence, good grace, and cooperation were a source of strength and support for me.

Dale Spender, originator and former editor of the Athene Series, early expressed her confidence in and her advocacy for the book. Renate Duelli-Klein, current Athene editor, has continued this support and encouragement. Angela Clark, until recently Social Sciences editor at Pergamon, skillfully and patiently guided me, and the manuscript, through to the production stage. Phyllis Hall's capable hands have taken over the work since. To Azizah al-Hibri a special thanks for saying to me, as I spoke about my proposed project yet again, "Stop talking about it—do it!" My thanks to Corky (Corlann Gee) Bush, Linda Henry, Margaret Rossiter, and Carol Brown for critical editing of my chapters for the book.

The women's studies community is the underlying support structure for much of the work herein—for ideas, for scholarship, for networks and feedback, for warm friendships. My thanks also to Victor Ferkiss who sustained my early critical interest in technology issues. Members of SHOT (Society for the History of Technology) and WITH (Women in Technological History) welcomed me into their organizations and encouraged my work on women and technology. My colleagues and my students at Lowell have also sustained my efforts, not the least through their curiosity and often provocative questioning.

To those I may have omitted from the above list, my thanks as well. All, named and unnamed, are absolved of responsibility for my politics and perspective, and for what I have finally let stand as written. Despite some long hours and hard work, putting the book together has proved to be a rewarding and stimulating experience. For those who shared in any way in the enterprise, I hope there have been similar pleasures and rewards.

Charlestown, MA

PART I
WOMEN, TECHNOLOGY, AND PRODUCTION

Introduction

Women and men have shaped their productive activities and have been affected by the productive forces and systems of the societies in which they live. But women and men have experienced production differently. Whether as childbearers and nurturers, workers or homemakers, women have interacted in special ways with production, and thus with tools, machines, and/or technological processes. Thus, a special relationship for women, technology, and production exists. Some of the dimensions of this relationship are explored in this section.

Autumn Stanley, in the opening essay, challenges the received wisdom that women have contributed little or nothing to the history of invention through the ages. Drawing examples from prehistory to modern machinery and medicine, she shows how women have definitively contributed to areas of invention and innovation often considered to be exclusively male. More significantly, she demonstrates that women's inventive achievements are much greater once we begin to include in our history the many productive activities and their associated technologies that are particularly the province of women. An example is women's traditional healing and remedies, some of which are still used or are being rediscovered, such as penicillin's antecedent, bread mold. Thus, Stanley suggests that our very definitions of technology and what we consider to be significant technology will change once we broaden our view to encompass women.

Many productive areas, especially technically and scientifically oriented professions, have been traditionally viewed as male, and women's accomplishments in such fields have largely been hidden from history. Martha Trescott, in the next essay, demonstrates the case in point of Lillian Moller Gilbreth whose prodigious contributions to the field of industrial engineering far outstripped those of her much better known husband, Frank Gilbreth. As Trescott shows, Lillian Gilbreth has been all but ignored in the literature of the field. In taking up a further theme—discussed from very different perspectives by Keller and King later in this volume—Trescott suggests that a female approach to her work may be significantly different from that of a male, with important human, technological, and social consequences.

Women have been systematically excluded from the engineering profession. Focusing particularly on engineering education, Sally Hacker, in the next essay, shows how mathematics has developed as a means to limit women and the field. Originally introduced as a means to stratify the profession for certain males, mathematics testing and requirements came to be employed to limit access of women, and of minorities as well. Noting that the advanced mathematics requirements in engineering education are often not needed for the practice of the profession, Hacker writes that the stress on mathematics reflects the attitudes and values of the white, Anglo-Saxon male leaders of the profession. They find in mathematics the abstract, depersonalized view of the world they are comfortable with, one to which the selected-out candidates and personnel who share this mathematical perspective will conform. Women don't fit the model.

The gender division of labor is also reflected in the different ways technology has affected various categories of women workers, especially those in traditionally female occupations. Denied the necessary training to use new technology, women have often been relegated to less-skilled occupations, then to be replaced by machines. But these patterns can vary. In the clerical field discussed in the next chapter, Roslyn Feldberg and Evelyn Glenn find that in some ways the effects of office automation have followed the critical theory model of increasing worker degradation and proletarianization. But in looking at the insurance industry in particular (with its very high proportion of clerical employees), the authors also found a mixed picture. While job supervision and routinization often increased with the introduction of new technology and job and work process reorganization, for some workers there was also growth in job autonomy and job opportunities.

The effects of technology on household labor have undergone similar analysis and reappraisal. Reviewing some of the current literature, the Rothschild chapter probes the myth and the reality of the claim that household technology liberates women. Although the most burdensome aspects of household work have been eliminated or greatly eased for the woman doing unpaid household labor in the home, Rothschild finds that technology has not freed women from their housewife role. In serving the dominant political and social order, technology has helped to lock women more firmly into their traditional roles in the home. But in easing work and providing material benefits, technology also helps to provide a pre-condition for women's liberation, especially among the more privileged classes.

The chapters in Part I have several implications for the field of technology studies. In calling attention particularly to productive activities associated with women, they indicate areas of research that have been neglected by the standard literature. They also illustrate further ways that women have been omitted from this literature: as individuals contributing to technological change, and as important segments of the workforce often differentially affected by technological change. The work represented here also suggests new ways of looking at the history of technology—broadening its scope and dimensions and altering its focus—and new approaches to the sociology of technology and work that modify accepted findings and offer new frameworks for analysis.

1

Women Hold Up Two-Thirds of the Sky: Notes for a Revised History of Technology

Autumn Stanley

Over two centuries ago, Voltaire declared, "There have been very learned women as there have been women lawyers, but there have never been women inventors" (1764, *s.v.* "Femmes"). Just three decades ago, Edmund Fuller wrote, "For whatever reason, there are few women inventors, even in the realm of household arts. . . . I cannot find a really conspicuous exception to cite" (1955, p. 301). Although Voltaire and Fuller were both mistaken, their view permeates most available accounts of human technological development. A revised account of that development, fairly and fully evaluating women's contributions through the ages, is long overdue.

What would such a revised history of technology look like? In the first place, the very *definition of technology would change*, from what men do to what *people* do. We would no longer find anthropological reports using the active voice to describe male activities (the men *choose* the wood for their bows with care) and the passive voice to describe women's activities (cooking *is done* in water-tight baskets: But by whom? And how did the baskets get to be water-tight?) Nor would any anthropologist say, as George Murdock did in 1973, "The statistics reveal no technological activities which are strictly feminine. One can, of course, name activities that are strictly feminine, e.g., nursing and infant care, but they fall outside the range of technological pursuits" (Murdock & Provost 1973, p. 210). The ethnologist doing a book on cradles (Mason 1889) would no longer be an oddity; and the inventions of the digging stick, child- and food-carriers, methods of food-processing, detoxification, cooking, and preserving, menstrual absorbers and other aspects of menstrual technology, infant formulas, trail foods, herbal preparations to ease (or prevent) childbirth would receive their proper share of attention and be discussed as technology (see, for example, Cowan 1979).

In the second place, *the definition of significant technology would change*. In prehistory, for example, the main focus would shift from hunting and its weapons to gathering and its tools (Tanner 1981)—gathering provided 60 to 80 percent by weight, and the only reliable part, of foraging peoples' diet (Lee & DeVore 1968, p. 7)—and eventually to horticulture and its tools and processes. In later times, the focus would shift from war and its weapons, industry and its machines, to healing and its remedies, fertility and antifertility technology, advances in food production and preservation, child care, and inventions to preserve and keep us in tune with our environment. Again, the change would be from what men do to what people do, with the added dimension of a shift in priorities.

To the degree that these major changes were slow in coming, two further or interim changes would take place. First, the *classification of many women's inventions would change*. For example, the digging stick would be classed as a simple machine, the first lever; the spindle whorl, the rotary quern, and the potter's wheel would be credited with the radical breakthrough of introducing continuous rotary motion to human technology; and women's querns (hand-operated grain mills) would be better known as bearing the world's first cranks. Herbal and other remedies would no longer be classified as "domestic inventions" when invented by women and as medicines or drugs when invented by men. Cosmetics would be classed as the chemical inventions they are, and built-in, multi-purpose furniture, moveable storage walls or room dividers, and the like would no longer be classed as architectural when invented by a man and as domestic when invented by a woman. The nineteenth century's inventions inspired by the Dress Reform Movement could be classed not as wearing apparel but as health and medicinal inventions; and food-processing in all its aspects, including cooking, would fall under agriculture.

Second, *women's creation of or contributions to many inventions significant by either or both definitions would be acknowledged*. In prehistory, women's early achievements in horticulture and agriculture, such as the hoe, the scratch plow, grafting, hand pollination, and early irrigation, would be pointed out. Architecture would grow out of weaving, chemistry out of cooking and perfumery, and metallurgy out of pottery. In more modern times, Julia Hall's collaboration with her brother in his process for extracting aluminum from its ore (Trescott 1979), Emily Davenport's collaboration with her husband on the small electric motor (Davenport 1929), Bertha Lammé's contribution to early Westinghouse generators and other great machines (Matthews n.d.), and Annie C-Y. Chang's contribution to genetic engineering (Patent 1981) would all be recognized.

As a result, we would almost certainly see females as primary technologists in proto- and early human societies, especially in any groups whose division of labor resembled that of the Kurnai ("Man's work is to hunt and fish and then sit down; women's work is all else," Reed 1975, p. 106); as at least equal technologists in such societies as those of the North American Indians and the African !Kung; and as highly important technologists in much of the so-called developing world today. Even in recent Western culture, when women's technological areas regain their true status and significance, and "Anonymous" is no longer so often a woman, women's contributions to technology emerge as much greater than previously imagined. In short, if we consider both history and prehistory, women hold up at least two-thirds of the technological sky.

To see how such a new view of technology might work out in practice, let us look at three areas of human technological endeavor—two that have traditionally been considered significant, but male, preserves; and one originally female preserve that began to be considered significant (i.e., worth including in histories of technology) only when males began to dominate it.

SIGNIFICANT, ASSUMED MALE, TECHNOLOGIES: FIRE AND MACHINES

The taming of fire is one of the most important technological advances of prehistory. Coming as it did (in Europe) in the midst of an ice age, between 75,000 and 50,000 years ago, it enabled Neanderthals to compete with large animals for cave dwellings, and in those dwellings to survive the ice-age winters. It also transformed early human technology. Food could for the first time be cooked, softening it for toothless elders and allowing them to survive longer to transmit more of their culture. Foods could be created out of toxic or otherwise inedible plants, opening up entire new food supplies, and so on. Although this revolutionary advance is usually ascribed to men, Elise Boulding suggests "it seems far more likely that the women, the keepers of home base and the protectors of the young from wild animals, would be the ones whose need for [fire] would overcome the fear of it" (1976, p. 80).

Mythological evidence connects women strongly with the taming of fire. The deities and guardians of the hearth and of fire are often female, from Isis and Hestia, Unči Ahči (Ainu), Chalchinchinatl, and Manuiki (Marquesas) to the Vestal Virgins and the keepers of Brigit's sacred flame in Ireland (Corson 1894, pp. 714–15; Frazer 1930, p. 83; Graves 1955, I, pp. 43, 75; Ohnuki-Tierney 1973, p. 15). The ancient aniconic image of the Great Goddess herself was a mound of charcoal covered with white ash, forming the center of the clan gatherings. A hymn to Artemis tells how she cut her first pine torch on Mysian Olympus and lit it at the cinders of a lightning-struck tree (Graves 1955, I, pp. 75, 84). In Yahi (American Indian) myth, an old woman stole a few coals of fire from the Fire People and brought them home hidden in her ear (Kroeber 1964, p. 79). In Congo myth, a woman named Favorite brought fire from Cloud Land to Earth (Feldman 1963, pp. 102–03).

Several myths show women, particularly old women, as the first possessors of fire, and men stealing fire not from the gods but from women. Examples come from Australia, the Torres Straits, mainland New Guinea, Papua, Dobu Island, the Admiralty Islands, the Trobriand Islands, from the Maori, the Fakaofo or Bowditch Islands north of Samoa, Yap, and Northern Siberia. In a Wagifa myth (Melanesia) the woman, Kukuya, gives fire willingly to the people (Frazer 1930, pp. 5, 15, 18, 23–28, 40, 43–45, 48–49, 50, 55–57, 74, 90–91, 104).

Other myths connect women directly with the making of fire, of course coming later than the taming of existing fire. A rather confusing and probably transitional Guiana Indian explanatory tale begins with an old woman who could vomit fire. At her death, "the fire which used to be within her passed into the surrounding fagots. These fagots happened to be hima-heru wood, and whenever we rub together two sticks of this same timber we can get fire" (Roth 1908–09, p. 133). From the Taulipang of northern Brazil comes a very similar myth representing perhaps a more nearly complete transition: An old woman named Pelenosamo had fire in her body and baked her manioc cakes with it, whereas other people had to bake their cakes in the sun. When she refused to share fire with the people, they seized and tied her, collected fuel, than set Pelenosamo against it and squeezed her body till the fire spurted out. "But the fire changed into the stones called *wato*, which, on being struck, give forth fire" (Frazer 1930, p. 131).

Among the Sea Dyaks of Borneo, a lone woman survived a Great Flood. Finding a creeper whose root felt warm, she took two pieces of this wood, rubbed them together, and thus kindled fire. "Such was the origin of the fire-drill" (apparatus for making fire by friction). Biliku, ancestress of the Andaman Islanders and a creator figure, made fire by striking together a red stone and a pearl shell. In this case, a dove stole fire for the people. Among the Nagas of Assam, two women invented the fire-thong (another fire-making device where the friction comes from pulling) by watching a tiger (or an ape) pull a thong under its claw. The ape, having lost fire, is all hairy, whereas people, having fire to keep them warm, have lost their hairy covering. In the New Hebrides, a woman discovered how to make fire while amusing her little boy by rubbing a stick on a piece of dry wood. When the stick smoked and smoldered and finally burst into flame, she laid the food on the fire and found it tasted better because of it. From that time on, all her people began to use fire (Frazer 1930, pp. 51, 94–95, 99, 105–06).

In the Torres Straits, the very operation of fire-making is called "Mother gives fire," the board from which the fire is extracted by the turning of the stick or drill upon it seen as "mother," and the drill as "child" (Frazer 1930, pp. 26–27). More common is a sexual analogy. Commenting on some of these myths, Frazer (1930) says:

> The same analogy may possibly also explain why in the myths women are sometimes represented as in possession of fire before men. For the fire which is extracted from the board by the revolution of the drill is naturally interpreted by the savage as existing in the board before its extraction . . . or, in mythical language, as inherent in the female before it is drawn out by the male. . . . (pp. 220–21).

This of course would not explain myths ascribing fire first to women in cultures using other fire-making methods.

Whatever the origins of fire in various cultures, women put fire to more uses in their work than men did: protecting infants from animals, warming their living area, fire-hardening the point of their digging sticks, cooking, detoxifying and preserving food, hollowing out wooden bowls and other vessels, making pottery, burning vegetation for gardens. Our familiar Prometheus myth may need a footnote.[1]

When Prometheus was on Olympus stealing fire from Hephaestus, he also stole "mechanical skill." Significantly enough, he stole it from a goddess, Athena, who shared a workshop with Hephaestus (Frazer 1930, p. 194). This seldom-cited Platonic version of the myth takes on new meaning when we reflect that women almost certainly invented the first lever, the digging stick (Stanley 1981, pp. 291–92; Tanner and Zihlman 1976, p. 599), that the crank may have appeared first in the West on women's querns (Lynn White 1978, p. 18; Mason 1894, p. 23), and that at least one historian of technology rates the crank second only to the wheel in importance (Lynn White 1978, p. 17). Women also invented a cassava-processing device called a *mapiti* or *tipiti*, combining the principles of press, screw, and sieve (Mason 1902, pp. 60–61; Sokolov 1978, pp. 34, 38).

In the development of many mechanical processes, the first stages imitated human limb action in using reciprocal (back-and-forth) motion, as for instance in an ordinary hand-saw. Real advances came with continuous or rotary motion, as in the wheel and the circular saw (Singer et al. 1954, chap. 9; Smith 1978, p. 6).[2] Women seem to have introduced rotary motion to human technology; at least three important early examples of rotary motion pertain unmistakably to women's work: the spindle whorl, the rotary quern, and the potter's wheel. In the spindle whorl, women invented the flywheel (Mason 1894, pp. 57–58, 279–80; Lynn White 1978, p. 18n). These early examples of axial rotary motion would certainly have influenced the invention of the vehicular wheel—which may have been women's doing in some cultures. In Meso-America (Mexico and Central America) wheeled vehicles appeared only as miniatures that may be either children's toys or religious objects (Doster et al. 1978, p. 55; Halsbury 1971, p. 13). If toys, they could easily have been made by women.

As we move into the industrial era, we find further evidence refuting stereotypes about women and machines. Women invented or contributed to the invention of such crucial machines as the cotton gin, the sewing machine, the small electric motor, the McCormick reaper, the printing press, and the Jacquard loom. Catherine Greene's much-debated contribution to the cotton gin may never be proven conclusively; but note that Whitney did arrange to pay her royalties and, according to a Shaker writer, once publicly admitted her help (*Shaker Manifesto* 1890, Stanley 1984). In his most famous lecture, "Acres of Diamonds," nineteenth and early twentieth century journalist and lecturer Russell H. Conwell has Mrs. Elias Howe completing in two hours the sewing machine her husband had struggled with for 14 years. Conwell's source was impressive—Elias Howe himself (Conwell 1968, p. 46; Boulding 1976, p. 686). It was also a woman, Helen Augusta Blanchard (1839–1922) of Portland, Maine, who invented zig-zag sewing and the machine to do it (Willard & Livermore 1893, p. 97). The nineteenth century patent records show literally dozens of sewing machine improvements by women.

Emily Goss Davenport's role in the invention of the small electric motor usually ascribed to her husband Thomas—her continuous collaboration with him and her crucial suggestion that he use mercury as a conductor—is best described by Walter Davenport (1929, pp. 47, 55, 62). Other sources merely sentimentally praise her for sacrificing her silk wedding dress to wind the coils of Thomas' first home-made electromagnet.

In the case of the reaper, Conwell (1968) cites "a recently published interview with Mr. McCormick," in which the inventor admitted that after he and his father had tried and failed, "a West Virginia woman . . . took a lot of shears and nailed them together on the edge of a board. Then she wired them so that when she pulled the wire one way it closed them, and . . . the other way it opened them. And there she had the principle of the mowing machine" (pp. 45–46). Another American woman, Ann Harned Manning of Plainfield, New Jersey, invented a mower-reaper in 1817–18. This was apparently a joint invention with her husband William, who patented and is usually credited with inventing it. Ann and William also invented (and he patented) a clover-cleaner (U.S. Patents of Nov. 24, 1830 and May 3, 1831; Hanaford 1883, p. 623; Mozans 1913, p. 362; Rayne 1893, pp. 116–17). The Manning Reaper, predating McCormick's by several years, was important enough to be mentioned in several histories of farm machinery.

Russell Conwell (1968) and Jessie Hayden Conwell (1962) state baldly that farm women invented the printing press and that Mme. Jacquard invented the loom usually credited to her husband.

SIGNIFICANT TECHNOLOGY WHEN TAKEN OVER BY MALES: MEDICINE

As keepers of home base and then of the home, as preeminent gatherers and then propagators of plants, and as caretakers of children until puberty, women traditionally cared for the sick, creating the earliest form of medicine—herbal medicine. The original deities of healing were probably female. Many such deities and reports of their attributes survive, from Neith, Isis, and Gula in the Middle East to Panacea in Greece and Brigit in Ireland. Minerva Medica parallels Athena Hygeia—Great Goddesses worshipped in their healing aspect (Graves 1955, I, pp. 80–81; Hurd-Mead 1938, pp. 11, 32—33; Jayne 1925, pp. 64–68, 71–72, 121, 513; Rohrlich 1980, pp. 88–89).

Except for contraceptives, abortifacients, preparations to ease labor, and other elements of women's or children's medicine, it is difficult to state unequivocally that women invented or discovered any specific remedy or procedure. However, in general, the more ancient any given remedy, the likelier it is to be a woman's invention; and, of course, if a remedy occurs in a group where the healers are women, the presumption is strong.

Many plants are both foods and medicines: asparagus, whose species name *officinalis* means that it once stood on apothecary shelves; clover, a styptic (Weiner 1972, p. 144) and heart stimulant and also a food; rhubarb, both a stewed dessert and an effective laxative. Plants may be both foods and contraceptives: wild yams, Queensland matchbox bean (Himes 1970, pp. 28–29; cf. Goodale 1971, pp. 180–81). Or they may serve as food, medicine, and contraceptive, depending on method of preparation, dosage, and concomitant regimen. An example of this triple usage is the Indian turnip or jack-in-the-pulpit, *Arisaema triphyllum*. The root or corm of this North American wildflower contains needle-like crystals of calcium oxalate (oxalate of lime). After proper preparation, however—drying and cooking or pounding the roots to a pulp with water and allowing the mass to dry for several weeks—the Iroquois and other Indians used it as food. The Pawnee also powdered the root and applied it to the head and temples to cure headache, and the Hopi used it to induce temporary or permanent sterility, depending on the dosage (Jack-in-the-pulpit 1958, p. 851; Weiner 1972, pp. 41, 64–65).

The most ancient medical document yet discovered, a Sumerian stone tablet, dates from the late third millennium BC, when Gula was Goddess of healing and medicine, and most healers were probably still women. The tablet's several prescriptions call for plants and other natural curatives, mentioning not a single deity or demon, and giving no spells or incantations. A tablet from the time of Hammurabi (around 1750 BC) by contrast—when medicine had become a male profession serving mainly elites—blames diseases on demons and suggests incantations as cures. But women healers still ministered to the lower classes, probably continuing to use herbal remedies (Kramer 1963, pp. 93–98; Rohrlich 1980, pp. 88–89).

Precisely parallel developments occurred centuries later in Greece (see, e.g., Graves 1955, I pp. 174–ff.) and still later in Northern Europe, where male doctors trained mostly in theology in Church-run universities wrested control of medicine from their herbally trained female counterparts, some of whom still practiced the old religion. These male usurpers were aided, intentionally or unintentionally, by the Christian Church, which threatened the wise women they called witches with both hell- and earthly fire. Innumerable precious medical secrets no doubt burned with these women at the stake.[3]

To get some idea of what may have been lost in that medieval holocaust, we need only reflect that European peasant women bound moldy bread over wounds centuries before Alexander Fleming "discovered" that a *Penicillium* mold killed bacteria; that medieval wise women had ergot for labor pains and belladonna to prevent miscarriage; and that an English witch discovered the uses of digitalis for heart ailments (Ehrenreich & English 1973, p. 14; Raper 1952, p. 1). Ergot derivatives are the main drugs used today to hasten labor and recovery from childbirth; belladonna is still used as an antispasmodic, and digitalis is still important in treating heart patients (Ehrenreich & English 1973, p. 14). Medieval wise women knew all this at a time when male practitioners knew little to prescribe except bleeding and incantations. Edward II's physician, for example, boasting a bachelor's degree in theology and a doctorate in medicine from Oxford, recommended writing on a toothache patient's jaw "In the name of the Father, the Son, and the Holy Ghost, Amen," or touching a needle first to a caterpillar and then to the tooth (Ehrenreich & English 1973, p. 17). Ladies of medieval epic poetry, repeatedly called upon to treat the ghastly wounds of errant knights, worked their miraculous-seeming cures not through prayer but through deep herbal knowledge and careful nursing (Hughes 1943).

Indeed, these women were the repositories of medical knowledge coming to them in a line of women healers from the days when Hecate the Moon Goddess invented aconite teas for teething and children's fevers, when Rhea invented liniments for the pains of children, when the Egyptian Polydamna gave her pupil Helen the secret of Nepenthe, and when Artemisia of Caria—famed for knowing every herb used in medicine—discovered the uses of artemisia to cause (or in other combinations to prevent) abortion and to expel a retained placenta, the value of wormwood, and the delights of absinthe (Hurd-Mead 1938, pp. 32, 37n, 40; Jayne 1925, p. 345). Thus, we should not be surprised to hear that in the sixteenth century Paracelsus burnt his text on pharmaceuticals because everything in it he had learned from "the Sorceress," i.e., from a wise woman or women he had known (Ehrenreich & English 1973, p. 17).

Although women are connected most intimately with herbal medicine, ancient women healers had accomplishments in other areas. The only surgery mentioned in the Bible is gynecological or obstetrical surgery—or circumcisions—done by women with their flint knives (Hurd-Mead 1938, p. 19). Flint in pre-Hellenic Greek myth was the gift of the Goddess (Spretnak 1978, p. 42). Ancient Scandinavian women's graves contain surgical instruments not found in men's graves. And California Indian medicine women used a technique only now being rediscovered, and still controversial in modern medicine—visualization, for focusing the body's own mental and physical powers of healing on the illness, tumor, or pain (Hurd-Mead 1938, pp. 6, 14).

In late medieval and early modern Europe, women healers continued to work unofficially. The most outstanding of them, such as Trotula, Jacoba or Jacobina, Felicie, and Marie Colinet, sometimes were given more or less recognition by the male medical profession or protected by wealthy patients. Marie Colinet learned surgery from her husband, the renowned surgeon Fabricius of Hilden, but by his own admission she excelled him. For shattered ribs she opened the chest and wired together the fragments of bone—this in the seventeenth century. Her complex herbal plasters prevented infection and promoted healing. She also regulated the postoperative diet and used padded splints. Marie Colinet was first to use a magnet to remove fragments of iron or steel from the eye. Though most sources credit Fabricius with this invention, he credits her (Boulding 1976, pp. 472–75; Hurd-Mead 1938, pp. 361, 433).

During the American colonial period, it is thought that more women practiced medicine than did men (Hymowitz & Weissman 1978, p. 7). Even in the nineteenth century, women healers still ministered to a great many American families, especially in rural areas. Some operated as informally as the Misses Roxy and Ruey Toothacre portrayed in Harriet Beecher Stowe's *Pearl of Orr's Island* (1862, pp. 17–18), and some more formally or professionally. But they relied on time-tested herbal knowledge brought from the Old World and enriched by contact with Indian women healers, while male practitioners relied heavily on bleeding and the poisonous calomel (containing mercury). Moreover, like Lady Aashild in *Kristin Lavransdatter*, like the medieval ladies in the epics, like the German Mother Seigel (b. *ca.* 1793), and like Sister Kenny in the Australian Outback in the twentieth century, they not merely made house calls, but stayed with their seriously ill patients for weeks at a time, personally conducting or supervising their care, medication, and diet (Kenny 1943, e.g., pp. 21–29, 71–72; Stage 1979, chap. 2, pp. 45–63; Anna J. White 1866). Women who observed their patients day and night, watching every symptom and the effect of every remedy, quite naturally gained more practical knowledge than the doctor who spent just a few moments with a patient.

Although the twentieth century finds male practitioners firmly in control of formal Western medicine, women doctors and healers still have important inventions and innovations to their credit.

For example, although three men received the Nobel Prize for penicillin, women participated significantly in the team effort that brought the drug to medical usefulness. Women had discovered the mold's usefulness centuries or perhaps millennia earlier (Halsbury 1971, p. 19; Raper 1952, p. 1), and one nineteenth-century Wisconsin woman, Elizabeth Stone, an early antibiotic therapist, specialized in treating lumberjacks' wounds with poultices of moldy bread in warm milk or water: she never lost an injury patient (Stellman 1977, p. 87). In the twentieth-century development of the drug, it was a woman bacteriologist, Dr. Elizabeth McCoy of the University of Wisconsin, who created the ultraviolet-mutant strain of *Penicillium* used for all further production, since it yielded *900 times as much penicillin* as Fleming's strain (Bickel 1972, p. 185; O'Neill 1979, p. 219).[4] And as Howard Florey, leader of the British penicillin team, was quick to point out, it was Dr. Ethel Florey's precise clinical trials that transformed penicillin from a crude sometimes-miracle-worker into a reliable drug. It was also a woman, Nobel laureate and X-ray crystallographer Dr. Dorothy Crowfoot Hodgkin, who finally determined the precise structure of the elusive penicillin molecule (Bickel 1972, p. 216; Opfell 1978, pp. 211, 219).

Women were also involved in developing the sulfa drugs that preceded penicillin. For instance, it was a married pair of chemists, Prof. and Mme. Tréfouël, and their colleagues at the Pasteur Institute in Paris who split red azo dye to create sulfanilamide (Bickel 1972, p. 50).

At least two women have invented new antibiotics for which they receive sole credit. Dr. Odette Shotwell of Denver, Colorado, came up with two new antibiotics—duramycin and azacolutin—during her first assignment as a research chemist at the Agriculture Department laboratories in Peoria, Illinois. She has also invented new methods for separating antibiotics from fermentation byproducts, and in doing so has played an important role in the development of two other antibiotics: cinnamycin and hydroxystreptomycin. Dr. Marina Glinkina of the USSR directed the laboratory effort that produced a new antigangrene antibiotic during World War II. Her postwar work as a senior scientist has been theoretical (Dodge 1966, p. 226; O'Neill 1979, p. 32; Ribando 1980).

Follies-girl-turned-scientist Justine Johnstone Wanger (1895–) was the laboratory part of the team that developed the slow-intravenous-drip method of administering drugs and other substances to the human body. She then joined a different medical team in applying this new method to the treatment of early syphilis, in an advance that was called the "greatest step since Ehrlich" (Hobson 1941, p. 298).

The DPT vaccine that protects virtually all infants in the developed world against three of their former mass killers (diphtheria; pertussis, or whooping cough; and typhus) was invented by Dr. Pearl Kendrick (1890–1980) and Dr. Grace Eldering (1900–) in the early 1940s. In 1939 they had invented a whooping cough vaccine. Unlike Drs. Salk and Sabin, they refused to allow their vaccines to be named for them. In the 1920s, Dr. Gladys Henry Dick (1881–1963) and her husband conquered another great childhood killer, scarlet fever. They not only isolated the streptococcus causing the disease, but created the toxin and the antitoxin that prevent and cure it, respectively. They then went on to develop the Dick test, a skin test showing susceptibility to the disease. They were recommended for the Nobel Prize in 1925, but no prize was given in medicine for that year. They did, however, receive the Mickle Prize of the University of Toronto, the Cameron Prize of the University of Edinburgh, and several honorary degrees (Dr. Kendrick . . . 1980–81, p. 12; Kendrick 1942; O'Neill 1979, p. 217; *Notable American Women* 1980, pp. 191–92; *Time* 1980, p. 105).

Although two male doctors are credited with developing the vaccines that conquered polio in the developed world, it was a woman, Sister Elizabeth Kenny (1886–1952) of Australia, who invented the only treatment useful once the disease had struck. Whereas the doctors of her day were splinting the affected limbs to prevent spasm—but also causing the damaged muscles to waste away and become useless for life—Sister Kenny used moist hot packs, massage, and daily gentle exercise, plus muscle reeducation. About 87 percent of her patients escaped paralysis, while about 85 percent of the doctors' patients were paralyzed for life. In spite of these results, the established medical profession long rejected her treatment. It was in the United States that she finally found acceptance. By the early 1940s, the National Infantile Paralysis Foundation had officially endorsed her treatment, and she saw the opening of the Elizabeth Kenny Institute in Minneapolis. Awarding her an honorary Doctor of Science degree, the President of the University of Rochester said, "In the dark world of suffering you have lit a candle that will never be put out" (Kenny 1943, *passim* and p. 267; Marlow 1979, pp. 259–65).

In still more recent times, women have contributed significant inventions or innovations in the battle against cancer, on many fronts. Outstanding examples are Drs. Charlotte Friend and Ariel Hollinshead. While working as a virologist at the Sloan-Kettering Institute for Cancer Research in the 1950s, Dr. Friend (1921–) not only demonstrated the viral origins of leukemia (the Friend mouse-leukemia virus), but developed the first successful anticancer vaccine for mammals. She won a *Mademoiselle* magazine achievement award for her work in 1957, and has since then won many other honors, including the Alfred P. Sloan Award (1954, 1957, and 1962), the American Cancer Society Award (1962), and the Virus-Cancer Progress Award from the National Institutes of Health (1974). In 1966, she became director of the Center for Experimental Cell Biology at New York's Mt. Sinai School of Medicine, where her work continues at this writing (Achievement awards 1958, p. 68; *American Men and Women of Science* 1979, p. 1602; O'Neill 1979, p. 224).

Dr. Hollinshead (1929–) is Professor of Medicine at George Washington Medical Center in Washington, DC, and director of its Laboratory for Virus and Cancer Research. Doing both basic and clinical research on cancer, she has helped develop immunotherapy for breast, lung, and gastric cancers as well as melanomas. But she may be best remembered for her lung-cancer vaccines. In the process of inventing these vaccines, which are made from antigens in cancer-cell membranes and are specific for their cancer of origin, she also invented a method of getting antigens out of membranes without destroying their structure, using low-frequency sound. Completed clinical tests show an 80 percent survival rate among those receiving the antigens as opposed to a 49 percent survival rate among the controls. Dr. Hollinshead's work, which opens possibilities for preventing as well as treating cancer, has been called brilliant, "the most advanced and exciting in the world" (*American Men and Women of Science* 1979, p. 2238; Arehart-Treichel 1980; Cancer vaccines . . . 1979, p. 248).

Severely neglected by medical research is the field of menstrual disorders. Although this health condition affects 35 million people in the United States alone, and not just once but every month, in 1974 only eight articles on menstrual pain appeared in the entire world medical literature. Quipped Thomas Clayton, Vice-President for Medical Affairs at Tampax in 1979, "If men had cramps, we'd have had a National Institute of Dysmenorrhea for years" (Thorpe 1980, p. 36; Twin 1979, p. 8).

Dr. Penny Wise Budoff, a family practitioner and medical school professor at the State University of New York (Stony Brook), undertook some dysmenorrhea research. Beginning in the 1970s with new findings on antiprostaglandins (drugs resembling aspirin but much stronger), she experimented first on herself. Most effective was mefenamic acid, and she next recommended mefenamic acid to a few women in her practice. When these patients also reported some relief, Dr. Budoff set up further experiments. By 1980 the U.S. Food and Drug Administration had approved mefenamic acid for treating menstrual pain. Eighty-five percent of the women tested so far have reported significant relief not only from pain but from nausea, vomiting, dizziness, and weakness. Dr. Budoff has also studied premenstrual tension, and recommends a simple dietary change that may give relief without drugs (Budoff 1980; Thorpe 1980, p. 36).

It seems fitting to climax and close this brief review of women inventors and innovators in health and medicine with Nobel laureate Dr. Rosalyn Sussman Yalow. Born in the Bronx in 1921, a brilliant and strong-willed child, she took Marie Curie for a role model at age 17, and seems to have moved with unswerving purpose ever since. She graduated from Hunter College with a physics major at age 19. If she was discouraged at being refused a graduate assistantship at Purdue because she was a New Yorker, Jewish, and a woman—or at being told at Columbia that she must start as secretary to a medical school professor—she did not reveal it. She received her Ph.D. in physics from the University of Illinois in 1945.

After working briefly as an electrical engineer, and teaching physics at Hunter College, she became interested in nuclear medicine and took a research position at the Bronx Veteran's Administration Hospital. Thus began the collaboration with Solomon Berson, M.D., that lasted until Berson's death and produced one of the most powerful research techniques, and one of the most powerful diagnostic tools, of the twentieth century: radioimmunoassay (RIA). RIA is a measurement technique so sensitive that it could detect a teaspoon of sugar in a lake 62 miles long, 62 miles wide, and 30 feet deep. In more practical terms, it has allowed doctors for the first time to measure the circulating insulin in a diabetic's blood.

Physicians and researchers continually find new and exciting uses for RIA. Pediatricians can prevent one kind of mental retardation by detecting and treating an infant thyroid deficiency. The RIA test uses only a single drop of the baby's blood, and costs only about a dollar. Thousands of blood banks now screen their blood with RIA to prevent transfusion hepatitis (the test can detect Hepatitis-B virus). RIA can also detect deficiencies or surpluses in human growth hormone in children so that they can be treated to prevent certain kinds of dwarfism and gigantism; can help explain high blood pressure and infertility; can detect hormone-secreting cancers and other endocrine-related disorders. It can detect heroin, methadone, and LSD in the bloodstream; it can gauge circulating vitamins and enzymes to shed light on human nutrition. It can make antibiotic treatment more precise and even help catch murderers, by revealing minute traces of poison in their victims' bodies. RIA was recently used to diagnose Legionnaires' Disease at an early stage, by detecting *Legionella* antigen in the urine.

Had Yalow and Berson decided to patent RIA, they could have been millionaires. Laboratories selling RIA kits do some $30 million in business each year. Thinking like scientists, however, instead of like entrepreneurs, the two freely published their work.

In awarding Rosalyn Yalow the Nobel Prize for Physiology and Medicine in 1977, the Prize Committee specifically recognized RIA as "the most valuable advance in basic research directly applicable to clinical medicine made in the past two decades" (Levin 1980, p. 135). In her acceptance speech she said:

> We still live in a world in which a significant fraction of people, including women, believe that a woman belongs and wants to belong exclusively in the home; that a woman should not aspire to achieve more than her male counterparts, and particularly not more than her husband. . . . But if women are to start moving toward [our] goal, we must believe in ourselves, or no one else will believe in us; we must match our aspirations with the competence, courage, and determination to succeed, and we must feel a personal responsibility to ease the path for those who come afterward (Stone 1978, p. 34).

Rosalyn Yalow has come a long way from the South Bronx to the chair of Distinguished Professor of Medicine at Mt. Sinai School of Medicine in New York City, where her outstanding work continues (Levin 1980, pp. 133–37; Opfell 1978; Rapid diagnosis . . . 1981, p. 358; Stone 1978, pp. 29–34ff; Yalow 1979).

Through examples from the taming and making of fire to the development of machines and medicine, we have glimpsed the history and prehistory of technology as they would be if women's contributions were included.[5] Most historians of technology to date, looking backward through the distorted glass of a prevailing cultural stereotype that women do not invent, have found, not surprisingly, that women never did invent. If, instead, we examine the evidence—from mythology, anthropology, and history—we find that, as H. J. Mozans wrote nearly 70 years ago:

> More conclusive information respecting woman as an inventor is . . . afforded by a systematic study of the various races of mankind which are still in a state of savagery [sic]. Such a study discloses the interesting fact that woman has . . . —*pace* Voltaire—been the inventor of all the peaceful arts of life, and the inventor, too, of the earliest forms of nearly all the mechanical devices now in use in the world of industry (1913, p. 338).

Our task now is to carry that systematic study of woman's achievement through to the present so that we can, once again, let her own works praise her in the gates.[6]

NOTES

1. Or indeed, a full-scale companion myth. The Prometheus myth is late and literary. The name Prometheus apparently comes from the Sanskrit word for the fire-making drill, or for

the process of making fire by friction. Thus it may be saying only that by inventing fire-making devices, humans stole fire from the realm of the gods and brought it down to the realm of the human (Corson 1894, p. 714).

2. In a striking nineteenth-century recapitulation of this ancient breakthrough, Sister Tabitha Babbitt (d. 1858) of the Harvard, Massachusetts, Shakers independently invented the circular saw about 1810. After watching the brothers sawing, she concluded that their back-and-forth motion wasted half their effort, and mounted a notched metal disk on her spinning wheel to demonstrate her proposed improvement (Deming & Andrews 1974, pp. 153, 156, 157; Anna J. White & Taylor 1904, p. 312). Joseph and Frances Gies reveal that Sister Tabitha intended the blade to be turned by water power (1976, pp. 255–56).
3. Mary Daly (1978) presents the most radical view of this tragic event in human history, accepting the highest reported figure for the almost entirely female deaths: 9,000,000. More conservative scholars have estimated as high as 3,000,000; and calmly rational Elise Boulding (1976) says:

> One could argue that there never was any overt decision to "get the women out," that it all happened by default. On the other hand, given the number of instances in which the church combined with various economic groups from doctors to lawyers to merchant guilds, not only to make pronouncements about the incapacities of women, but often to accomplish the physical liquidation of women through witchcraft and heresy trials, one can hardly say that it all happened without anyone intending it. The exclusion of women was a result of impersonal and intentional forces (p. 505).

4. Had she done this today, she could have patented the organism (*Diamond* v. *Chakrabarty* 1980).
5. For further discussion, see Stanley (1984).
6. "Give her of the fruit of her hands, and let her own works praise her in the gates" (Proverbs 31:31).

REFERENCES

Achievement awards, Dr. Charlotte Friend. 1958. *Mademoiselle*. (January):68.

American Men and Women of Science. 1979. ed. Jacques Cattell Press. 14th ed. New York: Bowker.

Arehart-Treichel, Joan. 1980. Tumor-associated antigens: Attacking lung cancer. *Science News* 118 (July 12):26–28.

Bickel, Lennard. 1972. *Rise up to life: A biography of W. H. Florey*. New York: Scribner's.

Boulding, Elise. 1976. *The underside of history: A view of women through time*. Boulder, Colo.: Westview Press.

Budoff, Penny Wise. 1980. *No more menstrual cramps and other good news*. New York: Putnam.

Cancer vaccines in the works. 1979. *Science News* 117 (April 14):248.

Conwell, Jessie Hayden. 1926 (c. 1865). Inaugural editorial, Ladies' Department, *Minneapolis Daily Chronicle*, weekly ed., *Conwell's Star of the North*. *Russell H. Conwell and his work*. ed. Agnes Rush Burr. Philadelphia: J. C. Winston: 141–44.

Conwell, Russell H. 1968 (1877). *Acres of Diamonds*. Kansas City, Mo.: Hallmark.

Corson, Juliet. 1894. The evolution of home. *Congress of Women*. ed. Mary K. Eagle. Chicago: Conkey. Vol. II:714–18.

Cowan, Ruth Schwartz. 1979. From Virginia Dare to Virginia Slims: Women and technology in American life. *Technology and Culture* 20, 1 (January):51–63.

Daly, Mary. 1978. *Gyn/ecology: The metaethics of radical feminism*. Boston: Beacon Press.

Davenport, Walter Rice. 1929. *Biography of Thomas Davenport, the "Brandon blacksmith," inventor of the electric motor*. Montpelier, Vt.: The Vermont Historical Society.

Deming, Edward; and Andrews, Faith. 1974. *Work and worship: The economic order of the Shakers*. Greenwich, Conn.: New York Graphic Society.
Diamond v. *Chakrabarty*. 100 US 2204 (1980).
Dr. Kendrick dies. 1980–81. *National NOW Times* (Dec./Jan.):12.
Dodge, Norton T. 1966. *Women in the Soviet economy: Their role in economic, scientific, and technical development*. Baltimore: Johns Hopkins.
Doster, Alexis III; Goodwin, Joe; and Ross, Jane M. 1978. *The Smithsonian book of invention*. Washington,DC: Smithsonian Exposition Books.
Ehrenreich, Barbara; and English, Deirdre. 1973. *Witches, midwives, and nurses: A history of women healers*. Old Westbury, N.Y.: Feminist Press.
Feldmann, Susan, ed. 1963. *African myths and tales*. New York: Dell.
Frazer, Sir James George. 1930. *Myths on the origin of fire*. London: Macmillan.
Fuller, Edmund. 1955. *Tinkers and genius*. New York: Hastings House.
Gies, Joseph; and Gies, Frances. 1976. *The ingenious yankees*. New York: Crowell.
Goodale, Jane C. 1971. *Tiwi wives: A study of the women of Melville Island, North Australia*. Seattle: University of Washington Press.
Graves, Robert. 1955. *The Greek myths*. Baltimore: Penguin. 2 vols.
Halsbury, Earl of. 1971. Invention and technological progress (fourth annual Spooner Lecture). *The Inventor* (London). (June):10–34.
Hanaford, Phebe A. 1883. *Daughters of America*. Augusta, Maine: True and Company.
Himes, Norman E. 1970 (1936). *Medical history of contraception*. New York: Schocken.
Hobson, Laura Z. 1941. Follies girl to scientist. *Independent Woman* 20 (October):297–98ff.
Hughes, Muriel Joy. 1943. *Women healers in medieval life and literature*. New York: King's Crown Press.
Hurd-Mead, Kate Campbell. 1938. *A history of women in medicine*. Haddam, Conn.: Haddam Press. [1973. Boston: Milford House.]
Hymowitz, Carol; and Weissman, Michaele. 1978. *A history of women in America*. New York: Bantam.
Jack-in-the-pulpit. 1958. *Encyclopedia Britannica* 12.
Jayne, Walter Addison. 1925. *The healing gods of ancient civilizations*. New Haven, Conn.: Yale University Press.
Kendrick, Pearl L. 1942. Use of alum-treated pertussis vaccine, and of alum-precipitated combined pertussis vaccine and diphtheria toxoid for active immunization. *American Journal of Public Health* 32 (June):615–26.
Kenny, Elizabeth. 1943. *And they shall walk*. New York: Dodd Mead.
Kramer, Samuel N. 1963. *The Sumerians: Their history, culture, and character*. Chicago: University of Chicago Press.
Kroeber, Theodora. 1964. *Ishi, last of his tribe*. Berkeley, Calif.: Parnassus.
Lee, Richard B.; and DeVore, Irven, eds. 1968. *Man the hunter*. Chicago: Aldine.
Levin, Beatrice S. 1980. *Women and medicine*. Metuchen, N.J.: Scarecrow.
Marlow, Joan. 1979. *The great women*. New York: A & W Publishers.
Mason, Otis T. 1889. *Cradles of the North American Indians*. Seattle: Shorey.
Mason, Otis. T. 1894. *Woman's share in primitive culture*. New York: D. Appleton.
Mason, Otis T. 1902 (1895). *Origin of inventions*. London: Scott.
Matthews, Alva. n.d. Some Pioneers, unpub. speech delivered to the Society of Women Engineers, n.p.
Mozans, H. J. 1913. *Woman in science*. New York: D. Appleton.
Murdock, George P.; and Provost, Caterina. 1973. Factors in the division of labor by sex. *Ethnology* 12 (April):203–25.
Notable American Women: the modern period. 1980. eds., Barbara Sicherman and Carol Hurd Green. Cambridge, MA: Harvard Univ. Press.

Ohnuki-Tierney, Emiko. 1973. The shamanism of the Ainu. *Ethnology* 12 (March):15ff.
O'Neill, Lois Decker, ed. 1979. *The women's book of world records and achievements*. Garden City, N.Y.: Doubleday/Anchor.
Opfell, Olga S. 1978. *The lady laureates; Women who have won the Nobel prize*. Metuchen, N.J.: Scarecrow Press.
Patent for gene-splicing, cloning, awarded Stanford. 1981. *Stanford Observer* (January):1f.
Raper, Kenneth B. 1952. A decade of antibiotics in America. *Mycologia* 45 (Jan.-Feb.):1–59.
Rapid diagnosis of legionellosis. 1981. *Science News* 6 (June):358.
Rayne, Martha Louise. 1893. *What can a woman do: Or, her position in the business and literary world*. Petersburgh, N.Y.: Eagle.
Reed, Evelyn. 1975. *Woman's evolution: from matriarchal clan to patriarchal family*. New York: Pathfinder.
Ribando, Curtis P. 1980. Personal communication, March 26; Patent Advisor, United States Department of Agriculture Northern Regional Research Center, Peoria, Illinois.
Rohrlich, Ruby. 1980. State formation in Sumer and the subjugation of women. *Feminist Studies* 6 (Spring):76–102.
Roth, Walter E. 1908–09. An inquiry into the animism and folk-lore of the Guiana Indians. 30th Annual Report, Bureau of American Ethnology, Washington, DC.
Shaker Manifesto. 1980. American women receiving patents. Vol. 2, no. 7, July, n.p.
Singer, Charles; Holmyard, E. J.; and Hall, A. R. 1954. *A history of technology*. Oxford, Eng.: Oxford University Press.
Smith, Denis. 1978. Lessons from the history of invention. *The Inventor* (London). (January):6ff.
Sokolov, Raymond. 1978. A root awakening. *Natural History* 87 (November):34ff.
Spretnak, Charlene. 1978. *Lost goddesses of ancient Greece: A collection of pre-Hellenic mythology*. Berkeley, Calif.: Moon Books.
Stage, Sarah. 1979. *Female complaints: Lydia Pinkham and the business of women's medicine*. New York: W. W. Norton.
Stanley, Autumn. 1981. Daughters of Isis, daughters of Demeter: When women sowed and reaped. *Women's Studies International Quarterly* 4: 3:289–304.
Stanley, Autumn. 1984. *Mothers of invention: Women inventors and innovators through the ages*. Metuchen, N.J.: Scarecrow.
Stellman, Jeanne M. 1977. *Women's work, women's health: Myths and realities*. New York: Pantheon.
Stone, Elizabeth. 1978. A Madame Curie from the Bronx. *The New York Times Magazine*, April 9, pp. 29–34ff.
Stowe, Harriet Beecher. 1862. *The pearl of Orr's Island*. Boston: Houghton Mifflin.
Tanner, Nancy M. 1981. *On becoming human: A model of the transition from ape to human and the reconstruction of early human social life*. Cambridge, Eng.: Cambridge University Press.
Tanner, Nancy; and Zihlman, Adrienne. 1976. Women in evolution. Part I: Innovation and selection in human origins. *Signs* 1 (Spring):585–608.
Thorpe, Susan. 1980. The cure for cramps: It took a woman doctor. *Ms*. (November):36.
Time. 1980. [Kendrick obit.] (Oct 20):105.
Trescott, Martha Moore. 1979. Julia B. Hall and aluminum. *Dynamos and virgins revisited*, ed. M. M. Trescott.: 149–79.
Trescott, Martha Moore, ed. 1979. *Dynamos and virgins revisited: Women and technological change in history*. Metuchen, N.J.: Scarecrow Press.
Twin, Stephanie L., ed. 1979. *Out of the bleachers: Writings on women and sport*. Old Westbury, N.Y.: Feminist Press.
Voltaire. 1764. *Dictionnaire philosophique*. Paris: Garnier.

Weiner, Michael A. 1972. *Earth medicine—earth foods: Plant remedies, drugs, and natural foods of the North American Indians.* London: Collier Macmillan.
White, Anna J. 1866. The mystery explained. *Shaker Almanac*:6 ff.
White, Anna J.; and Taylor, Leila S. 1904. *Shakerism, its meaning and message.* Columbus, Ohio: Fred J. Heer.
White, Lynn, Jr. 1978. *Medieval religion and technology.* Berkeley: University of California Press.
Willard, Frances E.; and Livermore, Mary A., eds. 1893. *A woman of the century.* Buffalo: Moulton.
Yalow, Rosalyn. 1979. Speech delivered to the American Physical Society Convention, January, New York City.

2

Lillian Moller Gilbreth and the Founding of Modern Industrial Engineering*[1]

Martha Moore Trescott

HISTORICAL OVERVIEW

Dr. Lillian M. Gilbreth (1878–1972) has been called "America's first lady of engineering" (SWE 1978, p. 1). Yet, many of Dr. Gilbreth's impressive intellectual contributions and much of their true significance have been lost to history.

Lillian M. Gilbreth began her pioneering research in human relations during the first decade of the twentieth century, in the heyday of the rise of scientific management. Frederick W. Taylor, known as the "Father of Scientific Management," had been engaged in time studies and the rationalization of various industrial work processes, serving as a consultant in the reorganization of many different kinds of factories, for about two decades when Lillian began serious research into the psychology of work. As mass production grew and spread to so many American industries, Taylor and his disciples, including Frank Bunker Gilbreth, were seeking to improve the efficiency and productive capacity of the worker by innovation of different arrangements of work, elimination of unnecessary motions, and subdivision and specialization of labor. In these efforts, Taylor and his colleagues focused minutely on the physical aspects of work—bending, lifting, walking, and so on—and misunderstood or ignored the psychology of workers. Taylor felt, for example, that better pay through wage incentives and the simpli-

* The author gratefully acknowledges the assistance of Mr. Keith Dowden, Chief Archivist, Gilbreth Collection, Purdue University. Without his help and access to the Gilbreth Collection, this essay could not have been prepared. Also, she wishes to acknowledge the Rockefeller Foundation, which provided grant funds for her study of the history of women engineers in the United States, 1850–1975.

fication of workers' jobs would provide workers a vested interest in Taylorism. Yet, labor complained bitterly and organized against Taylor's stopwatch, the monotony of work and the meaninglessness of overly simplified jobs over which there was little control by labor, particularly on the assembly line.

Into this relatively insensitive approach, Lillian Gilbreth brought her interpersonal presence and understanding of human behavior. In 1904 she married Frank B. Gilbreth (1868–1924), a disciple of Taylor and an expert in motion study. The Gilbreths worked together in scientific management—in their consulting firm advising companies which were to become the most important firms in the United States; in research and writing (together they authored hundreds of documents); in lectures at companies, universities, professional societies; in conducting the Gilbreth summer schools on management topics; and in raising their twelve children (*Cheaper By the Dozen* is their story, written by a daughter, Ernestine, and a son, Frank, Jr.) (Gilbreth, Jr. and Carey 1948; also see, e.g., Gilbreth Collection,* Gilbreth, L. M., Address, and correspondence, Rich; GC, Minutes). However, Lillian has received far less credit than Frank by engineers and historians alike. She has been considered an adjunct of Frank, even though he died at the age of only 56 in 1924, while she headed Gilbreth, Inc. for decades afterward. She has been considered primarily his assistant or disciple, even though he never earned a college degree and she attained the Ph.D.

Her own expertise lay in the realm of integrating psychology and considerations of mental processes with time-and-motion work, while it is recognized among their colleagues that "if Frank Gilbreth slighted any discipline in his consideration, it was psychology" (Barnes 1968, p. 15; Caples 1969, p. 72; Gomberg 1969, p. 77; Potter 1969; Spriegel & Myers 1953; Vaughn 1977). If she is cited by historians, discussions are often limited to her contributions to domestic engineering (e.g., design of kitchens and appliances), as in Siegfried Giedion's *Mechanization Takes Command*. Giedion also attributes to Frank work on the psychology of management (Giedion 1948, pp. 121, 525, 615–16). Historians, hailing Elton Mayo's studies of the Hawthorne plant of Western Electric in the 1920s as the beginning of "the human relations movement" in industrial engineering, usually fail to cite Lillian Gilbreth's relevant ideas and publications which preceded by over a decade Mayo's important study, and which were recognized as pioneering by her colleagues by at least 1921 (Guest 1967, pp. 61–63). Indeed, Robert Guest emphasizes that "the challenge for tomorrow's enlightened management" is to combine the "advantages of Scientific Management with the contributions of behavioral science to the understanding

---

* cited hereafter as GC.

of the nature of human work" and to help release "the great potential of the mind" (Guest 1967, pp. 63–64). Yet, 54 years before Guest's comments and before the rise of "sensitivity training" in management, that is just what Lillian Gilbreth embarked upon.

Historians of technology, business, industry, and management have typically not dealt at all, or at best in only superficial way, with either Lillian or Frank Gilbreth, despite the exhibit on their work shown at the Smithsonian Institution in Washington, D.C., in 1980. It is especially frustrating that such obscurity and lack of real understanding continues to surround her work.

David F. Noble has discussed the Gilbreths briefly in *America by Design*, claiming that "the single most important proponent of a broader view of the 'human factor' within the scientific-management movement was Frank Gilbreth" and that "the most significant contribution Gilbreth made to the revisionist movement within scientific management . . . was his marriage to Lillian Moller." The historian Milton Nadworny, as Noble also notes, rightly credits Lillian with emphasis on "the human element" and psychological matters in management (Noble 1977, pp. 274–75). Various other historians such as David Landes (1969), and also contributors to the two volumes of *Technology in Western Civilization* (including Guest), do not mention the Gilbreths at all, while citing Frederick W. Taylor, who is most often claimed to be "*The* Father of Scientific Management" (Kranzberg & Pursell 1967, Landes 1969). In his *Bibliography of the History of Technology*, Eugene Ferguson does cite sources on or by the Gilbreths, especially in his section on "Scientific Management and Systems Analysis" (Ferguson 1968, pp. 301–03, 116–17), but Alfred D. Chandler in *The Visible Hand* mentions Frank Gilbreth only once (Chandler 1977, p. 466). Both Gilbreths deserve more attention from historical research; Lillian more so, as she was vigorous and professionally active almost until the time of her death at the age of 94 in 1972, having outlived Frank by nearly fifty years. During this time, she not only headed Gilbreth, Inc. (in effect, she had been at its helm during much of Frank's lifetime, too), but also became a full professor of management in the School of Mechanical Engineering at Purdue in 1935, head of the Department of Personnel Relations at Newark School of Engineering in 1941, and visiting professor of management at the University of Wisconsin at Madison in 1955. Also, her humane approach to scientific management, which now seems considerably ahead of her time, not only aimed sincerely to improve human relations among workers and managers (her approach, consistent with Adlerian psychology, can also be seen in her works on the home and family) but also affected women workers positively (Appel 1982; Gilbreth, L. M. 1927, 1928; Gilbreth, L. M., Thomas, and Clymer 1954. See also Gilbreth, L. M., Schlesinger Library file, and further discussion later in this chapter).

THE PSYCHOLOGY OF MANAGEMENT *AND ENGINEERING THOUGHT AND PRACTICE*

According to the Society of Women Engineers, Lillian Gilbreth "pioneered in the field of time-and-motion studies, showed companies how to improve management techniques and how to increase industrial efficiency and production by budgeting time and energy as well as money" (SWE 1978, p. 1). Her major contributions lie in two directions: (1) the incorporation into time and motion analysis of psychological considerations, as conceived in broad terms (problem-solving and the behavior of individuals and related topics such as incentives, the nature of the work environment, monotony, and the transference of skill among jobs and industries); and (2) the establishment of industrial engineering curricula in engineering schools in this country and abroad. The first of those will be the focus here, with some comments on the second.

With graduate studies in psychology at the University of California, Berkeley, and Brown University (she obtained her Ph.D. in 1915), Lillian Gilbreth was perhaps the best trained psychologist dealing with time-and-motion study at the time. Neither Frederick W. Taylor nor Frank Gilbreth had had any special training in psychology. Lillian's insights and those of her students and others (both male and female) whom she inspired, helped reduce workers' resistance to scientific management. Complementing Frank's work in physiological areas, her work helped to establish forerunners for the study of human factors in engineering design.

Of her great volume of writings and lectures, her early book, *The Psychology of Management* (1914), which stemmed from her Ph.D. research, is the most important in the history of engineering thought. This book was termed "a golden gift to industrial philosophy" by George Iles (who had subsumed her work under Frank's in a book he compiled in 1917) (Iles 1917, pp. ix–x). When the Society of Industrial Engineers made her an honorary member in 1921 (she was the second person to be so honored; Herbert Hoover was also made an honorary member of SIE), it was commented that:

> she was the first to recognize that management is a problem of psychology, and her book, *The Psychology of Management*, was the first to show this fact to both the managers and the psychologists. . . . Today it is recognized as authoritative (SIE 1921, pp. 2–3).

In the literature of scientific management prior to World War I, there was little coverage of topics which Lillian treated in depth, such as the psychology of work and management, and it was in this relative vacuum at the early date of 1914 that *The Psychology of Management* appeared. Others such as

Hugo Munsterberg had studied industrial psychology at about the same time as Lillian's work appeared. However, as Robert T. Livingston, a professor of industrial engineering at Columbia, commented in 1960, "Munsterberg's writings went largely unrecognized" for a long while (1960, p. 126). Secondly, no one prior to Lillian Gilbreth in *The Psychology of Management* had brought together the basic elements of management theory, which are:

1. Knowledge of individual behavior.
2. Theories of groups.
3. Theories of communication.
4. Rational bases of decision-making (Livingston 1960, p. 126).

Although not always addressed in this modern terminology, Dr. Gilbreth dealt with these areas, some in more depth than others. The subtitle of her book, *The Function of the Mind in Determining, Teaching and Installing Methods of Least Waste*, more nearly captures the scope of her concerns than to think of her work strictly in the sense of industrial psychology. Her concern was not primarily with industrial psychology as we might understand that field today. She was writing in the context of scientific management which had previously focused almost entirely on the physiological, rather than the mental and emotional, characteristics of workers and managers. Her book deals in depth with the "function of the mind," or problem-solving, decision-making, planning, communicating, measuring, and evaluating in various work and managerial environments. She particularly revised Taylor not only in dealing with workers' feelings. She also focused on group behavior and the coordination of activities among work groups, critical for the functioning of the modern corporation (as Alfred D. Chandler and others note), but which was unaddressed by Taylor (Chandler 1977, pp. 276–77; and Guest 1967, p. 60–63).

In *The Psychology of Management*, Lillian dealt as minutely with the psychology of the worker as Frank did with the worker's physiology. She pioneered in considering the "individuality" of the worker, and devoted a whole chapter to that topic, commenting on individual teaching, incentives, and welfare. The approaches of both Taylor and Frank Gilbreth left much to be desired in enabling each worker to feel himself or herself a unique individual. Lillian's insight on and sensitivity to the needs of individuals had been honed by graduate work in psychology, as well as by years of raising a large family (a sense of her human insight emerges in her works on homemaking and child-raising) (Gilbreth, L. M. 1928, e.g., pp. 54–55; and Gilbreth, L. M. 1927).

Throughout *The Psychology of Management*, she is able virtually to transform time-and-motion study into the rudiments of modern managerial practices. While she does draw on the literature available, including her husband's work, it is clear that her analysis represents a new point of departure in management. At various points, her analysis demonstrates her empathy with how workers *feel*, about which there is little in the literature of scientific management at that time.

Her chapter on individuality, especially on "knowledge of individual behavior," clearly demonstrates her innovative work in management theory. And yet not even this most obvious contribution is noted in the American Society of Mechanical Engineers (ASME) volume covering *Fifty Years Progress in Management, 1910–1960*. Munsterberg, Gillespie, Lecky and other psychologists are cited but not Mrs. Gilbreth (who, incidentally, was co-author of the introductory, overview essay).

As early as 1911, Lillian Gilbreth had introduced the first mention of the psychology of management at any management meeting at the Dartmouth College Conference on scientific management (GC, Dartmouth), presenting aspects of the material that formed the basis for her dissertation and her book. Thus, she was truly among the earliest of those studying the interfaces between psychology and management—both in industry and in the home, a foremost pioneer (GC, Gilbreth, L. M., Discussion of Dr. Person's paper).

In the extensive Gilbreth Collection at Purdue, perhaps the richest in engineers' papers I've seen, one finds her own brief career sketch of her work, differentiating her contributions from Frank's. (She wrote this as part of her application for membership in the ASME, which had not exactly sought her as a member, despite her renown.) Between 1904 and 1914, when Frank B. Gilbreth, Inc. operated as a construction company, she said, "I was chiefly employed in the systems work, standardizing practice. The results were published in *Field System*, *Concrete System*, and *Bricklaying System*," all of which show only Frank's authorship. She continued:

> I was also engaged in the perfecting of the methods and devices for laying brick by the packet method, and in the design and construction of reinforced concrete work. This work had to do with the management as well as the operating end.
>
> In 1914 our company began to specialize in management work. I was placed in charge of the correlation of engineering and management psychology, and became an active member of the staff making visits to the plants systematized in order to lay out the method of attack on the problems, being responsible for getting the necessary material for the installation into shape, working up the data as they accumulated, and drafting the interim and final reports. I was also in charge of research and teaching, and of working up such mechanisms, forms and methods as were needed for our type of installation of scientific management, motion study, fatigue study and skill study. These had to do not only with the handling of men, but with the simplification and standardization of the machinery and tools, for the use of both the normal and the handicapped. During Mr. Gilbreth's frequent and prolonged absences, both in this country and abroad,

> I was in responsible charge of all branches of the work. This was also the case while he was in the service, and while he was recovering from his long illness incurred therein.
>
> Since Mr. Gilbreth's death, June 14, 1924, I have been the head of our organization, which consisted of Consulting Engineers and does work in management, and I have had responsible charge of the research, installation and the teaching, in this country and abroad (GC, Gilbreth, L. M., Biog. memo).[2]

Lillian considered herself—and was considered by others—an expert in fatigue study, in the study of skill and its transference among industries and jobs, in precision in measurement, and in standardization of the work of both managers and laborers, as well as in the more narrowly defined psychological areas. She was also known as both a researcher and teacher. *The Psychology of Management* shows her early interest in many of these areas, with entire chapters on measurement, standardization, and teaching, stemming from her original Ph.D. work.

CONTRIBUTIONS TO EDUCATION AND EFFECTS ON WOMEN

As both Lillian and Frank conceived scientific management, teaching was integral to implement and disseminate its practice. Even though instruction of employees within given firms was crucial to the spread of scientific management practice, educational effort of a different order was needed to integrate scientific management with engineering disciplines intellectually for the academic community. A brilliant researcher and teacher with a grasp of theory and practice and of the evolution of the field, Lillian Gilbreth brought her experience with workers and managers and as an academic to this task. Her reputed tact and diplomacy also served her well in integrating developments in industry and the universities.

Her upper-level undergraduate and graduate courses in management at Purdue in the 1930s and 1940s were "open only to graduate students and to seniors of outstanding ability" and covered "investigation of specific management problems in the fields of organization, time-and-motion study, industrial accounting, factory layout, economic selection and equipment, and similar topics" (*Bulletin of Purdue University* 1934–35—1949–50).

She authored papers and spoke about encouraging women to go into industrial engineering and management in this country and abroad. And at the Gilbreth Summer Schools, which she conducted, at least half the participants from various countries (mostly European) were women (GC, Gilbreth Summer Schools).

Lillian's work with and on behalf of women—from the handicapped homemaker to the female worker in the factory and office to the professional in management and engineering and to women consumers in general—is a forgotten chapter in women's history.

Although an upper-middle-class housewife and professional herself, her work and its effects extended beyond that of her own class to benefit lower-class women as well, women whose lives had not necessarily improved with the thrust of industrial and technological change. This work included her research into the improvement of housework and, most significantly, a focus on the handicapped homemaker; her work for this dispossessed group was part of her long-standing research on jobs for the handicapped generally (Berch 1980; Gilbreth, F. B. & L. M. 1920; Rusk 1969, p. 89; Yost & Gilbreth, L. M. 1944, 1945. Also see GC, Gilbreth, L. M., various process charts, and The Engineer in the Home).

We also tend to forget the onerous conditions which prevailed in the nineteenth and well into the twentieth centuries for industrial workers, especially females, before modern managerial practices were introduced. When scientific management is criticized for fostering control over workers, we need to remind ourselves that women workers particularly have been tightly controlled and dominated by their supervisors since the inception of the factory system. Many times they labored under a domineering male who summarily fired them, or worse, if they refused his advances or otherwise displeased him. Their fate was largely left to the whim of one man. Under scientific management—and especially as it was revised by Lillian Gilbreth and others—managerial tasks were more specialized and subdivided, just as were all areas of work. Therefore, workers, including women, were more likely to be and were, in fact, judged by more than one manager. (The record shows that such abusive behavior is inhibited when a male supervisor is subjected to peer scrutiny.) (Gilbreth, L. M. 1914; Gilbreth, L. M. & Cook 1947).

Lillian's concern with the subdivision of management meant that one foreman would not be both disciplinarian and supervisor. Standardization of ways of reporting and evaluating workers' progress and established grievance procedures meant that firing a person would not be left to the whim of just one man. In *The Psychology of Management*, Lillian was primarily concerned with such standardizing of managerial practices so that workers operated under precise, well-articulated, as opposed to unpredictable, conditions. We can argue that such practices benefited women workers—subject as they were to sexual harassment—much more than male workers. Clearly, when assessing the effects of scientific management, as modified by Lillian Gilbreth, it is important to differentiate between female and male workers, as Mary H. Blewett shows we should in earlier industrial history (Blewett 1981, p. 82).

Lillian's work also included improved lighting, reduced pollution, rest intervals and breaks, incentives for workers, and, along with Frank, greater control by workers over their own speed and tasks. She studied chairs and positions in which women worked, so as to reduce fatigue and backache.

Gilbreth, Inc. often consulted with firms that either employed mostly female workers (both clerical and factory operatives) or made products that would be used mostly by women. No doubt having a woman at the helm was instrumental for the Gilbreth firm's obtaining these contracts. For example, in the 1920s, Gilbreth, Inc. completed a monumental and strongly pro-female study of the sanitary pad, plus a report on menstruation and fatigue, for Johnson & Johnson. There were very few studies on menstruation, and very little was known about fatigue during a woman's period, particularly effects on women at work; many employers assumed that menstruating women could not work well, if at all. Lillian's study was a lengthy inquiry; it carefully delineated the characteristics of the various sanitary pads on the market, and contained recommendations about how to increase the women's comfort and protection during menstruation. Growing out of her own expertise, her study on fatigue here helped refute myths that women were incapacitated at such times and unable to work (GC, Report of Gilbreth, Inc.; Gilbreth, F. B. and L. M. 1916).

Other important Gilbreth customers were Burroughs, whose machines were operated mostly by women in financial institutions; Macy's, most of whose sales force and certain managers were women by the 1920s; and the Green Line Cafeteria, managed and run by women. The Gilbreths also made studies for laundries, typically employing women, on such motions as handkerchief-folding, Lillian having studied such operations in detail in her own home. We may speculate that a woman-led Gilbreth, Inc. could work more effectively and sensitively with firms oriented to women as workers and/or consumers (as many companies still are) (GC, Green Line, Burroughs, Macy, Remington, Lies, Sealy, and Typing, Shorthand).

The new jobs that opened up in offices, stores, and factories in this period increased the range of options for women for work outside the home. Although many of these jobs have since become dead-end, they were seen then as new frontiers for paid work by groups, such as women and the handicapped, whose work opportunities were far more limited before. Specialization was the key to the hiring of these new groups of employees. In the context of the rise of specialization, the effect of Lillian Gilbreth's humane rendering of scientific management was to improve working and managerial conditions, and to improve relations between workers and managers. Thereby, she felt, productivity and the welfare of all would be enhanced. Unlike men in her field such as Taylor, who may well have primarily sought greater control of workers, Lillian Gilbreth was concerned with the overall welfare of individuals, whether male or female, homemakers or factory workers, handicapped or able-bodied, young or old, upper class or poor (a view never disputed by her acquaintances whom I have interviewed). She was a *woman* researcher in scientific management, and that meant a very different approach and concern than that of male colleagues. She was holistic and interested in people's health and well-being. Largely because of her influence and of those who followed, management theory and practice evolved away from the strict, stern scientific management of Frederick Taylor and his disciples.

In her work with young people, she encouraged women as well as men into the increasingly important field of industrial engineering. She wrote papers, for example, on "Industrial Engineering As a Career for Women" and on "Opportunities for Women in Industrial Engineering," the latter for the Women's Engineering Society in Britain in 1924. She also initiated a survey of all female members of the Society of Industrial Engineers in 1924 (a grand total of eight at that time) to encourage their more active participation in the Society. Each of these eight women was interested in and/or working in personnel work at the time of the survey (GC, Gilbreth, L. M., Opportunities, pp. 2–3; correspondence, Dent; Industrial Engineering).

She taught women at the university level and served as mentor to women such as Anne Shaw of Britain, Irene Witte of Germany, and Charlotte Thumen of France, all of whom were involved in scientific management.[3] Anne Shaw studied under Lillian Gilbreth at the Gilbreth motion study laboratory and was known in management and engineering circles for her use of the chronocyclograph technique in England (GC, Gilbreth, L. M., correspondence, Faunce, Marts; GC, Gilbreth Summer Schools, Thumen, van Kleeck).

In the manuscripts of Lillian Gilbreth, there is a paper on "The Industrial Engineer" by a woman who felt in 1933 that, since to become an industrial engineer "requires a long and rigid training, a four-year course in mechanical engineering at a technical college is a great asset, especially to a woman who will want to have her preparation for the work beyond question" (GC, Pilune, p. 1. See also ASME 1960, pp. 136, 138–39; Witte 1969, p. 109). Although Lillian Gilbreth told the Women's Engineering Society in 1924 that the SIE, the American Management Association, ASME, and other professional groups were open to women and already had a few women members, she had to go to some lengths to become a member of ASME in 1926. She noted, too, that some of the courses in industrial engineering and business administration in the men's colleges were still closed to women in the 1920s (continuing, we might add, in some schools into our own day) (GC, Gilbreth, L. M., Opportunities; correspondence, ASME).

TOWARD A NEW PARADIGM

Not only Lillian Gilbreth's work with and for women, but also her various contributions to industrial engineering and its precursors, spanning nearly seven decades, have been only partly and vaguely acknowledged. Although she helped formulate much of the theoretical underpinnings of the field, she has been too narrowly labeled a "psychologist." This is not to say that she did not treat such topics as the study of "psychopathic types in industry," for she did that as well (GC, Gilbreth, L. M., Possible psychopathic types). It is to say that her work covered the study and measurement of a wide range of mental (and physical) processes involved in work and management. The precursors of the modern notion of "the work of a professional manager," in terms of "planning, organizing, integrating and measuring," in Harold Smiddy's conception, can be seen in Lillian's published works, including *The Psychology of Management*, and in the records of studies she did for various firms, held in the Gilbreth Library. Yet, when Smiddy and other modern writers view the evolution of ideas about the function of the mind in management, Lillian Gilbreth's work is typically ignored (Smiddy 1960).

After Frank's death in 1924, she continued to be a prolific writer and to participate in meetings of professional groups such as the ASME, presiding over sessions as one on "Management Research" in 1933. Even before her husband died, the Gilbreths together authored well over fifty papers on scientific management topics, not including those written by each of them as sole author, nor including their books and consulting reports. While Lillian's name alone appears on a few of these papers, she is the likely main author of at least such works as "The Place of the Psychologist in Industry," "The Individual in Modern Management," "Psychiatry and Management," "The Relation of Posture to Fatigue of Women in Industry," and similar papers. She may well have been the principal investigator and author of articles credited to them both in the areas of fatigue, standardization, and transference of skill (GC, Gilbreth, Frank, N File, pp. 124-3 through 125).

Her original work and contributions have been buried not only by the circumstance of marriage to a man in the same general field (even though her career also obviously benefited in many ways from this close association with Frank, in terms of directions her interests took, just as Frank's work benefited from the marriage, though his contributions were not so obscured by marriage). Her work has also been partially obscured because of Frank's wish that both their names appear on all they wrote, even though this did not always happen. Yet, because her own expertise and that of her husband were so clearly differentiated in many areas, and because she outlived him so long, establishing authority "in her own right," it is possible to resurrect her unique contributions, at least in part.

It is important that we remember the context of Lillian's work which emphasized the "human element" in scientific management. Being among the first to be so concerned with the human factor meant that she undertook to explore a frontier. Many subject areas were legitimate topics of her research, since the human element is pervasive in all areas of her work. As she, and others who came after her, worked, an increasing number of avenues for investigation were opened and a certain definition of the field evolved. *The Psychology of Management* was an entering wedge, opening whole new areas to scientific management, which have later evolved into mainstream topics in industrial engineering. *The Psychology of Management* was a departure from classical scientific management and from which much modern management theory has taken shape.

Lillian Gilbreth's path-breaking research would likely have not been as influential as it was in molding industrial engineering had she not lived and been so active in as many areas of the field in its formative stages. Of the early pioneers of scientific management, Lillian Gilbreth was a key figure among the surviving members of the pre-World War I investigators during most of this century. She not only lived longer than the others, but was active in industrial engineering longer. Also, of those who lived into mid-century (and beyond), she was among the few who became outstanding and productive academics as well as businesspersons and consultants. Thus, as a liaison from the early pioneering group of researchers to later generations, and as a "gatekeeper" of knowledge about scientific management and industrial engineering between academia and business, she played a central role in interpreting the shape and directions of industrial engineering as the field evolved. In fact, because of her consulting work, research and publications, lectures, courses and workshops and, therefore, her prestige and popularity, she may have contributed more in the first four decades of this century than any other *one* person to determining what comprises industrial engineering and its major areas of investigation and analysis.

It is alarming that history has buried many of the most significant contributions of Lillian Moller Gilbreth, "Member No. 1" of the Society of Women Engineers and perhaps the foremost woman engineer in history.

NOTES

1. The definition of modern industrial engineering, as adopted by the American Institute of Industrial Engineers, is as follows:

   > Industrial engineering is concerned with the design, improvement, and installation of integrated systems of people, materials and equipment; drawing upon specialized knowledge and skill in the mathematical, physical and social sciences together with the principles and methods of engineering analysis and design, to specify, predict, and evaluate the results to be obtained from such systems (Hicks 1977, p. 37).

   Industrial engineers deal with the design of production systems in a wide variety of manufacturing and service industries. The use of process and timestudy charts and other techniques, many of the forerunners of which stem from the period of the Gilbreths and their colleagues, is important in this work. Also, as Hicks comments, operations research, management science, systems engineering, and computer science are closely related fields used in conjunction with industrial engineering today (Hicks 1977, p. 37).

2. A search of the *Official Gazette* of the U.S. Patent Office for Gilbreth patents is ongoing, along with a search of the Gilbreth Collection for reference to patents. However, notwithstanding Frank Gilbreth's chronocyclograph, the Gilbreths primarily contributed to the history of engineering through the creative innovation of techniques and arrangements of work and management based on their research into motion study, fatigue, incentives, standardization, and other matters. Their ideas were captured and disseminated in their consulting reports, articles, books, and other writings.
3. Witte also wrote a book on Taylor, Gilbreth, and Ford (Witte 1925).

REFERENCES

American Society of Mechanical Engineers (ASME), Management Division. 1960. Fifty years of progress in management. New York: ASME.

Appel, Carole S. 1982. Conversation with author, July 22, and letter to author, July 23.

Barnes, Ralph M. 1968. *Motion and time study: Design and measurement of work.* 6th ed. New York: J. Wiley & Sons.

Berch, Bettina. 1980. Scientific management in the home: The empress's new clothes. *Journal of American Culture* 3 (3):440–45.

Blewett, Mary H. 1981. Shared but different: The experience of women in the nineteenth century work force of the New England shoe industry. *Essays from the Lowell Conference on Industrial History 1980 and 1981.* Lowell, Mass.: Lowell Conference on Industrial History:77–85.

Bulletin of Purdue University. 1934/35-1949/50. Purdue University: Purdue University Press.

Caples, William G. 1969. Comment on More Bricks, Less Sweat, American Society of Mechanical Engineers. *The Frank Gilbreth Centennial.* New York: ASME:71–72.

Chandler, Alfred D., Jr. 1977. *The visible hand, the managerial revolution in American business.* Cambridge, Mass.: Belknap Press of Harvard University Press.

Ferguson, Eugene S. 1968. *Bibliography of the history of technology.* Cambridge, Mass.: MIT Press.

Giedion, Siegfried. 1948. *Mechanization takes command.* New York: Oxford University Press.

Gilbreth, Frank B.; and Lillian M. 1916. *Fatigue Study.* New York: Sturgis and Walton.

Gilbreth, Frank B.; and Lillian M. 1920. *Motion study for the handicapped.* London: G. Routledge.

Gilbreth, Frank B., Jr.; and Carey, Ernestine Gilbreth. 1948. *Cheaper by the dozen.* New York: T. Y. Crowell.

Gilbreth, Lillian M. 1914. *The psychology of management: The function of the mind in determining, teaching and installing methods of least waste.* New York: Sturgis and Walton.

Gilbreth, Lillian M. 1927. *The home-maker and her job.* New York: D. Appleton.

Gilbreth, Lillian M. 1928. *Living with our children.* New York: W. W. Norton.

Gilbreth, Lillian M.; and Cook, Alice Rice. 1947. *The foreman in manpower management.* 1st ed. New York: McGraw-Hill.

Gilbreth, Lillian M.; Thomas, Orpha Mae; and Clymer, Eleanor. 1954. *Management in the home: Happier living through saving time and energy.* New York: Dodd, Mead.

Gilbreth, Lillian. 1878–1972. Biography file. Cambridge, Mass.: Schlesinger Library, Radcliffe College (including her resume).

Gilbreth Collection, Purdue University:

Burroughs Company. Materials on file NGRB B5 0696.

Dartmouth College Conference. File NHZ 0830-23, with typewritten note by Lillian, 2113–41, n.d.

Gilbreth, Frank. Index, N file. pre-1924.
Gilbreth, Lillian M.
Address by Dr. Lillian Moller Gilbreth, President of Gilbreth, Inc., IBM Schoolhouse, Endicott, NY. January 27, 1940. Box 0 (also contains two other speeches at IBM in 1946 to sales classes).
Around the World. Tapes on and by Lillian Gilbreth from the 1960s about her international travels, interests, speeches, and other activities.
Biographical memo. 1926. File NHZ 0830-1.
Correspondence with
Anthony, Richard L., February 26, 1941. File NHZ 0830-5.
ASME. 1925–26. File NHZ 0830-1.
Dent, George C. September 19, October 1, and November 29, 1924. File NHZ 0830-42.
Dyer, Dorothy. February 13, 1941. File NHZ 0830-5.
Faunce, W. H. May 7, 1928. File NHZ 0830-4.
Marts, Arnaud C. December 12, 1940 and January 8, 1941. File NHZ 0830-5.
Rich, A. B. 1924–29. File NHZ 0830-7.
Devilled eggs, process chart. File NGVCP, n.d. (pre-1924).
Discussion of Dr. Person's paper—Industrial psychology. Taylor Society, Boston, Mass. April 25, 1924. File NHZ 0830-11.
Dishwashing, showing effect of fragility on time, process chart which covers four types of dishes—unbreakable, cheap grade, china, and better china. File NGVCP, n.d. (pre-1924).
Dishwashing, showing left- and right-hand motions, process chart. File NGVCP, n.d. (pre-1924).
The engineer and the home. File NHE.
Fatigue elimination in hair combing, remarkable process diagram. File NGVCP, n.d. (pre-1924).
Industrial engineering as a career for women. Mimeo, n.d., File NHZ 0830-67.
Opportunities for women in industrial engineering. Mimeo, October 20, 1924. File NHZ 0830-60.
Possible psychopathic types in industry; Psychiatry and management, n.d. File NAPEGTG 0099.
Gilbreth summer schools. 1927. File NHZ 0830-3. See also Thumen and van Kleeck below.
Green Line, Inc. File NGRG 2 0701.
Lies, B. Eugenia (Director of planning, R. H. Macy & Company). Research as applied to retailing. Mimeo, March 28, 1928. Box 0.
Macy, R. H. & Company. File NGRM 0707. See also Lies and Sealy.
Minutes of the research group meeting held in room 2438, General Electric Company, New York City. March 27, 1929. File NHZ 0830-10.
Pilune, Catherine. The industrial engineer. Mimeo. File NHZ 0830-112.
Remington Company. File NGRR 2 0712.
Report of Gilbreth, Inc. January 1, 1927. (for Johnson & Johnson) File NGRH 3 0704-2.
Sealy, Marie P., Macy's Planning Department, memo to Mrs. Gilbreth, October 20, 1925. Also various Macy job descriptions developed with Gilbreth, Inc.) Box 0.
Thumen, Charlotte B. The elimination of unnecessary fatigue in France. June 19–25, 1927. Meetings of the Gilbreth summer school in Baveno, Italy. File NHZ 0830-3.
Typing, shorthand, and dictation machines. Files NBCG and NAPNLE 4 0324.2 (the latter with chronocyclographs showing women typing and working other office machines and also folding handkerchiefs).

van Kleeck, Mary. Notes for Mrs. Gilbreth. 1927. Memo on method of conducting Gilbreth summer schools. File NHZ 0830-3.

Gomberg, William. 1969. Discussion on more bricks, less sweat. American Society of Mechanical Engineers. *The Frank Gilbreth Centennial*. New York: ASME:76–78.

Guest, Robert H. 1967. The rationalization of management. *Technology in Western Civilization*, 2nd vol., eds. Melvin Kranzberg and Carroll W. Pursell, Jr. New York: Oxford University Press:52–64.

Hicks, Phillip E. 1977. *Introduction to industrial engineering and management science*. New York: McGraw-Hill.

Iles, George. 1917. Introduction to Frank B. Gilbreth and L. M. Gilbreth, *Applied motion study, a collection of papers on the efficient method to industrial preparedness*. New York: Sturgis and Walton.

Kranzberg, Melvin; and Pursell, Carroll W., Jr., eds. 1967. *Technology in western civilization*. New York: Oxford University Press.

Landes, David. 1969. *The unbound prometheus*. Cambridge, England: Cambridge University Press.

Livingston, Robert T. 1960. The theory of organization and management. In ASME: 123–28.

Noble, David F. 1977. *America by design: Science, technology, and the rise of corporate capitalism*. New York: Knopf.

Potter, Andrey A. 1969. Frank Gilbreth—a pioneer. *The Frank Gilbreth Centennial*. New York: ASME: 97–99.

Rusk, Howard A. 1969. Rehabilitation of the handicapped. *The Frank Gilbreth Centennial*. New York: ASME: 88–89.

Smiddy, Harold F. 1960. Management as a profession. In ASME: 26–41.

Society of Industrial Engineers (SIE). 1921. Honorary member no. 2, *Society of industrial engineers bulletin* 3 (May):2–3.

Society of Women Engineers (SWE). 1978. Lillian Moller Gilbreth: Remarkable first lady of engineering. *Society of Women Engineers Newsletter* 25 (November-December):1–2.

Spriegel, William R.; and Myers, Clark E. 1953. *The writings of the Gilbreths*. Homewood, Ill.: R. D. Irwin.

Vaughn, Richard C. 1977. *Introduction to industrial engineering*, 2nd ed. Ames, Iowa: Iowa State University Press.

Witte, Irene M. 1925. *Taylor, Gilbreth, Ford*. Munich: R. Oldenbourg.

Witte, Irene M. 1969. Frank Gilbreth—a philosopher. *The Frank Gilbreth Centennial*. New York: ASME:102–09.

Yost, Edna; and Gilbreth, Lillian M. 1944. *Normal lives for the disabled*. New York: Macmillan.

Yost, Edna; and Gilbreth, Lillian M. 1945. *Straight talk for disabled veterans*. New York: Public Affairs Committee.

3

Mathematatization of Engineering: Limits on Women and the Field*

Sally L. Hacker

The main function of mathematics in advanced capitalist society is the maintenance of social stratification. Our courses . . . are the feature of formal education which performs the most decisive winnowing of students. Society tells the student, even the working class student, you may be a dentist if you pass the test, you may be a military officer if you pass the test . . . and the decisive test is in math. . . . The aridity of our courses, their remoteness from students' human concerns—together, of course, with their difficulty—make them especially forbidding, hence especially good as selectors of students with superior capacity for self discipline (sometimes called repression).

—Professor Chandler Davis,
Department of Mathematics,
University of Toronto, 1980.

MATHEMATICS AND ENGINEERING: BACKGROUND AND AN ARGUMENT

Several years ago, I began studying how technological change affected women workers in a number of industries. These studies led me to explore the culture of engineering, the field which directs and implements technological change—and helps determine the nature of women's work by planning the organization and structure of work itself. Engineering seemed to be undergoing a process of work degradation (Braverman 1974) similar to what I had found automation causing in telecommunications, agribusiness, printing and publishing, and insurance (Hacker 1977, 1979, 1980). Lower status visual and manual skills were being routinized, consigned to cheaper

* Supported in part by an NEH Summer Seminar Grant: History of Engineering, directed by Eugene Ferguson, University of Delaware. My thanks for editorial assistance to Joan Rothschild and Barton Hacker, and to Eugene Ferguson for critical review of an earlier draft.

help, then automated; the more abstract and managerial skills were left to engineers. As engineering undergoes these processes of degradation and stratification, disproportionately large numbers of women are being shunted into the newer jobs of engineering technician or technologist, which differ from engineer chiefly in resting on degree programs less heavily invested in calculus and theory courses.

My effort to understand these developments began with questions about what shaped engineers' thinking, about their training (i.e., engineering education), and particularly about what attracted engineering educators to their fields (Hacker 1981). Among the most striking results of my research at a prestigious American institute of technology was my observation of the faculty's pervasive attraction to abstraction, elegance, and simplicity—the qualities embodied in mathematics. Faculty members approached mathematics with playful insight and appreciation. The pleasure and ease with which men at the top exercise these skills is one reason mathematics weighs so heavily in engineering educational success.

When later I attended engineering and technical courses, at this and other institutions, I learned something else important about engineering and mathematics. A world of difference separated the pleasures of mathematics at the top from the grind at the bottom, where engineering students struggled to achieve the required "C" or better in calculus or statics examinations. Clearly, mathematics and the methods of teaching it served to stratify access to the profession—to "weed out" those not proficient in taking mathematics tests, or not delighted in the abstract, from those who were. Only the good test takers pursued the program successfully, won their degrees, and gained access to the profession. Mathematics tests serve as a major criterion for success in today's educational system—particularly engineering education—and more generally in the world of work. Selecting successors by the criterion of math-testing may, perhaps inadvertently, assure cultural homogeneity in the field. Such a one-dimensional perspective in this significant profession affects us all.

I have not here addressed the issue of gender-differentiated ability in mathematics, a subject fully treated by others (Russo 1981, Sells 1978, Tobias 1978). Contrary to popular misconceptions, the data suggest that women are just as competent as men in mathematics. Yet, women continue to be grossly underrepresented in the math-based *professions*, such as engineering. Women's mathematical ability went unquestioned in the early twentieth century reports by the U.S. Bureau of Education, one of which (no. 7, 1911) noted that women were outperforming men in college mathematics. The search for sex-related differences proved largely fruitless, although men displayed a more "rugged" attitude toward the subject. Interestingly enough, the report suggested stressing courses which would "develop that proper sex difference which is so generally recognized" (p.

30). Things have not changed that much since. In showing how mathematics testing has operated to stratify and structure the engineering profession, this study may add an important piece toward solving the puzzle of women's technological exclusion.

Women can surmount the barriers to male dominated professions, in this case, perhaps, by "overcoming math anxiety"—as Sheila Tobias (1978) titled her excellent work on the subject. But, if a primary function of mathematics courses is limiting the number and kind of applicants to a field, then large numbers of women (and men disadvantaged by race or class) mastering mathematical test-taking would simply cause the criteria to shift. (I discuss below the possibility that this may, in fact, be a shift now occurring.) So, at the same time we learn "how-to"—today's fashion in literature, courses, programs—we also need to understand how and why the professions select the standards of excellence they do. Otherwise, most women will remain at least a step behind. A second commanding reason for this broader perspective challenges the criteria themselves—we must understand not only their creation but also their subsequent impact on the field, its services, and its products.

Thus, two issues seemed vital to pursue further: First, how and why—beyond technical considerations—did mathematics become so important to engineering education? Second, how does this link between mathematics and engineering education affect the practice of engineering in our society generally, and the structure and organization of the workforce in particular?

THE DISCIPLINE OF MATHEMATICS AND ITS ROLE IN ENGINEERING EDUCATION

In this section, I shall examine the discipline of mathematics and explore some of the nontechnical reasons why it became integral to engineering education. Mathematics tests serve as major determinants of success or failure in today's educational system, particularly in engineering education. This bias extends to programs outside formal education, where a growing number of people actually receive training, as in apprenticeship programs. Scores on mathematics tests (as well as high school shop courses and "attitude") play major parts in assigning the points that determine whether or not an applicant will enter a program.[1] One reason for these practices lies in the real and growing technical demands of science-based industry, which makes mathematics seem particularly important. But mathematics is not quite the arid, neutral subject of some critics—"the most objective, most coercive type of knowledge, and therefore . . . least affected by social influences" (Mehrtens et al. 1981, p. ix). Critical scholarship has begun to show how strongly social factors affect the content and direction of mathematics (Ernest 1976, Grabiner 1981, Mehrtens et al. 1981). The impact of social factors on engineering is even more pronounced, mathematization itself being one such social factor affecting the nature of engineering.

Mathematics has long been emphasized for nontechnical, or "cultural," reasons. In nineteenth-century France, for example, mathematics "represented rationality." Its study was not for the masses but for the "relatively large and unformed elite" (Hodgkin 1981, p. 63). In England, "mathematics was used to educate gentlemen, not to train mathematicians" (Enroc 1981). Historically, other courses have served the stratifying function Davis assigned mathematics (in the epigraph, above)—"weeder" courses, the students call them. When the Church controlled higher education, Latin was the obstacle. Theology gave way to aristocratic classical studies, then science, as control shifted from one ruling segment to another. Classicists, then the bourgeoisie challenged Church control: education should "promote the everyday interests of society rather than the welfare of the church" (Artz 1966, p. 67). Critics felt "the stress placed on Latin rhetoric seemed particularly absurd" (Artz 1966, pp. 66–67).

Change came slowly; as late as 1802, matriculation at Harvard University demanded proficiency in Latin but not mathematics. But by century's end, the emphasis on mathematical requirements had increased markedly (U.S. Bureau of Education no. 8, 1911, p. 15). In continental Europe and England, as in the United States, mathematics became the chief reliance for measuring educational success through self-discipline (or repression, as Davis would have it). Mathematics superseded not only Latin and theology, but also moral philosophy and logic (Cardwell 1957). As Tobias remarks, "Quantitative method, if not math itself, has become the Latin of the modern era" (1978, p. 42).

Belief in the antagonism of mind and body is as old as civilized society (Rothschild 1981). Medieval religion associated passion with women and the devil. Seeking to hold the passionate body in check, the Church promoted abstraction against empiricism, or learning through the senses (Ehrenreich & English 1973). By the eighteenth century, reason had replaced faith as the dominant ideology (Artz 1966). In the nineteenth century—the century wherein "the sense of limitation [was] the common sense" (Hodgkin 1981, p. 67)—reason, morality, and self-discipline joined to control the unruly passions.

Samuel Smiles wrote his famous mid-nineteenth century *Lives of the Engineers* to prescribe the good and productive life, and his readers welcomed his prescriptions. "The Smiles engineer . . . cultivated first the world within and then externalized the forces of his [self-disciplined] character" (Hughes 1966, pp. 12–13). Smiles believed an engineer could not fulfill his major task, bringing order from chaos, if he were sensuous, self-indulgent, reckless, untidy, or emotional. A time of rapid social change promoted an ideal vision of nature under disciplined control, a control which encompassed the unbridled nature of man himself. "Science . . . is the habit [of mind] recognizing that there is a rational way of doing things as over against a passionate, inpulsive, instinctive or partisan way of doing things" (F. J. E. Woodbridge, as quoted in Finch 1948, p. 43). Another scholar spoke of the "solid and certain reasoning" induced by the study of mathematics, which prevents "youthful conceits and presumptuousness' (Finch 1948, p. 43).

Mathematics, especially in technical education, would teach a rational mode of thought. The 1763 national plan of education for France stressed mathematics because, according to Magistrate La Chalotais, "It is very possible and very common to reason badly in theology, in politics; it is impossible in arithmetic and geometry. The rules will supply accuracy and intelligence for those who follow them" (Artz 1966, p. 68). A nineteenth-century British cleric argued that mathematics "induces habits of industry" even if later cast aside; such study would be beneficial for nontechnical professionals such as lawyers as well (Cardwell 1957, p. 44).

Then as now, however, doubters wondered whether science and mathematics education could quench the fires of youth. As one British professor of philosophy and opponent of increasing mathematics and science in the curriculum questioned: "Should young men, at an age when their passions should be restrained, be introduced to the study of such a subject as 'the reproductive functions?' " Doing so might, he felt, "corrupt the youthful mind. It would make all students medical students" (Cardwell 1957, p. 38). (I asked a friend, a mathematics professor, if indeed his study "cooled the passions." "Hell, no," he said, "but it allows you to sidestep them.")

To others, science and mathematics showed as little promise in teaching reason as in cooling passion. In an 1826 issue of *The Edinburgh Review*, a writer asked of the mathematician, "He can reason?" and answered himself: "But no one reasons so ill as the mathematicians!" Another critic questioned the most important presumed value of mathematical study, disciplined thought: "To say that discipline is the object of a place in education, is much the same thing as to say that the object of an army is to be drilled" (Hugh Wyatt, as quoted in Cardwell 1957, p. 77). And yet another critic cited the mistake of "teachers who value grammar higher than literature itself," and science teachers who value "mathematics preliminary to a knowledge of the laws of nature . . . higher than the knowledge itself" (Thomas Clarke 1875, p. 257). Clarke also claimed:

> Much time is wasted in our colleges and technological schools over the higher mathematics. Every engineer here will agree with me that the times where the use of the higher calculus is indispensable are so few in our practice, that its study is not worth the time expended upon it (1875, p. 257).

Controversy surrounded both the value of mathematics and how best to teach it; both remained subjects of continuing debate. In the United States, it emerged most strongly in the "shop culture" versus "school culture" struggle to control engineering education. Like England, the United States in the nineteenth century relied on the shop floor for most engineers. Training through apprenticeship still characterizes the British approach to engineering education. Engineering status and pay are notably lower there than here, largely because a greater degree of professional muscle in the United States keeps salaries high and limits access to the field.[2]

Relatively early in the nineteenth century, however, American engineering diverged toward the French model, beginning with education in the military academies (Calvert 1967). The American transition was not an easy one, as Noble's brilliant 1977 book illustrates. Corporate capitalism demanded control over this new, dynamic, and often unruly technical elite. With the help of the military, engineering/management in powerful science-based industries came to direct engineering education. Eventually, this extended even to the minutiae of preferred character traits (see Noble 1977, pp. 176ff, for this "boy scout" list), and the personality tests to discern them.

In the mid-nineteenth century beginnings of the movement for engineering professionalism, entrepreneurs and other "practical men" preferred what Calvert (1967) calls "shop culture." They hand-picked young men to learn technical and social skills, work with machines and get their hands dirty, meet future clients, get to know future subordinates. Support for shop culture also came from other sources—elite educators, for one, or Navy officers who complained that school graduates might know mathematics but had never touched a machine. These proponents of shop culture, according to Calvert, represented the cream of mechanical engineering located or trained in elite institutions. They selected young men most like themselves to be the next generation of engineers. Their arguments for the shop approach were couched in terms of work quality and democratic principle. Hands-on experience produced better engineers, and mathematical requirements for engineering degrees might exclude many young men without previous mathematical experience. (And too many degreed engineers would raise the cost of labor.)

The representatives of "school culture"—largely land grant college engineering educators—also argued for quality and democracy. They claimed that mathematics skills had become necessary for good engineering, given the increasing fusion of science and technology (Merritt 1969). Mathematics criteria, they hoped, would also open engineering to the average middle class young man, making it no longer a field restricted to those hand-picked by entrepreneurs. School culture triumphed over shop culture. This was not, however, a product merely of more persuasive argument. Behind the demise of the shop approach lay several factors. Educators themselves campaigned successfully for schooling credentials. Perhaps more decisive, shop training could not readily accommodate the process requirements of large-scale, science-based industries, notably electrical and chemical. Processes of mass production also increased demand for cheaper technical workers educationally "inferior" to engineers. Mathematics became a means of differentiating shop workers from engineers, as shown, for example, in the pages of *American Machinist* at the turn of the century (1899–1900; see especially Halsey).

Supply did not long exceed demand. Perceived overcrowding in the engineering field quickly brought raised admissions standards to limit and reduce the number of entering students. As critics had foreseen, the result disadvantaged those young men whose education had not earlier emphasized mathematical skills. Neither shop nor school culture very closely matched professed democratic ideals. The mismatch scarcely aroused great concern when the emergent profession took stock of itself early in the twentieth century. The Society for the Promotion of Engineering Education commissioned reports from Charles Mann, W. E. Wickenden, and other prominent science and engineering educators. A significant issue was the growing number of young men seeking engineering degrees and threatening to "overcrowd" the field. The midwestern land grant colleges, funded under the provisions of the 1862 Morrill Act, became the major source of the rapid influx of degreed engineers. By the 1920s, it seemed that "every technical student wants a degree" and that "a prestige hunger sought to claim a prairie college 'the same as Cornell' or a YMCA school a university" (Wickenden 1934, pp. 1078, 1112–13).

The younger states seemed particularly pushy, seeking to "telescope the entire span of social evolution from sod-breaking to a system of complex economic interchange into fifty years or less" (Wickenden 1934, p. 1079). They often required nothing but a high school diploma for entrance to college engineering. In 1926, the profession proposed enrollment limits "to protect and elevate professional standards rather than to increase the number of engineering colleges"; the "excess" students might attend technical or trade schools (Wickenden 1930, p. 94). "Many who ought not to try to become engineers are permitted to undertake a course of study for which they have little natural ability" (Mann 1918, p. 47). That ability proved to be primarily mathematical test-taking.

Engineers, in fact, viewed education as "the most important branch of the engineer profession in that the development of the profession depends upon it more than any other branch" (Wadell as quoted in Stine 1980, pp. 15–16). The profession watched over the status and pay of its members, staked out a body of knowledge it could call its own, controlled access, and measured merit on its own terms. (The issues of concern have not, in fact, changed much; then as now they centered on status and money. Within education, the clear problem was attracting high quality men to teaching, when professorial salaries fell far below industrial, and even a new graduate might expect to receive more than the professor who had trained him.)

The profession was aware that engineering differed from "one-level" professions such as law and medicine. No linear route leads from nurse to doctor, or from legal secretary to attorney. Engineering support workers, however, were male; the path from craftsman, technician, or mechanic to engineer lay open. This might help prevent technicians from unionizing, but such mobility also "lessens their [engineers'] chance of public recognition as members of a professional aristocracy" (Wickenden 1934, pp. 1109–10; see also Calhoun 1960). This is the contradiction between democracy and merit inherent in professionalism. Educators had hoped that school culture, using mathematics as filter, would be more democratic than shop culture. Their concern, however, centered on young, middle-class, white Protestant males alone. Women were excluded, non-Anglo-Saxon men unwelcome. In the 1920s, the profession wondered if the infusion of Eastern and Southern European immigrants might account for failure rates in mathematics. Research laid this concern to rest; mathematics courses also weeded out those of "sound extraction" (Wickenden 1930, p. 168).[3]

In the United States, requirements varying from school to school provoked demands for standardization (see, e.g., U.S. Bureau of Education no. 9, 1911). The Joint Council on Engineering Education commissioned Charles R. Mann to assess the status of engineering education. The so-called Mann Report of 1918 was but the first such effort. From the beginning, engineering educators preferred to claim scientific and mathematical expertise, in contrast to practical skills. Mathematics, physical science, and English formed the essential core of engineering preparation. So the high schools were told in 1930: "The misconception that preparation for engineering should be based chiefly on . . . manual training . . . should be dispelled" (Wickenden 1930, p. 175). The profession, as a result, was more than once challenged to show how it differed from the sciences.[4]

The standardized curricula began to reflect this image cleaning. In one early study, engineering teachers and graduates ranked mathematics, physics, chemistry, and graphics (largely descriptive geometry) as the four most important courses. The first three waxed, while graphics declined (Mann 1918, pp. 35–36). Wickenden (1930, p. 549) summarized engineering curriculum trends from the late nineteenth century to 1930 as:

1. A gradual transfer of mathematics from requirement for graduation to requirement for entry;
2. Gains in physical science with losses in graphics;
3. Less emphasis on foreign language;
4. Increased emphasis on the need for economics and management.

Mathematics and science remained in the curriculum; graphics did not. Graphics was siphoned off for less highly trained and less well paid people, eventually emerging as a separate field called drafting, or drawing. Increasingly, women entered this occupation. Much of this work is currently automated, while engineering has retained the abstract skills. Baynes and Pugh (1978, 1981) describe both how women entered such jobs as engineering-drawing copiers in the 1880s, and how a century later copying machines have replaced the women.[5]

How mathematics was to be taught and how performance was to be evaluated concerned practitioners as well as educators. A "mania" for examination had swept British institutions in the mid-nineteenth century in a reform movement to eliminate patronage in the professions, and in response to the clamor for admittance from middle class men. There was considerable criticism of the attempt to replace such means of student evaluation as research projects, reports, displays, or fieldwork with rationalized, specialized, and expert examinations. Opponents noted the injurious consequences of relying on something as useless as a test in assessing talent. Examination addressed professional rather than industrial needs (Cardwell 1957, pp. 119–20). The best suffered most in testing, while only the lazy majority benefited; examinations were the "poison of education" (Cardwell 1957, p. 13). They would never give "a love of things of the mind" (Cardwell 1957, p. 114). Yet the 1850s and 1860s saw a heightened enthusiasm for examination (Cardwell 1957, p. 112). The overwhelming appeal of an examination system lay both in its claims to eliminate personal bias in evaluation, thus promoting democracy, and in its "efficiency." In British science education, mathematics examinations were first to be subject to rationalization (Cardwell 1957, p. 114).

During the first decades of the twentieth century, freshman-sophomore engineering college curricula in the United States were largely limited to basics—calculus, mechanics, higher algebra, coordinate geometry. From 1899 through the 1920s, varying little from year to year, 60 percent of students flunked out, with calculus and science courses weeding out the most (Wickenden 1930, p. 200). Some voices called for efforts to reduce the rate of failure, and perhaps enhance understanding, by integrating theory with practice. Students might benefit from modeling, visualizing, drawing, building, testing pieces of technology. Others wondered whether measuring a student's ability to pass mathematics tests really served the best interests of engineering education. "Is the ability to pass current school and college examinations a valid criterion of engineering ability?" Mann asked (1918, p. 48).

In 1913 he approached General Electric for help in attacking the question empirically. Mann asked the actual employers of engineering graduates to rate them on technical ability, accuracy, industry, ability to get things done, and personality. Granted, such traits may seem particularly useful to those seeking a profit in a competitive system while enjoying a troublefree workforce (Noble 1977). Yet, to the extent that engineering skills could be defined, Mann's list fairly represented then-current views of what they were. Subsequent studies included evaluations of the graduate's work by foremen and peers as well. Mann found *no correlation* between grades and job performance. A similar study of forty graduates employed by Westinghouse produced the same results.

Mann, Thorndyke, and others also undertook extensive research on engineering skills tests. At least eight components failed to correlate with grade-getting ability within engineering education as it was (and is). Some of these skills were verbal; most were visual or manual—matching or completing diagrams, solving laboratory problems, constructing devices from unassembled parts. These skills, they suggested, were not so much unimportant as simply not measured in college (Mann 1918, pp. 50–52). For all that, however, Mann favored retaining mathematics requirements and tests—students "will 'soldier' just like workers" unless forced to study for an exam; they "know as well as anybody that college grades are very ineffective measures of the type of abilities that win recognition in the world's work" (Mann 1918, p. 69). A decade later, Wickenden found nothing amiss in this pattern either; he urged maintaining the system as it was, and even raising admission standards. Once again, the perception of overcrowding controlled. To those whose concerns centered on building and protecting professional status, and on preserving engineering against industry's drive for cheaper, nonprofessional help, nothing else served the purpose as well as mathematics examinations.

Such abilities as visualizing physical phenomena, drawing them, or manipulating physical objects presented problems of evaluation. They may not, in fact, best be learned in the classroom. Mathematics tests, on the other hand, fitted smoothly and easily into the newly bureaucratized way of becoming an engineer—mass professional education in large bureaucratic institutions. High school grades and entrance examination scores predicted a student's ability to win good grades in the early years of college. Grades in the first two years, in turn, predicted grades in later years. But such measurements—grades—do not predict how well one performs as an engineer. Large classes and limited time still encourage teachers to rationalize grading and record-keeping as much as possible. A set of calculus problems I submitted in one course, for example, received a grade reduced by 10 percent because the pages had not been stapled together. A statistics professor, asked why students could not have two hours instead of one for an examination, responded: "If we gave people more time, anyone could to it. The secretaries could even pass it." (Tobias [1978] suggests that timed tests are one of the strongest barriers to understanding and appreciating mathematics.)

This problem—the value of test scores for predicting a good engineer—plagues researchers today, largely because the definition of a good engineer remains obscure. Mann acknowledged the absence of such a definition. Income, he noted, might identify the most successful, but not necessarily the best. The Dean of Engineering at an Eastern university recently told me much the same thing: Defining a good engineer remains the crux, and income makes a poor gauge; it perhaps reflects less quality of engineering than quality of contacts derived from proper family background and matriculation at the proper school.[6]

Engineering faculty members when interviewed admitted that calculus and other forms of higher mathematics may have little relevance to job performance. But they insisted on the importance of such courses, often echoing arguments current for a century or more. Passing calculus, they felt, was important "to show that you can do it," or to "develop a proper frame of mind." But others saw mathematics as not only irrelevant but harmful. Engineering, they argued, not only can but should avoid higher mathematics, which "separates you from the physical reality," or gets in the way of knowing "what is happening, physically." Interviews with mathematicians who teach "weeder" courses such as engineering calculus show they find the chore as distasteful as do the students. Many mathematics and engineering teachers, no less than their students, continue to question the justice or wisdom of allowing mathematics tests and similar criteria to decide who succeeds and who fails in engineering.

THE ROLE OF MATHEMATICS IN STRATIFYING THE TECHNICAL WORKFORCE— A CONTINUING PHENOMENON

The late twentieth century may be a particularly good time to look at the mathematization of engineering. As the ratio of engineers to technicians declines, women and minorities are being actively recruited to become the technicians—that is, engineering aides—who form a growing proportion of the new technical workforce (Harris & Grede 1977). Engineers tend increasingly to work in sophisticated, science-based industries, with technologies that require knowledge and skills in mathematics. The distinction between engineering and technically related occupations rests heavily on college calculus courses. Following the pattern set in the earlier days of engineer training, mathematics continues to play an important role in stratifying the technical workforce. And once again, there are strong, nontechnical reasons why.

Industrial processes—the search for enhanced productivity through less expensive labor and automation—call for new occupations below engineer:

industrial technician, engineering technician, engineering technologist. Educational and training programs geared to produce this varied workforce provide the basis for these stratified engineering and technical occupations. Women are actively recruited for the lower levels (and often counted as engineering majors in national data files); calculus serves as a major filter between lower and upper levels (Hacker & Starnes, 1981).

As the literature of engineering and career education makes abundantly clear, complex problems surround the development of the new engineering-related occupations and paraprofessions. Questions of demand, definition, training, curricula, accreditation, and standards have been easier to raise than answer. Equally knotty, and perhaps even touchier, has been the issue of status and pay appropriate for workers whose skills might be termed "subprofessional." New levels added to the hierarchy of occupations impose an intricate, often puzzling, pattern of relationships among training programs, educational institutions, professional societies, industry needs, and students.

Theoretically, any of the three newest paraprofessionals—industrial technician, engineering technician, engineering technologist—works under the direct or indirect supervision of an engineer, ordinarily the holder of a bachelor's or higher degree from an accredited college of engineering. Engineers, again in theory, must sign off on the work of subordinate technical personnel, and in doing so assume ultimate responsibility for that work. As this new occupational structure developed, funding and accreditation of engineering aide programs became the subject of a prolonged struggle between vocational training and engineering (*Technician Education Yearbook* 1963–64). Vocational education lost. The Engineering Council on Professional Development (ECPD)—later renamed the Association for Bachelors' in Engineering and Technology (ABET)—became the official accrediting body for most such programs. The engineering profession now finds itself in the uncomfortable position of attempting to oversee a process that produces its own competition.

Industry prefers cheaper help than engineers. According to analyses by the National Science Foundation, much engineering work is fairly routine and may be performed as well by those with less education and training (Dubin 1977, Katz 1977). Unless these technicians are well organized, the work will also be performed more cheaply. Recent issues of *Engineering Manpower Bulletin* show the holder of a B.S. in engineering earning 11 percent more than the BET (Bachelor of Engineering Technology), on average, and 55 percent more than the engineering technician. The 55 percent pay differential between engineer and engineering technician approximates the distance between men's and women's earnings generally (women earn 59¢ for every $1.00 earned by men). The real question may be: "Do employers substitute one specialty for another [technicians for engineers, for example] when relative salaries make it attractive, or are occupational demands relatively stable regardless of relative salaries?" (Kramer Associates 1978).

Unsettled criteria pose problems for those who set standards. In a case that came before a State Board of Engineering Examiners, BET's who had taken and passed the state engineering examination claimed professional status as engineers, a practice no longer allowed in several states. A Dean of Engineering testified in the case that his College of Engineering required three calculus courses, equating that requirement with higher quality graduates. The Administrator of the BET institution countered that his program not only required three calculus courses, but also provided more hands-on work experience. Yes, replied the Dean of Engineering, but the *last* course in the BET calculus sequence approached the level of difficulty only of the *first* course required in the engineering calculus sequence. (My calculus is bigger than your calculus.)

An interesting new development is occurring in mathematical criteria. In the summer of 1982, an elite, invitation-only conference of educators and mathematicians met at the Sloan Institute for Management in New York to explore the displacement of calculus—the mathematics of continuous change—by forms of discrete mathematics more appropriate to digital computers. Discrete mathematics concerns itself with individual on-off, yes-no functions, more suitable to the study of probability than the analysis of continuous functions. Many educators feel "calculus . . . may be going the way of Latin—more honored than taught," according to science writer Lee Dembart (1982):

> The pending eclipse of calculus which has been the handmaiden of science and technology practically since the Renaissance, is one more example of the pervasive influence of computers on the way society works and on the ways in which we interpret reality (p. 3).

Citing scholars pro and con, Dembart nonetheless found spokespersons from such institutions as Berkeley and Dartmouth strongly supporting the Sloan Foundation and discrete mathematics. As it happens, discrete math is "easier for many students than calculus . . . an easy way to satisfy a requirement."

As women struggle to overcome their inexperience in such forms of mathematics as calculus, computer-related substitutes can gain in importance for them. Less prestigious institutions, with women and minorities increasingly seeking admission, may persist in stressing calculus much longer than elite institutions. Professional/technical positions may also begin to require other skills—skills now important at the cutting edge of technology, but not yet integrated into the bureaucratized engineering curriculum. (For example, a technical job notice in the *Los Angeles Times* in July 1982 ended: "Prefer someone good at video games.")

Technical fields today offer opportunities far superior to traditional options for women and minorities. Not surprisingly, according to community college counselors, women and minorities express high satisfaction with the programs, jobs, and salaries. While this is a welcome development and we should seek to overcome remaining barriers, such progess should be viewed within a larger context. As Joan Acker (1980) remarks in her recent review of the literature on sex stratification: "The interesting and useful questions are not how individuals get into certain slots, but how the structure itself is formed and what its changing contours are." The ongoing question must be how mathematics testing helps form the new contours and composition of the technical workforce and affects the barriers faced particularly by women in engineering education. Applying what we know about the role of education in maintaining social stratification (Bowles & Gintis 1976, Collins 1979, Pincus 1980) and about the processes of stratification within engineering education (Brittain & McMath 1977, Noble 1977) to career training generally (Grubb & Lazerson 1975), we can ask with Karabel (1972) if career education in community colleges may be a device to keep women and minorities in low status occupations. DeVore (1975) observes that the case for occupationally linked education is proliberal and prodemocratic, but the results are too often illiberal and undemocratic.

In emphasizing abstract mathematical criteria for professional engineering education, educators eliminate other criteria—the hands-on and visual skills. These choices reflect tastes and skills of men at the top, and the boundary maintenance needs of the profession. But overemphasis on abstract criteria may warp the practice of engineering, an effect that will be explored in the next section.

THE IMPACT OF THE MATHEMATIZATION OF ENGINEERING

When systems of stratification emerge, those near the top of the pyramid generally establish the standards for success. Although they tend to justify such standards on rational or technical grounds, they may well have other reasons for their choices, perhaps covert, perhaps unconscious, but in any case notably less objective. Rosabeth Moss Kanter (1975) tells us that several decades ago the tough, aggressive, competitive, independent people who held management positions unconsciously elevated just such characteristics to criteria of excellence. Only later did much of the business community begin to recognize the dysfunctions of overemphasizing these qualities at the expense of others, such as cooperation and sensitivity. Something similar marks the structure of engineering and engineering education: too great an emphasis on mathematical criteria may adversely affect the field and its products.

Some engineering faculty have judged that over-attention to mathematics at the expense of visual and manual skills threatened good engineering. Cooley (1982), a British engineer, traces the impact of automation and abstraction on creativity in engineering design. Rosenbrock (1977) argues that mathematics in general, calculus in particular, represents only one aspect of engineering: engineering as algorithmic, mathematical, scientific technique. Indispensable and intellectually appealing as that fact may be, Rosenbrock warns, it is not the whole of engineering, nor does technical expertise encompass everything the engineer must possess. Such important qualities as judgment, experience, understanding of social complexity, to name a few, must not be neglected.

Ferguson (1977) carries this argument a step further. Large systems failures, he suggests, may stem from the engineer's decreased contact with physical reality. He is particularly concerned that engineers no longer receive the extensive training in visual and drawing skills they once did:

> Two results of the abandonment of nonverbal knowledge in engineering colleges can be predicted; indeed, one is already evident. The movement towards a 4-year technician's degree reflects a demand for persons who can deal with the complexities of real machines and materials and who have the nonverbal reasoning ability that used to be common among graduates of engineering colleges. In the longer run, engineers in charge of projects will lose their flexibility of approach to solving problems as they adhere to the doctrine that every problem must be treated as an exercise in numerical systems analysis. The technician, lower in status than the systems engineer, will have the ability but not the authority to make the "big" decisions, while the systems engineer in charge will be unaware that this nonverbal imagination and sense of fitness have been atrophied by the rules of a systematic but intellectually impoverished engineering approach (p. 835).

Noble (1979) also notices the problems engineers face when they are several layers of workers removed from the sounds and smells, the sensual input of the shop floor. Out of touch with the real machines and materials, the engineer is left with too little "feel" for what he designs. Ida Hoos offers a witty and cogent study of systems thinking applied to social problems (1972), and Lilienfeld's analysis of its ideological role also addresses these issues (1978). These works provide a healthy balance for Tobias' uncritical acceptance of the increasing use of systems analysis in many fields (1978, pp. 35 ff).

As engineering tends toward abstraction and managerial tasks, mental labor departs still further from physical labor. Engineers and scholars alike note the adverse effects, not only on the profession and its practitioners but on the organization of technology itself. Mathematical skills receive even greater stress as engineering strives to protect the field from challenges verging on crisis. For example, mathematics may serve to distinguish the technician and the technologist from the engineer; it may serve to prevent industry's potentially inappropriate use of lesser trained workers; and it may select the students for contracting numbers of places in colleges of engineering.

The process has its ironies. More elite institutions, for example, seem least likely to adopt the most extreme division of labor, formally separating mind and hand work. Published (*Leonardo* 1978) and private correspondence stimulated by Ferguson's (1977) remarks on the damage engineering suffers from deemphasized visual skills tells much the same story as interviews with engineering faculty members (Hacker 1981). Elite institutions such as MIT are more likely than others to retain such training, to stress hands-on experience and laboratory contact with expert craftspeople (see also U.S. Bureau of Education no. 8, 1911, p. 37, for interdisciplinary efforts in elite schools). Asked why such institutions might place less emphasis than others on separating mind from eye or hand, Professor Ferguson thought they might be more secure in their status. It should be added they may also feel less enrollment pressure.

SUMMARY AND CONCLUSION

Now as in the late nineteenth century, both the structure of technology and the institutions which provide its workforce are changing. Failing to recognize this fundamental fact, we are all too likely to misinterpret what we see—women once again breaking into male-dominated areas of engineering and technology, especially in technical support of engineers. But, if women are to take advantage of contradictions between capital and patriarchy—patriarchy here structured in professionalism (Brown 1979, Hartmann 1976, Sokoloff 1980)—we must bear in mind Acker's call to understand how new structures form, and what their changing contours are. Because capitalism needs cheap labor and the system can routinize and cheapen engineering tasks, women benefit in the short run as new technical jobs open to them. The more patriarchal profession (that is, engineering) appears to be declining—again, in the short run—unless technicians can be persuaded to view themselves as professionals. This may not prove difficult. Paraprofessional status offers prestige, all the more attractive given the newcomers' otherwise disadvantaged place in the labor market; the "real" professions virtually exclude women, chiefly through the peculiar manipulation of mathematics as a standard. The result is women channeled toward the lower range of the job market, while men enjoy less competition for the better jobs (Sokoloff 1980).

As their work becomes more routinized, engineers begin to complain about its "factory-like" quality (Cooley 1982, National Science Foundation

1977). Less costly technical workers take over routine engineering as automation looms. A U.S Bureau of Labor Statistics report (1966, p. 48) called for a long-term (through 1975) increase in the ratio of technicians to scientists and engineers, in part due to "rising salaries of . . . engineers." This plan did not include raising the ratio of drafting positions to engineering ones (the area attracting many women today) because of greater projected use of photoreproduction, mechanized drafting equipment, and automation. Women assume the role of technician, and the gap between the pay of technician and engineer begins to approximate that between female and male workers in society generally. If technicians identify with other workers in unions, rather than with their own paraprofessional technical societies, they may in fact become better technical workers. Not only may they thus increase their income, they may also prevent further degradation of nonverbal and nonmathematical skills, the otherwise vanishing essence of good engineering.

Tensions between business and the profession of engineering have waxed and waned over the past century. The early twentieth century saw such tensions alleviated (Layton 1969), but now we may again see contradictions emerging (see, e.g., Gouldner 1976). This article suggests the need to alter the structure of engineering in ways that might benefit us all. Professional criteria, especially for access to the field, developed as the product of a small, technically trained elite. In particular, special kinds of testing have allowed engineering to maintain its homogeneous positions. Mathematical examinations became the powerful filters of entry to engineering.

In stressing nontechnical or nonrational reasons for this use of mathematics, my intention is not so much to imply that such reasons are necessarily the most important (although they may be). Rather, I wish to draw attention to the unexpected: seemingly technical standards for a technical field which are imposed for reasons having little to do with the field's technical demands. This suggests one way to desegregate and improve engineering: Remove scores on mathematics tests as the major standard of success in engineering education. Though small, given the vested interests of the educational gatekeepers, such change will not likely be easy. Further, as suggested in *Social Problems* (Benét & Daniels 1976), the smallest adjustments in the direction of greater equity in education may ultimately require basic changes in the institutional fabric of society. The efforts of women to enter male-dominated professions as engineering must be joined with a struggle for structural change in the field, especially given the power of engineering to shape the direction of technology, and thus our lives (Ferguson 1977, Hacker 1983).

NOTES

1. Feminist attorney Marlene Drescher of Eugene, Oregon, and others have filed creative legal actions to eliminate discrimination in apprentice training programs (*Cormier* v. *Central*

Electrical JATC et al., Civil No. 82-607E, U.S. District Court for the District of Oregon 1983; *Judy Marlene Parks and Deborah Marlye Grossberg* v. *San Mateo County JATC for the Electrical Construction Industry*, Case No. C-81-3389 WHO, U.S. District Court for the Northern District of California).

2. It may also slow the proletarianization of engineering, which appears to be moving much more quickly in England than the United States (Cooley 1982; *New Scientist* 1979–80).
3. Tables report percentage of students whose parents and grandparents were born in the United States, and industry urged schools to note graduates' "heredity," "parents' occupation, education and nationality" (Wickenden 1930, p. 251).
4. Layton (1969) has suggested that the distinction may be chiefly point of view—engineering seeks to do, science to understand.
5. Eugene Ferguson, an engineer and historian, notes the continuation of this process today: "The sad fact is that the status of non-verbal knowledge is lower than the verbal-mathematical in the powerful councils of the New Mandarins of scientific technology" (*Leonardo* 1978, p. 350).
6. Someone else at that college of engineering, trying to discover whether good grades promised a good engineer, took income—measured in the amount of alumni contributions—as the index of engineering success, equating success with quality. Size of donation proved to be significantly correlated with former grade-point average, but negatively—the larger the donation, the poorer the grades.

REFERENCES

Acker, Joan R. 1980. Women and stratification: A review of recent literature. *Contemporary Sociology* 9:25–39.

American Machinist. 1899–1900.

Artz, Frederick B. 1966. *The development of technical education in France, 1500–1800*. Cambridge, Mass.: MIT Press.

Baynes, Ken; and Pugh, Francis. 1978. Engineering drawing: Origins and development. In Welsh Arts Council, *Art of the Engineer* (Cardiff: The Council), pp. 3–12.

Baynes, Ken; and Pugh, Francis. 1981. *The art of the engineer*. Woodstock, N.Y.: Overlook Press.

Benét, James; and Daniels, Arlene Kaplan. 1976. Education: Staitjacket or opportunity? *Social Problems* 24:143–307. (Entire issue).

Bowles, Samuel; and Gintis, Herbert. 1976. *Schooling in capitalist America: Educational reform and the contradictions of economic life*. New York: Basic Books.

Braverman, Harry, 1974. *Labor and monopoly capital: The degradation of work in the twentieth century*. New York: Monthly Review Press.

Brittain, James E.; and McMath, Robert C., 1977. Engineers and the new south creed: The formation and early development of Georgia Tech. *Technology and Culture* 18:175–201.

Brown, Carol. 1979. The political economy of sexual inequality. Paper presented at the annual meeting of the Society for the Study of Social Problems, Boston.

Calhoun, Daniel H. 1960. *The American civil engineer: Origins and conflict*. Cambridge, Mass.: Technology Press, MIT.

Calvert, Monte. 1967. *The mechanical engineer in America, 1830–1910: Professional cultures in conflict*. Baltimore: Johns Hopkins University Press.

Cardwell, Donald S. L. 1957. *The organisation of science in England: A retrospect*. London: Heinemann.

Clarke, Thomas C. 1875. The education of civil engineers [and discussion]. *Transactions of the American Society of Civil Engineers* 3:255–66.

Collins, Randall. 1979. *The credential society: An historical sociology of education and stratification*. New York: Academic Press.

Cooley, Michael. [1980] 1982. *Architect or bee? The human/technology relationship*. Boston: South End Press.

Davis, Chandler. 1980. Where did twentieth-century mathematics go wrong? Paper presented at the joint annual meetings of Society for the History of Technology, History of Science Society, Philosophy of Science Association, and Society for the Social Study of Science, Toronto.

Dembart, Lee. 1982. Computer era threatens pre-eminence of calculus. *Los Angeles Times*, May 25, part 1, pp. 3, 16.

DeVore, Paul W. 1975. Review of *American education and vocationalism: A documentary history, 1870–1970*, ed. Marvin Lazerson and W. Norton Grubb (New York: Teachers College Press, 1974). *Technology and Culture* 16:113–14.

Dubin, Samuel S. 1977. The updating process. In National Science Foundation. *Continuing education in science and engineering*: Appendix C, pp. 165–88.

Ehrenreich, Barbara; and English, Deirdre. 1973. *Witches, midwives and nurses: A history of women healers*. Old Westbury, N.Y.: Feminist Press.

Enroe, Phillip C. 1981. Cambridge university and the adaptation of analytics in early 19th century England. *Social history of nineteenth century mathematics*, eds. Herbert Mehrtens, Henk Bos, and Ivo Schneider, Boston: Birkhäuser: 135–48.

Ernest, John. 1976. Mathematics and sex. Unpublished paper, Mathematics Dept., University of California at Santa Barbara.

Ferguson, Eugene S. 1977. The mind's eye: Nonverbal thought in technology. *Science* 197:827–36.

Finch, James Kip. 1948. *Trends in engineering education: The Columbia experience*. New York: Columbia University Press.

Gouldner, Alvin W. 1976. *The dialectic of ideology and technology: The origins, grammar, and future of ideology*. New York: Seabury Press.

Grabiner, Judith V. 1981. *The origins of Cauchy's rigorous calculus*. Cambridge, Mass.: MIT Press.

Grubb, W. Norton; and Lazerson, Marvin. 1975. Rally 'round the workplace: Continuities and fallacies in career education. *Harvard Education Review* 45:451–74.

Hacker, Sally L. 1977. Farming out the home: Women and agribusiness. *The Second Wave* 5:38–49.

Hacker, Sally L. 1979. Sex stratification, technology and organizational change: A longitudinal case study of AT&T. *Social Problems* 26:539–57.

Hacker, Sally L. 1980. The automated and the automaters: Human and social costs of automation. Paper presented at annual meeting of the International Federation of Automatic Control, Rabat, Morocco (forthcoming *Proceedings*. New York: Pergamon).

Hacker, Sally L. 1981. The Culture of Engineering: Woman, Workplace and Machine. *Women's Studies International Quarterly* 4:341–53.

Hacker, Sally L. 1983. Engineering the shape of work. *Proceedings*, Conference on Ethics and Engineering—Beyond Whistleblowing, Illinois Institute of Technology, Chicago, 1982.

Hacker, Sally L.; and Starnes, Charles. 1981. The proletarianization of engineering. Presented at the annual meetings of the Society for the Study of Social Problems, Toronto.

Harris, Norman C.; and Grede, John F. 1977. *Career education in colleges*. San Francisco: Jossey-Bass.

Hartmann, Heidi. 1976. Capitalism, patriarchy, and job segregation by sex. *Women and the workplace: The implications of occupational segregation*, eds. Martha Blaxall and Barbara B. Regan. Chicago: University of Chicago Press: 137–69.

Hodgkin, Luke. 1981. Mathematics and revolution from Lacroix to Cauchy. *Social history of mathematics*, eds. Herbert Mehrtens, Henk Bos, and Ivo Schneider, Boston: Birkhäuser: 50–71.

Hoos, Ida R. 1972. *Systems analysis in public policy: A critique*. Berkeley: University of California Press.

Hughes, Thomas Parke, ed. 1966. *Selections from lives of the engineers, with an account of their principal works, by Samuel Smiles*. Cambridge, Mass.: MIT Press.

Kanter, Rosabeth Moss. 1975. Women and the structure of organizations: Explorations in theory and behavior. *Another voice: Feminist perspectives on social life and social science*. eds. Marcia Millman and Rosabeth Moss Kanter. Garden City, N.Y.: Anchor Press/Doubleday: 34–74.

Karabel, Jerome. 1972. Open admissions: Toward meritocracy or democracy? *Change* 4 (May): 38–43.

Katz, Israel. 1977. Continuing education in science and engineering: Audiences; non-academic. In National Science Foundation *Continuing education in science and engineering*. Appendix E: 197–234.

Kramer Associates, Inc. 1978. *Manpower for energy research: Design of a comprehensive manpower information system for energy research, development, and demonstration*. Washington: Department of Energy, Office of Education, Business, and Labor Affairs.

Layton, Edwin. 1969. Science, business, and the American engineer. *The engineers and the social system*, eds. Robert Perrucci and Joel E. Gerstl. New York: Wiley: 51–72.

Leonardo. 1978. Letters to the editor about the reprinted version of Ferguson, "Nonverbal thought in technology." 11:348–50.

Lilienfeld, Robert. 1978. *The rise of systems theory: An ideological analysis*. New York: Wiley.

Mann, Charles R. 1918. *A study of engineering education*. Prepared for the Joint Committee on Engineering Education of the National Engineering Societies. New York: Carnegie Foundation for the Advancement of Teaching, Bulletin no. 11.

Mehrtens, Herbert; Bos, Henk; and Schneider, Ivo, eds. 1981. *Social history of nineteenth century mathematics*. Boston: Birkhäuser.

Merritt, Raymond H. 1969. *Engineering in American society, 1850–1875*. Lexington: University Press of Kentucky.

National Science Foundation, Directorate for Science Education, Office of Program Integration. 1977. *Continuing education in science and engineering*. Washington: Government Printing Office.

New Scientist. 1979–1980. Oct. 25: 283–85; Nov. 22: 622–23; Nov. 29: 689–91; Jan. 10: 80–83.

Noble, David F. 1977. *America by design: Science, technology, and the rise of corporate capitalism*. New York: Knopf.

Noble, David F. 1979. Social change in machine design: The case of automatically controlled machine tools. *Case studies on the labor process*, ed. Andrew S. Zimbalist. New York: Monthly Review Press: 18–50.

Pincus, Fred L. 1980. The false promises of community colleges: Class conflict and vocational education. *Harvard Educational Review* 50:332–61.

Rosenbrook, N. H. 1977. The future of control. *Automatica* 13:389–92.

Rothschild, Joan, ed. 1981. Women, technology and innovation. *Women's Studies International Quarterly* 4:289–388.

Russo, Nancy Felipe. 1981. Mathematics and sex: The 19th century revisited. *National Forum* 61 (4):19.

Sells, Lucy. 1978. Mathematics—A critical filter. *The Science Teacher* 45 (2) (Feb.).

Sokoloff, Natalie J. 1980. *Between money and love: The dialectics of women's home and market work*. New York: Praeger.

Stine, Jeffrey K. 1980. Professionalism vs. special interest: The development of engineering education in the U.S. Unpublished paper, Department of History, University of California at Santa Barbara.

The Technician Education Yearbook. 1963–1964.

Tobias, Sheila. 1978. *Overcoming math anxiety*. New York: Norton.

U.S. Bureau of Education Bulletin No. 7. 1911. Undergraduate work in mathematics in colleges of liberal arts and universities. International Commission on the Teaching of Mathematics. The American Report, Committee No. X. Washington: Government Printing Office.

U.S. Bureau of Education Bulletin No. 8. 1911. Examinations in mathematics other than those set by the teacher for his own classes. International Commission on the Teaching of Mathematics. The American Report, Committee No. VII. Washington: Government Printing Office.

U.S. Bureau of Education Bulletin No. 9. 1911. Mathematics in the technological schools of collegiate institutions in the United States. International Commission on the Teaching of Mathematics. The American Report, Committee No. IX. Washington: Government Printing Office.

U.S. Bureau of Labor Statistics. 1966. Technician manpower: Requirements, resources, and training needs. Bulletin No. 1512, June. Washington: Government Printing Office.

Wickenden, William E. 1930–1934. *Report of the investigation of engineering education, 1923–1929, accompanied by supplemental report on technical institutes, 1928–1929*, 2 vols. Pittsburgh: Society for the Promotion of Engineering Education.

4

Technology and Work Degradation: Effects of Office Automation on Women Clerical Workers*

Roslyn L. Feldberg and Evelyn Nakano Glenn

Following World War II, computer technology was introduced into the office. The potential for revolutionizing office work was widely proclaimed. Both managers and social researchers expected widespread resistance on the part of office workers to the changes that would take place. As a result, numerous studies were undertaken to assess the responses of workers to the introduction of computers. Much of this research was predicated on a belief among technological optimists that negative responses were irrational, since computerization would, in the long term, benefit workers as well as managers. We call this the consensual research model.

In contrast, other observers, drawing the parallel to the tendency of mechanization in manufacturing to lead to reduction and deskilling of jobs, predicted largely negative consequences for office workers. This position has been developed systematically in recent theoretical and empirical work on the labor process (Braverman 1974, Edwards 1979, Stone 1975). We call this the critical research model.

In this article, we argue first that the critical model, with its emphasis on the way social relations affect the development and use of technology, offers a better framework for assessing the impacts of technology in the case of clerical work. It helps us to see what happens to the work over time.

* Research for this paper was supported in part by a grant (#MH-30292) from the Center for Work and Mental Health, National Institute of Mental Health. An earlier version was presented at the meetings of the American Sociological Association, New York, 1980. We thank Natalie Sokoloff and Sally Hacker for detailed comments. The paper also benefited from readings by Sharon Strom and Chris Bose; from discussions of the Women and Work Study Group, originally sponsored by a grant from the American Sociological Association Problems of the Discipline Program; and from careful review by Joan Rothschild.

Clerical work has become more subdivided, specialized, standardized. This argument is supported through a detailed review of the evidence on shifts in numbers and types of jobs within clerical work. Second, we argue that the critical model has at least the following major limitation. Analysts using this model, Braverman (1974) in particular, have assumed that changes in the work are experienced as changes for the workers who end up in subdivided/standardized jobs. They tend to concentrate solely on the division between capital and labor, ignoring the divisions within each. In particular, workers are presented as being a uniform group with an identical relationship to work; therefore, they are viewed as similarly affected by the capitalist use of technology. Our position is that, historically, labor has been divided into many segments, representing separate pools of workers who have access to different types of work and whose interests may be contradictory.[1] These segments reflect social divisions which are incorporated into the labor market. These divisions are based on ascriptive characteristics such as sex, race, and age; and, within these ascriptive segments, on social characteristics such as class, level of education, and previous job history.

An accurate assessment of the effects of technology requires identifying the social divisions within the labor force, describing the impacts for each group, and analyzing the connections and differences between what happens to one group and what happens to another group. We offer this kind of analysis for women in clerical work. Thus, we focus on gender as a fundamental division, arguing that men and women have different relations to the labor market due to the interaction of gender hierarchies in families with gender hierarchies and related practices in the labor market (see Feldberg & Glenn 1979). Because of these differences, we argue, men and women are differentially impacted by changes associated with the use of the new technology.

THE MODELS

The dominant research model in the early years of office automation was developed within a consensus framework that saw no fundamental opposition between the interests of workers and management. In this model, technology is viewed as a politically neutral tool contributing to progress for the benefit of all. This optimistic view rested on the assumption that technology would benefit management by increasing productivity and efficiency, and would benefit workers by relieving them of the more boring, routine tasks and by upgrading their jobs. Numerous studies were carried out to assess the responses of workers to automation and to evaluate programs for changeover (Cheek 1958, Hardin, et al. 1961). A smaller number of studies tried to assess the effects of automation on the occupational structure. These reported that job loss was concentrated among low-skilled jobs, while relative and absolute increases were found in higher skilled jobs. The observation, though accurate, was misleading, because it implied an upgrading of lower-skilled workers and drew attention away from job loss and displacement among particular groups of workers (Faunce, et al. 1962, Shepard 1971, Wolfbein 1962). As a result, such studies provided little insight into the transformation of clerical work or the impacts of this process on clerical workers.

The critical research model was developed within a conflict framework that posits an opposition between the interests of workers and management. In this framework, technology is viewed as a resource of the capitalist class (since they own and control its development, see Noble 1977), and is used by management to increase productivity through greater efficiency and rationality at the expense of the workers. This position was partly articulated earlier by Mills (1956) but has been more fully developed in recent years by Marxist analysts studying the labor process (Braverman 1974, Edwards 1979). Technology is viewed as one of the mechanisms used by managers to increase control over the work process by centralizing knowledge in the hands of management, thus reducing dependence on qualified, intelligent, committed workers. By implication, the impact of the use of technology within capitalism is to displace and downgrade workers.

Analysts in this tradition have spelled out the downgrading argument clearly and compiled evidence to support it. In line with our criticism of this model's limitations, we contribute to its development by giving special attention to differential impacts on men and women. We argue that gender hierarchies and related practices, in both the labor market and the family, structure the way in which men and women are allocated to jobs created around that technology. We find that in the technological transformation of the office to date, women are increasingly confined to lower paid jobs with fewer opportunities for mobility.

In assessing the models, we examine effects on work and workers at three levels: 1) the aggregate labor force and overall organization of work; 2) the labor force and the work process in an organization; and 3) the workers and work process in particular jobs.[2] Too frequently, analysts fail to differentiate these levels. Change at one level is assumed to indicate parallel change at another level; for example, the increase of new technical jobs in the occupational structure (level one/two) is taken to mean that there has been an upgrading of the work done in all jobs (level three). There is no necessary connection. Indeed, other jobs are as likely to remain unchanged or to be simplified as they are to be upgraded by such a shift in the occupational structure.

LEVEL ONE: OCCUPATIONAL STRUCTURE

We turn first to changes in the occupational structure which have occurred since the introduction and spread of automation.

The assessment of impacts of office technology on the occupational structure is complicated by other economic and organizational changes that occurred simultaneously with growing automation. Some of these developments have had as great, if not greater, effects on the size and distribution of the clerical work force; and, in many cases, these developments have had impacts opposite to those created by automation. Thus, while automated technology may have reduced the number of workers needed to carry out a given volume of a particular activity, business growth and shifts in the economy increased the volume of activity so greatly that many more workers were needed.

During the period of expanding automation, there was a general expansion of clerical occupations as the volume of record-keeping and communication grew. The growth in these activities can be attributed to increased size and complexity of organizations and the disproportionate growth of the service and financial sectors of the economy (see Glenn & Feldberg 1977).

As table 4.1 shows (pp. 64–5), for the period 1960–1981, employment in clerical and kindred occupations doubled. From the table, we can identify categories that grew more quickly than average, i.e., more than doubled, and those that grew more slowly, i.e., increased less than two-fold. Two expected patterns appear. First, there is dramatic growth in the categories associated with the new technology. For example, computer equipment operators grew more than two-hundred-fold during this period, while computer specialists grew fifty-fold. In part, this dramatic growth reflects the small size of these occupations in 1960; but, even in the years 1970 to 1981, these categories continued to experience faster-than-average growth. Second, there is a drastic decline in or complete elimination of categories of jobs that are displaced by the computer. Non-computer machine operators, such as tabulating or calculating machine operators, disappear while stenographers fall to less than one-third of their previous total.

Alongside these expected changes, however, are several anomalies. File clerks, expected to disappear with the growth of central data banks, declined only slightly. Other groups, expected at least to decline, have grown instead. It was thought that the spread of new technology such as word processing and semi-automatic dictating equipment would lessen the need for secretaries. However, the number of women employed as secretaries grew more rapidly than clerical work as a whole. One might speculate that the personal service and assistance rendered by secretaries remained critical to the operation of offices, as well as to the comfort and prestige of managers. These services may have had particular importance in the expanding field of personal, professional, and business services. Similarly, the number of receptionists and typists continued to grow—despite automated and semi-automated correspondence and telephone systems—due to continued expansion of communication in large organizations.

Finally, one interesting indicator of change in the office structure was the disproportionate growth in the number of clerical supervisors. This pattern may also be related to automation. Larger capital investment per worker and potentially greater productivity may foster greater concern with managerial control of the work process.

As these varying patterns indicate, the overall impacts of technology on the occupational structure are not homogeneous. Technology may increase productivity in certain areas, but the volume of activities can increase even more rapidly, thus offsetting declines in employment. At the level of the occupational structure, with data from different industries—some expanding and some shrinking, some undergoing change and others stagnating—it is difficult to separate the impacts of technology from other factors. In addition, technology may be used to reorganize work so that, although a job category remains stable or grows, the actual work activity may be different. If the same title does not necessarily mean the same work activity or the same place in the social relations of the workplace, then it is difficult to state precisely the degree of change or continuity.

To control for some of these factors (e.g., changing business patterns) among industries, we examined the aggregate pattern of occupational changes in a single industry—insurance. The Bureau of Labor Statistics conducted wage surveys of over 200 insurance companies in 13 metropolitan regions in 1961, 1966, 1971, 1976, and 1980. Using these data, we can examine changes in detailed occupational categories (see table 4.2, p. 66).

For the most part, the data in table 4.2 for the insurance industry correspond to the data for the clerical and related occupations in all industries. The fastest growing occupations in the insurance industry were the "professional technical," EDP (electronic data processing) related ones—programmers and systems analysts, most of whom were men. Other computer related jobs, such as keypunchers and computer operators, expanded after 1961, but leveled off with improvements in the systems which increased capacities, and speeded up and decentralized processing. The positions displaced included those involved in hand or mechanical processing: for example, tabulating machine operators had disappeared by 1976. Clerks involved in record-keeping, transcribing premium payments, assembling records, calculating values on policies, handling remittances (Assemblers, Policy Evaluation Clerks, Ledger Clerks, and Premium Acceptors) were reduced in number, again despite increase in the volume of activity.

In the meantime, most other positions dealing with transactions and communication remained at a stable level, including clerks in accounting and correspondence, while underwriters increased slightly in response to greater volume. Stenographers were rapidly disappearing and typists were becoming fewer; a new category of transcribing typist who worked with dictating machines made up for some, but not most, of the loss of these jobs. Although data on secretaries were not presented in 1961 and 1966, there was a substantial increase in secretaries between 1971 and 1976.

A related trend, not shown in either table, is the increased differentiation

Table 4.1. Employed Persons in Selected Office Occupations by Sex 1960–1981

Selected Occupations	1960[1]			1970[1]			1981[1]		
	Men	Women	Total	Men	Women	Total	Men	Women	Total[2]
Computer Specialists	8,528	765	9,293	204,656	49,945	254,601	457,083	169,917	627,000
Programmers	5,970	2,170	8,140	124,991	36,391	161,382	259,102	107,898	367,000
Systems Analysts	2,558	722	3,280	68,293	11,748	80,041	158,046	54,954	213,000
Bank Tellers	39,725	93,205	132,930	34,439	215,037	249,476	36,985	532,015	569,000
Billing Clerks	8,039	35,091	43,130	18,838	87,347	106,185	18,054	134,946	153,000
Bookkeepers	153,559	773,980	927,539	277,214	1,259,443	1,536,657	174,529	1,786,471	1,961,000
Cashiers	112,275	373,955	486,230	136,954	695,142	832,096	229,080	1,430,920	1,660,000
Clerical Assist. Social Welfare	—	—	—	261	942	1,203	—	—	—
Clerical Supervisor	28,393	25,824	54,217	64,391	48,389	112,780	73,000	177,000	250,000
Collectors, Bl. & Act.	26,137	6,485	32,622	32,947	18,537	51,484	34,038	48,962	93,000
Counter Clks., Except Food	47,483	74,156	121,639	76,584	152,667	229,251	84,960	275,040	360,000
File Clerks	23,426	121,591	145,017	65,221	294,678	359,899	51,030	263,970	315,000
Messengers	49,659	8,766	58,425	46,206	11,225	57,431	71,004	25,996	97,000

Office Machine Oper.	80,706	230,488	311,194	145,477	408,001	553,478	255,024	710,976	966,000
Bookkeeping/Billing	5,432	45,951	51,383	6,720	56,629	63,349	5,978	43,022	49,000
Calculating	671	36,406	37,077	3,071	31,880	34,951	—	—	—
Computer/Peripheral Equipment	671	1,257	1,928	83,072	34,241	117,313	204,168	359,832	564,000
Duplicating	8,066	5,650	13,716	8,788	11,609	20,397	—	—	—
Keypunch	43,691	117,376	161,067	27,964	244,957	272,921	16,120	231,880	248,000
Tabulating	18,143	7,530	25,673	4,128	4,042	8,170	—	—	—
Office mach. nec.	4,030	16,318	20,350	11,734	24,643	36,377	—	—	—
Payroll, Timekpg.	43,920	63,681	107,601	48,622	107,364	155,986	43,890	187,110	231,000
Receptionists	11,018	145,709	156,727	16,046	288,326	304,372	18,225	656,775	675,000
Secretaries	42,607	1,424,166	1,466,773	64,608	2,640,740	2,705,348	35,253	3,881,747	3,917,000
Statistical Clks.	59,042	78,124	137,166	89,204	160,492	249,696	72,890	297,110	370,000
Stenographers	11,625	258,554	270,179	8,097	120,026	128,123	11,026	62,974	74,000
Typists	25,468	496,735	522,203	57,272	922,804	980,076	38,147	992,853	1,031,000
Misc./Not Specified	448,521	1,085,922	1,534,443	201,255	610,017	811,272	451,836	1,504,164	1,956,000
All Clerical and Kindred[3]	2,921,912	6,203,858	9,125,770	3,452,281	9,582,440	13,034,691	3,619,980	14,944,020	18,564,000

Sources: for 1960 and 1970, U.S. Census Bureau 1970; for 1981, U.S. Department of Labor 1982.

[1] For 1960 and 1970, 14 years of age and over; for 1981, 16 years of age and over.

[2] Rounded to nearest thousand.

[3] Including all clerical occupations listed in census, but excluding computer specialists. This total includes occupations not listed above.

Table 4.2. Distributions of Employees in Selected Occupations in Offices of Life Insurance Carriers in Thirteen Selected Areas of the U.S.[1]

	1961			1966			1971			1976			1980
	Men	Women	Total	Men	Women	Total	Men	Women	Total	Men	Women	Total	Total*
Actuaries	983	83	1,066	499	18	517	527	35	562	755	100	855	1,090
Assemblers	56	1,294	1,350	44	1,002	1,046	—	—	—	—	—	—	—
Claims Approvers	—	—	—	391	338	729	402	491	893	363	866	1,229	1,882
Clerks, Accounting	346	3,174	3,520	278	2,702	2,980	202	3,530	3,732	—	3,887	3,887	4,261
Clerks, Correspondence	782	1,322	2,104	427	1,409	1,836	228	1,659	1,887	—	1,964	1,964	2,121
Clerks, File	156	4,637	4,793	99	4,494	4,593	55	3,725	3,780	—	3,629	3,629	3,218
Clerks, Policy Evaluation	144	1,397	1,541	89	1,045	1,134	43	945	988	—	951	951	935
Clerks, Premium Ledger	25	1,654	1,679	16	780	796	3	553	556	—	263	263	344
Console Operators	131	10	141	417	53	470	—	—	—	—	—	—	—
Computer Operators	—	—	—	—	—	—	1,765	481	2,246	2,104	257	2,361	2,315
Keypunch Operators	2	3,072	3,074	5	3,489	3,494	7	3,458	3,465	—	2,955	2,955	2,813
Premium Acceptors	62	672	734	9	518	527	5	606	611	—	570	570	563
Programmers	503	112	615	1,011	355	1,366	1,935	942	2,877	2,255	1,242	3,497	4,148
Secretaries	—	—	—	—	—	—	5	6,413	6,418	—	7,532	7,532	7,855
Stenographers	—	3,586	3,586	16	3,867	3,883	—	2,336	2,336	—	1,286	1,286	703
Systems Analysts	335	30	365	470	80	550	1,465	345	1,810	1,914	790	2,704	3,596
Tabulating Machine Operators	1,789	1,344	3,133	992	895	1,887	459	421	880	—	—	—	—
Tape Librarians	—	—	—	32	39	71	59	134	193	48	137	185	198
Transcribing Machine Typists	—	—	—	—	—	—	2	1,021	1,023	—	993	993	791
Typists	3	6,389	6,392	2	6,514	6,516	4	5,327	5,331		4,098	4,100	3,252
Underwriters	1,156	404	1,560	1,154	410	1,564	1,119	555	1,674	1,004	657	1,661	2,088

Sources: U.S. Department of Labor 1961, 1966, 1971, 1981. For each year, source is Average Weekly Earnings, Selected Occupations.

* No breakdown by sex given in 1980.

[1] The following metropolitan areas: Atlanta, GA, Boston, MA, Chicago, IL, Dallas–Fort Worth, TX, Des Moines, IA, Hartford, CT, Houston, TX, Jacksonville, FL, Los Angeles–Long Beach, CA, Minneapolis–St. Paul, MN, Newark, NJ, New York, NY, Philadelphia, PA.

of levels within occupations. For example, in the 1961 insurance industry survey, file clerks were differentiated into A and B categories based on degree of autonomy/responsibility (U.S. Department of Labor 1961, 1966, 1971). By 1966, there were three levels of file clerks. Similarly, in EDP occupations, the levels of programming and systems analysts increased from two to three by 1971.[3] These finer differentiations probably reflect greater rationalization of office procedures and more explicit definitions of duties, changes which are consistent with the analysis of the critical model (Kraft 1977, Greenbaum 1979).

Examining changes in gender composition of the various occupations within the insurance industry reveals a striking pattern. With the exception of keypunchers, all of the EDP-related positions, including that of computer operators, began and remained overwhelmingly male. In contrast, most of the shrinking and stable positions which began mostly female became increasingly feminized. Traditional clerical occupations (such as accounting clerks, correspondence clerks, policy evaluation clerks) which had a fairly sizable minority of men in 1961, had almost none by 1976. According to Hacker (1979), jobs in which females are concentrated, or have recently been allowed to enter, are most likely to be displaced by technology. The evidence in this case supports this claim. Although the largest category eliminated by automation, tabulating machine operators, had slightly more men than women in 1961; the other five occupations which declined 25 percent or more between 1961 and 1976 were occupations in which women were at least 90 percent of the 1961 labor force. As these occupations grew smaller, all five became 100 percent female. Overall, it appears that, with the exception of underwriting, the occupational structure in the insurance industry became more sex-segregated between 1961 and 1976, with the technical EDP jobs developing as male provinces, especially at the highest levels, while the routine clerical work became increasingly female.

Taking data on both the broad occupational structure and the distribution in one industry, what can we conclude about the relationship between office automation and the occupational structure? First, the introduction of the new technology was labor saving, and some occupations were eliminated completely—fewer workers were needed to accomplish certain tasks. Second, the continued expansion of clerical activity more than offset savings in labor; thus, the clerical labor force grew slightly overall. However, in insurance, a steadily growing industry that relies heavily on both automation and clerical labor, there has been a sizable reduction in the number of traditional clerical jobs. Third, the new technology has been used not only to reduce the total number of jobs but also to reorganize the work, with the result that occupations are narrower, more specialized, and more standardized, and rely less on workers' detailed knowledge of the particular office or business. Fourth, the expansion of computer related occupations has increased the total number of jobs and created some new, higher paid occupations. However, the workers displaced by automation do not appear to benefit: the new jobs are technical level and largely held by males. Women from traditional clerical jobs are unlikely to be moving up into these jobs. Rather, a new layer of largely male workers recruited from a different labor pool has been inserted into the office. The critical model correctly directs attention to the reorganization of the occupational structure, with displacement for some groups and more routinized occupations for others. It is clear that what benefits management does not benefit workers who are displaced or restricted. However, it is also clear that different segments of the work force experience different kinds and degrees of advantage and disadvantage from these changes.

LEVEL TWO: THE ORGANIZATION

Analysis of the aggregate level above offers a picture of the changing national occupational structure. In order to see how these changes interrelate, i.e., how changes in one occupation are linked to changes in another occupation, we must look at particular firms. Unfortunately, there are few studies which provide detailed information on the changing occupational structure within firms. Most studies at the organizational level deal with the problems managers face during the introduction of automation, especially with workers' attitudes toward automation.[4] Two early studies (Helfgott 1966, Rothberg 1969) that present full before-and-after pictures of the occupational structure in particular firms will be reviewed to see what light they shed on the relationships between technological change and the changes in the clerical occupations, including differential effects on men and women. Following that, we review findings of two more recent studies (Cummings 1977, Hacker 1979) that suggest how patriarchal relations in the labor market interact with technological innovations to produce the occupational structure in particular firms.

Helfgott (1966), in a case study of a large insurance company, shows that the number of clerks involved in tasks such as sorting, calculating, verifying, recording, and maintaining records was markedly reduced following the introduction of computers. In 1960, the company home office employed 4,475 clerical workers, accounting for two-thirds of the total employment in the home office. By 1964, that number had dropped to 3,872—a loss of 603 positions. In addition, the 1964 figure included the new job of keypuncher, which represented 154 new jobs (or 4 percent of the clerical category). Thus, a total of 757 traditional clerical jobs (16.9 percent) had been eliminated. At the same time, the company had added new technical employees (programmers, computer operators, systems analysts) and expanded the ranks of supervisory employees so that the combined category increased by 275 jobs or 15 percent. Managerial staff also increased during this period, by 78 jobs or 20 percent.[5] As of 1964, clerical workers had dropped from the original two-thirds to three-fifths of the work force in the home office.

How did these changes affect the sex composition of the office? Since traditional clerical jobs were almost entirely female, while the growing technical, supervisory, and managerial jobs were held largely by men,[6] there was a marked decline in female employment in the home office between 1960 and 1964. This decline was coupled with increased dominance of men in the upper levels of the office hierarchy.

Rothberg's (1969) report on automation in a branch of the Internal Revenue Service shows similar outcomes even in a context of expanding employment in clerical jobs. Before automation, the routine jobs were held primarily by women (80–95 percent, depending on the job), and the administrative jobs were held primarily by men (over 90 percent). During automation, the total labor force grew by 80 percent.[7] Some of the traditionally female jobs accounted for a large percentage of the increase. Examining and statistical jobs and sorting, classifying and filing jobs, which together accounted for 30 percent of employment under the old system, rose to 50 percent of employment in the new larger system. In addition, keypunch and other machine operators doubled in number. However, the new, upper level, technical jobs created during automation were filled almost entirely by men (95 percent). Although women continued to dominate in the total work force, men's domination of the higher levels of the office increased. Thus, with increasing automation, male/female stratification in the office became even more pronounced.

One other impact of change in the firm's occupational structure, also revealed by the studies of the Internal Revenue Service, was to reduce opportunities for upward mobility. Many high level, complex clerical jobs disappeared early in computerization (U.S. Department of Labor 1963). These changes compressed the occupational hierarchy, cutting off occupational mobility for employees in certain departments or specialties. Similarly, middle level jobs, previously viewed as training positions, were eliminated or changed in ways that reduced training opportunities. As a result, these jobs and the ones below them became virtual dead ends. Similar blocks to mobility of clerical workers after automation are found in other studies of the insurance industry (Cummings 1977, U.S. Department of Labor 1965), the cost accounting department in a steel company (Weber 1959), and other types of firms (Hoos 1961, Shepard 1971). Overall, women who already hold traditionally female clerical jobs are least likely to benefit from the changes accompanying automation. The available evidence indicates that these workers are more likely to find their work unchanged or to experience negative consequences, such as loss of employment, "deskilling," or diminished opportunities for advancement.

In addition to the overall effects on the occupational structure and the gender composition of jobs, technological changes can have different and sometimes contradictory effects on particular segments of the clerical labor force. A study by Cummings (1977) hints at the complex process by which gender hierarchies are incorporated into technological changes and work reorganization. In 1960, one unit of a large insurance company employed approximately 400 clerical workers, both men and women. Men were concentrated in the higher level jobs; women in the lower level jobs. Over the next 15 years, the work process was reorganized and new technology was introduced. The result was a more standardized work procedure, a lessening of specific knowledge required by the workers, and a loss of approximately 175 jobs. At the end of the period, the unit was 95 percent female. As the jobs were reorganized and downgraded, these jobs were made available to women. The consequences are difficult to assess. On the one hand, the reorganized jobs held by women were less valuable in salary, prestige, autonomy, and opportunity for advancement than the eliminated high level jobs held by men. On the other hand, the new jobs were better on these dimensions than most of the jobs previously held by women. The final ambiguity is that management is now planning to reorganize the work further—to eliminate over 100 additional jobs and to rationalize the remaining ones. It may turn out that the women have been used as a transitional labor force.[8] It is not clear whether management plans to transfer some of these same women into the further rationalized jobs, or to draw on a new labor pool, such as men or women from racial minorities, for whom even these jobs might represent an improvement over previous employment opportunities.

A similar process in which technological change differentially affected male and female segments of the work force is described in Hacker's (1979) analysis of technological displacement and employment shifts at AT & T. Here, significant technological changes were introduced when the company was under a court order to carry out affirmative action. Hacker finds that the combination of technological changes and the movement of white and minority women from their traditional occupations to ones that were "new" for women reduced them as a proportion of the total labor force. In addition, both groups of women were most likely to be hired into positions in which job security and skill requirements were being eroded by technological change. The company's ability to implement this strategy was enhanced by the barriers which male-dominated unions and individual husbands and fathers placed in the way of the women organizing in their own interests. Thus, patriarchal practices in family life, the unions, and the work organization influenced the way technological change affected specific segments of the work force.

LEVEL THREE: THE WORK PROCESS

Finally, we turn to the impacts of the use of technology at the work process level as it is experienced by the individual worker. Researchers of the consensus school (Blauner 1964, Shepard 1971) have pointed out that automation makes it possible to bring together in a single job functions which were separated out and divided among several jobs under mechanized technology. The presumption is that the resulting job is a more integrated whole, one which gives the worker greater autonomy and reduces alienation. Unfortunately, this claim has never been properly assessed in relation to clerical work. The major published investigation (Shepard 1971) deals with the topic primarily by examining the workers' attitudes. If workers sound less alienated on a number of dimensions, Shepard infers that their jobs in automated offices are more integrated and that they are more autonomous in their work; yet he fails to look at the actual content or organization of those jobs.

In contrast, those working within the critical tradition point out that bringing together several rationalized tasks does not necessarily increase worker autonomy or create more holistic tasks, and may serve primarily as a form of speedup (Rinehart 1978). Here, the argument is that automation requires the use of standardized formats which is likely to mean greater rationalization of work procedures and a loss of workers' autonomy in many aspects of the task (Braverman 1974; Glenn & Feldberg 1977, 1979; Hall 1975, p. 319; Rico 1967, p. 31). While this position seems credible in view of the logic of both mechanization and automation, once again, the argument is presented as if it were uniformly applicable across jobs and segments of the labor force. And, once again, we question that formulation. The way jobs are reorganized around the new technology is not a given. The forms of reorganization introduced appear to vary in relation to different segments of the work force. In particular, the reorganization may involve not only shifts in the composition of the work force, as discussed above, but also in the areas, as well as the degree, of worker autonomy.

To illustrate, we turn to case materials from our own research in a utility company: a detailed analysis of the reorganized job of "customer service clerk." This set of activities was once carried out by several clerks. Now, with the information available via computer terminal, it is carried out by one person. The customer service clerk handles complaints, inquiries, and requests for service, doing all phases of the work. Before the computer system was fully developed, customers called separate departments for specific types of questions. Each clerk provided information on a specific area: sales, bills, service/repair, etc. Separate files were maintained in each office and a complex question might require several phone calls to track down information. With computerization, the files were centralized. Now, one set of clerks, using computer terminals, has access to all the information. The clerks who answer these phones can look up a customer's account and explain a billing problem, can set up appointments for service calls, or tell a customer the balance due on a special service. In addition, the clerk can enter into the terminal any new information provided by the customer: the time someone will be home for the service call, the type of problem, a change in address, or other billing information.

The job involves a broader scope of information, but it is also more closely supervised. Several monitoring systems keep track of the work done by each clerk. An automatic call distributor distributes phone calls and records the number of calls answered and those lost (by customers hanging up) on each line. The clerk's code, entered into the computer terminal with every transaction, provides a tally and an error count on information processed. In this more rationalized system, each part of the job must be handled according to specific procedures and within a specified time frame. Although the clerk now has access to information for all areas of the company, less knowledge of the procedures in each area is required than previously. Thus, she is less able to judge what constitutes a reasonable modification of these procedures. Management is also attempting to make greater use of slack time. Clerks are being asked to do part of the work of their previous position, entering routine billing information through their terminals during slack hours when there are few calls. Finally, the clerk is now seated at her desk/terminal throughout the day.

It is difficult to evaluate whether there has been an increase or decrease in worker autonomy with reorganization. On the one hand, standardized procedures must be followed for taking care of routine customer requests. The clerk is also subject to close, though unobtrusive, supervision through the machine counts on her work and her errors. On the other hand, the clerks have broader information and are allowed more leeway in negotiating bill complaints/payments with customers. Management permits this discretion because it increases the likelihood that bills will be paid, without additional expenditure. Since this is the ultimate goal of the company, it is likely that this discretion will be maintained as long as it appears to contribute to that end.

This reorganization of the labor process brought about a shift from predominantly male to predominantly female clerks but, in the process, the job itself was changed. When men were in these jobs, the customer service clerk was the top position in a job ladder which began with outside work, a completely male specialty. The male customer service clerks, because of their previous work experience, were knowledgeable about the physical equipment and often advised customers on problems they were having with appliances. When women were brought into the job, they were specifically told not to give such advice. In any case, the new female clerks, coming from positions in accounting and bookkeeping, have not had any experience with the physical equipment and are given no training in this area; they are, therefore, not prepared to discuss these matters with customers. Thus, discretion in one area has been greatly reduced. At the same time, because of their experience in accounting, they are better prepared to discuss charges and payments, an area in which the male clerks had little expertise. Thus, autonomy in the financial area has been increased. Whether knowledge of the billing system represents a greater or lesser "skill" than knowledge of the equipment is debatable. At the moment, the job remains at the top of the non-managerial pay scale.

Given the change in company policy of discouraging customer clerks from discussing appliance problems, it would appear that the men remaining in the job, who constitute about a third of the category, have lost their area of autonomy, while the newer women clerks have gained autonomy. From our observations, this does not appear to be the case. It is true that the men's special knowledge has been declared "off-limits" and the areas of discretion have shifted to those in which they have little expertise and previous experience. However, because their practical knowledge remains useful, and because they have the most seniority, they continue to use this knowledge unofficially. Indeed, their "special" knowledge of the equipment and their longer experience in the job, perhaps reinforced by the cultural assumption that males are more authoritative, have combined to make the men informal consultants to the women. As a result, the men are viewed as the experts who "help the girls out" when they get a difficult question. At the same time, the men's lack of experience with billing has freed them from the obligation to do routine billing in slack time, presumably because they do not understand the system well enough to do it.

This example suggests that social characteristics of the workers, in this case "being male," may have an effect independent of the impact of technological change. The effect of gender is evident in differences in the supervisors' treatment of the men and women. As one woman complained: "When we come back from lunch or break a few minutes late, it's: 'Come on, girls, let's go,' shouted out across the floor. When the men do it, nothing is said." Observation corroborated her account on at least two occasions. The differences in discipline found in the utility company are consistent with the stricter enforcement of rules for women employees reported in other settings by Langer (1972) and by Acker and Van Houten (1975). It is also noteworthy that the accounting system, in which the women are expected to be most knowledgeable, is the aspect of the work process which is now subject to closest supervision. Thus, it appears that the impacts of a technologically based reorganization of work on workers' autonomy may differ according to the social characteristics of the workers.

CONCLUSIONS

Our examination of the effects of the changing organization of office work reveals that women have been differentially and more negatively affected than men by changes accompanying office automation. This finding, although consistent with the framework of the critical model which informed our research (Glenn & Feldberg 1977, 1979), had to be pieced together because much of the research on technological change has obscured the variation in effects. Such research does so in two ways. First, many studies focus at the aggregate level, analyzing the relationship between new technologies and skill level using statistics for a total labor force at the national or firm level. These studies do not usually investigate whether the same relationship holds at the firm or work process level respectively, nor do they examine whether the effects are systematically different for particular segments of the work force, such as men vs. women, white vs. minority workers. Second, studies of technological change in particular industries or firms usually focus on industries in which white men are the primary labor force. Yet, the findings of such studies are treated as if they provide a picture of trends affecting all industries and all workers. For example, many studies have been conducted on the automobile industry. The experiences of its workers are treated as if they were representative of mechanization in industry as a whole. In fact, however, the automobile industry and the associated assembly line experience represents only a fraction of industry and involves primarily a distinct segment of the labor force, white males. To understand the meaning of technological change for other groups or segments, including women, researchers need to look at the industries and work processes in which those groups are concentrated.

Is it important to analyze the varying meanings of technological changes? Does such detailed appreciation of variations affect the way we think about work and its relation to social structure? We think the answer to both questions is "yes." In an earlier period, many researchers assumed that the changes associated with the industrial revolution took place simultaneously, in a uniform fashion, across whole populations. With such a faulty picture of the nature and conditions of work, and the changes people were experiencing in their lives, these researchers found it difficult to understand why there were not more sustained uprisings by people whose entire lives were supposedly uprooted by the industrial revolution. Recent work, such as Strumingher's (1979), shows that men and women were affected differently by changes in the technology and the work organization of the French textile industry during the nineteenth century. Perhaps this is a clue to the absence of uniform response by workers. In similar fashion, the new technologies associated with computers are being hailed or decried as the basis of a new revolution. Yet now, too, there is reason to believe that the extent of change and the direction of change will differ by industry, by work process, and by the segments of the labor force. If, instead of studying the pattern and process of change, we assume what they are, then we will make erroneous predictions of workers' responses, and, having done so, will misinterpret their actual responses. For example, if we assume uniform downgrading of the jobs of women clerical workers, we might predict strong negative feelings about technological change. What we find instead is a range of feelings. A portion of the workers are positive about the use of new technology, some because it relieves them of routine operations and others, especially minority women, because the reorganization accompanying technological change has provided access to better paid, easier, or more secure jobs than those they had or had expected to get. If we did not understand these different effects, we might mistakenly conclude that the clerical workers did not mind having their work downgraded.

Only when we begin to study the actual changes taking place in particular industries, specific firms, and specific work processes and begin to analyze the way these changes differentially, yet systematically, affect particular segments of the labor force, will we begin to understand the many, contradictory meanings of technological changes and the problems and opportunities being created.

NOTES

1. Our use of the concepts of segment of the labor force differs from that associated with labor market segmentation theory (Barron & Norris 1976, Piore 1975). The labor market segmentation theorists stress the division of employment possibilities (the labor market) into two distinct types, representing different conditions of labor (core/primary vs. periphery/secondary). Our analysis stresses the division of the work force itself into distinct segments on the basis of social characteristics, with membership in a particular segment affecting the conditions of work that workers face, even in the same industry.
2. This point, derived independently, parallels Kasarda's in his analysis of the relationship between expanding size and administrative structure for three levels of social system. His research showed that the correlation between size and structural components differed for each of the three levels (Kasarda 1974, p. 24).
3. See Kraft (1977) and Greenbaum (1979) for analyses of this growing differentiation as the consequence of the "deskilling" of computer programming.
4. The case study literature was published primarily between 1955 and 1968, when the introduction of computers was expected to have dramatic effects on office employment. The chief concerns during this period were workers' reactions and personnel problems resulting from geographic and occupational shifts. This literature does not provide basic information

about changes in the tasks or the working conditions of specific occupations or about the numbers of people displaced. Thus, we found these studies of little value for our analysis.

5. Increase in the size of the managerial staff following the introduction of computers has been noted by several researchers (Helfgott 1966, Hoos 1961). Various reasons are suggested: each worker produces more and, therefore, needs to be more carefully supervised; new kinds of jobs require new kinds of supervision that need to be tied into the administrative hierarchy; and, as the remaining clerical tasks become "more qualitative and less quantitative," some of the work shifts to administrative personnel—this last according to one administrator of Inland Steel Company.
6. It is interesting that most jobs related to computer processing, such as computer operators, are classified as technical, but that keypunchers are classified as clerical. Perhaps the fact that keypunchers are overwhelmingly female influenced the classification, since existing female office jobs are defined as clerical.
7. Almost 30 percent of the labor force "chose" to retire or to quit during the transition period, and another 109 people accepted downgrading as an alternative to relocating. Thus, 36.7 percent of the original labor force was displaced. The previous occupations, sex, race, and age distribution are not given.
8. The practice of using women as a transitional labor force has been documented at least since the early introduction of electronic data processing. Mann and Williams (1960) note that employers believed women would have higher rates of (voluntary) attrition and consequently hired them to fill temporary jobs during the changeover.

REFERENCES

Acker, Joan; and Van Houten, Donald R. 1975. Differential recruitment and control: The sex structuring of organizations. *Administrative Sciences Quarterly* 20:152–62.

Barron, R. D.; and Norris, G. M. 1976. Sexual divisions and the dual labour market. *Dependence and exploitation in work and marriage*. Eds. Diana Leonard Barker and Sheila Allen. London and New York: Longman, 47–69.

Blauner, Robert. 1964. *Alienation and freedom*. Chicago: University of Chicago Press.

Braverman, Harry. 1974. *Labor and monopoly capital: The degradation of work in the twentieth century*. New York: Monthly Review Press.

Cheek, Gloria. 1958. *Economic and social implications of automation: A bibliographic review*, vol. 1, *Literature before 1957*. East Lansing: Labor and Industrial Relations Center, Michigan State University.

Cummings, Laird. 1977. The rationalization and automation of clerical work. Unpublished M.A. thesis, Brooklyn College, May.

Edwards, Richard. 1979. *Contested terrain: The transformation of the workplace in the twentieth century*. New York: Basic Books.

Faunce, William; Hardin, Einar; and Jacobson, Eugene H. 1962. Automation and the employee. *Annals of the American Academy of Political and Social Science* 340:60–68.

Feldberg, Roslyn; and Glenn, Evelyn Nakano. 1979. Male and female: Job vs. gender models in the sociology of work. *Social Problems* 26:524–38.

Glenn, Evelyn Nakano; and Feldberg, Roslyn L. 1977. Degraded and deskilled: The proletarianization of clerical work. *Social Problems* 25:52–64.

Glenn, Evelyn Nakano; and Feldberg, Roslyn L. 1979. Women as mediators in the labor process. Paper presented at the American Sociological Association Annual Meetings, Boston, Mass.

Greenbaum, Joan. 1979. *In the name of efficiency: Management theory and shop floor practice in data processing*. Philadelphia: Temple University Press.

Hacker, Sally L. 1979. Sex stratification, technology and organizational change: A longitudinal case study of AT & T. *Social Problems* 26:539–57.

Hall, Richard H. 1975. *Occupations and the social structure*. 2nd ed. Englewood Cliffs, N.J.: Prentice-Hall.

Hardin, Einar; Eddy, William; and Deutsch, Steven. 1961. *Economic and social implications of automation: An annotated bibliography*, vol. 2, *Literature 1957–1960*. East Lansing: Labor and Industrial Relations Center, Michigan State University.

Helfgott, Roy B. 1966. EDP and the office work force. *Industrial and Labor Relations Review* 19:503–16.

Hoos, Ida R. 1961. *Automation in the office*. Washington, D.C.: Public Affairs Press.

Kasarda, John D. 1974. Structural implications of social system size: A three level analysis. *American Sociological Review* 39:19–28.

Kraft, Philip. 1977. *Programmers and managers. The routinization of computer programming in the United States*. New York: Springer-Verlag.

Langer, Elinor. 1972. Inside the New York Telephone Company. *Women at Work*, ed. William O'Neill. New York: Quadrangle Press: 305–60.

Mann, Floyd C.; and Williams, Larry K. 1960. Observations of the dynamics of a change to electronic data processing equipment. *Administrative Science Quarterly* 5:217–56.

Mills, C. Wright. 1956. *White collar*. New York: Oxford University Press.

Noble, David F. 1977. *America by design: Science, technology and the rise of corporate capitalism*. New York: Alfred A. Knopf.

Piore, Michael J. 1975. Notes for a theory of labor market stratification. *Labor market segmentation*, eds. Richard C. Edwards, Michael Reich, and David M. Gordon. Lexington, Mass.: D. C. Heath, 125–50.

Rico, Leonard. 1967. *The advance against paperwork*. Ann Arbor: Graduate School of Business Adminstration, The University of Michigan.

Rinehart, James. 1978. Job enrichment and the labor process. Paper presented to New Directions in the Labor Process Conference, sponsored by the Department of Sociology, SUNY, Binghamton, N.Y., May.

Rothberg, Herman J. 1969. A study of the impact of office automation in the IRS. *Monthly Labor Review* 92:26–30.

Shepard, Jon M. 1971. *Automation and alienation: A study of office and factory workers*. Cambridge, Mass.: MIT Press.

Stone, Katherine. 1975. The origins of job structures in the steel industry. *Labor market segmentation*, eds. Richard C. Edwards, Michael Reich, and David M. Gordon. Lexington, Mass.: D. C. Heath: 27–84.

Strumingher, Laura S. 1979. *Women and the making of the working class: Lyon 1830–1870*. St. Albans, Vt.: Eden Press Women's Publications.

U.S. Census Bureau. 1970. Census of the population, characteristics of the population, Vol. 1, Part 1, Table 221; Detailed occupations of the experienced labor force and employed persons by sex: 1970 and 1960.

U.S. Department of Labor. 1961. Bureau of Labor Statistics, Industry wage survey, Life insurance, May-July. Bulletin No. 1324, Average weekly earnings, selected occupations.

U.S. Department of Labor. 1963. Bureau of Labor Statistics, Bulletin No. 1364. Impact of office automation in the Internal Revenue Service.

U.S. Department of Labor. 1965. Bureau of Labor statistics, Bulletin No. 1468. Impact of office automation in the insurance industry.

U.S. Department of Labor. 1966. Bureau of Labor Statistics, Industry wage survey, life insurance, Oct.-Nov. Bulletin No. 1569, Average weekly earnings, selected occupations.

U.S. Department of Labor. 1971. Bureau of Labor Statistics, Industry wage survey, life insurance, Dec. Bulletin No. 1971, Average weekly earnings, selected occupations.

U.S. Department of Labor. 1976. Bureau of Labor Statistics, Industry wage surveys: Banking and life insurance, December. Bulletin No. 1988, Table 67: Average weekly earnings, selected occupations.

U.S. Department of Labor. 1981. Bureau of Labor Statistics, Industry wage survey, Life insurance, Dec. Bulletin No. 2119, Average weekly earnings, selected occupations.

Weber, C. Edward. 1959. Impact of electronic data processing on clerical skills. *Personnel Administration* 22:21–26.

Wolfbein, Seymour L. 1962. Automation and skill. *Annals of the American Academy of Political and Social Science* 340:53–59.

5

Technology, Housework, and Women's Liberation: A Theoretical Analysis[1]

Joan Rothschild

Technology, it is often claimed, liberates women. We learn how the pill has freed women from childbearing, how myriad household appliances have liberated women from housework, and even how, indirectly, the typewriter once brought women into the labor force and thus led to their emancipation.[2] This chapter examines the liberation claim relative to housework, meaning women's unpaid labor in the home. Have women been liberated, or further controlled? What are the myths and what are the realities, and the realities that sustain the myths? What of the future?

I shall argue in this chapter that, in the United States, household technology as a liberating factor for women cuts two ways. Although technology has greatly eased the worst burdens of household labor, women have not been liberated from their housewife role. Technology has aided a capitalist-patriarchal political order to reinforce the gender division of labor and to lock women more firmly into their traditional roles in the home. Under the guise of freeing women, technology contributes to women's economic dependency, and to control by the political economy over women's household labor processes. However, technology can also provide a precondition for women's liberation. It has done so in the past, and can do so in the future, but only within the context of a broader feminist analysis.

Technology includes not only machinery and mechanized processes but also the organization of work, as in the following definition by Bernard Gendron (1977, p. 23):

> *A technology is any systematized practical knowledge, based on experimentation and/or scientific theory, which enhances the capacity of society to produce goods and services, and which is embodied in productive skills, organization, or machinery.*

As Noble (1977) demonstrates, technology is part of the social relations of production, a social process that "must inescapably reflect that particular social order which has produced and sustained it." It can have the power of ideology as it "assumes the particular forms given it by the most powerful and forceful people in society" (p. xxii).

As an interdependent variable, therefore, technology is tied to sociopolitical structure and to ideology. In the United States, this structure and ideology can be described as a capitalist-patriarchal political order. Capitalism and patriarchy are intertwined. *Capitalism* is a system of privately-owned production for private profit dependent, materially and ideologically, not only on class hierarchies but on gender, racial, and other social hierarchies to sustain the system. *Patriarchy* is a system of male supremacy, dependent, materially and ideologically, not only on a hierarchic gender division of labor but also on the "naturalness" of that division and its necessity to the political order in which the system is situated.[3] Capitalism and patriarchy intersect through the gender division of labor (Eisenstein 1979, Young 1981).[4]

The capitalist-patriarchal political order relates to women's domestic labor in the following way. Although the gender division of labor predated the Industrial Revolution, with the rise of industrial capitalism changes in both material conditions and ideology transformed "women's work" (Hartmann 1976, Kessler-Harris 1976, Sacks 1974, Zaretsky 1976). Home and workplace became separated: men's work moving increasingly outside the home, women's work remaining within it. Although many women worked for wages—as domestics in others' homes, as factory operatives, as home-based piece workers, and later as office workers—the unpaid work of maintaining the household came to be viewed as women's primary work, and women's work exclusively. As the middle class ideal of the two spheres took hold, the family,[5] and women's proper role within it, developed into a powerful ideology that persists to this day (Welter 1966). Women's work at home was deemed natural to women because of their biology and, by extension, temperament. Women's entry into the labor force was rationalized as temporary, even though this flew in the face of the experience of poor and working class women, black and white. Women were relegated to marginal, reserve, ill-paying jobs, and to feminized occupations (Abbott 1918, Oppenheimer 1970).

Capitalism and patriarchy together benefited from this strengthened gender division of labor. Women's unpaid domestic labor in the home reproduced the labor force, literally through biological reproduction, and through care of household and family members. Through women's work at home, workers were enabled to sell their labor power in the marketplace. As the nineteenth century advanced, emotional support was added to women's domestic labors. The patriarchal nuclear family became integral to industrial capitalist production. Profits were enhanced by the existence of a marginal, reserve labor force that could be ill-paid and limited to certain jobs not only because women's place was in the home and women were therefore classed as temporary workers. Women were so categorized in the labor force also because patriarchal ideology held that women were limited by nature and temperament only to certain skills. Women's economic dependency was thereby strengthened. As an unpaid worker in the home, a woman was dependent upon her husband or other male head of household, which meant her dependency as well on the political economy. If a wage worker, marginal and poorly paid, she could not sustain herself or her family and was forced to seek male protection and to come under his direct authority.[6] The patriarchal family and patriarchal authority were thereby strengthened as well.

Women's unpaid labor in the home thus was and is a linch-pin of the capitalist-patriarchal political order.

In the following section, I shall first show both the liberating and controlling effects of technology on women's household labor. I shall then discuss how, despite the liberatory aspects, technology for the home, functioning within this sociopolitical order, has played a key role in sustaining and strengthening the place of women's domestic labor within it.

FREEDOM AND CONTROL

Liberation means both "freedom from" and "freedom to." If liberatory, technology would free women from housework, ultimately from doing it at all, and thus from the "housewife" role. It would also free woman to have more choices about her work, for example, to enter the labor force, and to have control over her labor processes. Let us examine these "freedoms."

To claim in the 1980s that technology has not eased women's household work over the years would be an absurdity. Although slower in coming to the home than to the factory or other workplace, technological changes began to reach into the household even in the nineteenth century (Strasser 1982).[7] Items such as soap, candles, and textiles and clothing, once produced in the home, were now manufactured and offered for sale. The cast-iron stove replaced the open hearth for cooking and heating as well, coal replacing wood, especially in urban areas. But, with the exception of the more affluent homes, major technological changes affecting the household did not arrive until the twentieth century (Cowan 1976). Gas and electricity for cooking, heating, and lighting; indoor plumbing; and the washing machine dramatically reduced filthy and back-breaking labor for the housewife. Appliances such as vacuum cleaners, refrigerators, dishwashers, freezers, plus convenience foods have saved cooking and cleaning time and made such work easier. Changes did not come uniformly. Middle and upper class homes, especially in Northern and Midwestern cities were equipped with indoor plumbing, central heating, electrification, and appliances long before those of the poor and working classes. Most farm homes were not electrified until the rural electrification programs of the 1930s and 1940s. Nevertheless, as we enter the final decades of the twentieth century, the technologizing of the home has become fairly widespread, reaching across class, regional, and urban/suburban/rural lines. According to the U.S. Bureau of the Census (1981), only 2.8 percent of all housing units in 1979 (86.4 million total) lacked some or all plumbing facilities (p. 760). Among occupied units (78.6 million), only .7 percent had no heating equipment at all (p. 766), while 91.6 percent had telephones (p. 760). In those housing units wired for electricity (meaning most at 79.4 million), there is the following equipment: 99.9 percent with radios and black and white (89.8 percent color) TVs; 99.9 percent with vacuum cleaners, toasters, coffeemakers, and irons (98.8 percent steam and spray); 77.3 percent with washers and 61.5 percent with clothes dryers; 55.5 percent with room air-conditioners; 44.7 percent with freezers; 43 percent with dishwashers and food waste disposers; 92.8 percent have mixers, 64.2 percent electric blankets, 63.6 percent automatic can openers, and 52.4 percent electric blenders (p. 766). By the 1970s, possession of household appliances was no longer an indicator of social status (Vanek 1978). The tremendous growth in and use of fast food establishments in the last decade (Strasser 1982), presumably meaning less cooking at home, must also be added to this technologizing process.

What appeared puzzling to researchers in the 1970s was that, despite greatly improved equipment as well as wider diffusion of it, the full-time housewife was spending as much time in housework as her grandmother did 50 years earlier (Thrall 1982, Vanek 1974). Although a woman employed outside the home spends less time, she remains the household member primarily responsible for housework; she thus puts in more total hours of work than any other adult household member (Thrall 1982). Contrary to popular myth, women, by and large, are not receiving help from others in the household; evidence suggests that the gender division of labor in the home has even increased in recent years (Bose 1979, Thrall 1982). Full-time servants have long been a thing of the past for almost all of those who ever had them; part-time domestic help (except for child care) is not statistically significant (and such workers are almost exclusively women, mostly poor and minority).

Women have not been liberated from their housewife role. The *housewife*, meaning "unpaid domestic laborer," remains the social role as developed under industrial capitalism (see Glazer-Malbin 1976, Lopata 1971, Oakley 1975), integral to the sociopolitical order. The work and the person doing it are inextricably linked. Although the number of full-time housewives has decreased markedly in recent years, most women are unpaid domestic laborers, "housewives" in this sense, whether or not they are full-time, and whether or not they are actually wives. Technology has not changed this social fact.

Furthermore, technology did not liberate women to work. Poor and working class women—running water and electricity or no—have always worked (Kessler-Harris 1981). Single women from the middle classes have frequently been employed as well. In the past, as today, the major impetus for women to enter the labor force has been economic need (Cowan 1976, Kessler-Harris 1976, Oppenheimer 1970, Sokoloff 1980). The recent substantial influx of married women into the labor force—over 50 percent of married women are now in the labor force compared to 40 percent in 1970[8]—is due to inflation pressures necessitating a two-income household, and/or to recession and consequent male breadwinner unemployment. Since these women, as noted above, are primarily responsible for the housework, technology can make life easier; but it hardly liberates them. Thus, household technology does not multiply women's choices. Women are not, as claimed, freed to work or not; rather, if they end up with two jobs, the unpaid one is necessarily cut back and can be eased through technology.

Technology does affect housewives' choices, however, in other ways. Like most consumers in our economy, the housewife is faced with the "choice" among an array of goods, none of which she has designed, or created, or perhaps even needs. Her influence on such manufactures and services is limited to marketing polls and the negative sanction of refusing to buy. Her choices are limited by what is available on the market, and by her and/or household income. Products carry minute, step-by-step instructions, leaving little room for initiative or ingenuity, and programming women to be docile consumers and workers (Baxandall et al. 1976). Housewives become dependent on company experts to fix malfunctioning machinery that women are to operate but not understand. A consumer-oriented economy encourages dependency on these tools, products, and machinery, including the seemingly indispensable automobile.

The puzzle of why more time did not accrue to the household worker as the result of improved, more sophisticated household technology can be explained in several ways. "[H]ousework is inefficient and small scale because capitalist organization of industry has not yet penetrated here" (Hartmann 1974, p. 226). The woman, working alone, works very much as her grandmother did, performing many jobs, a "veritable jane-of-all-trades" (Cowan 1976, p. 23). Some of the jobs have changed, however; the content of housework has shifted. Instead of scrubbing, polishing, and scouring, women spend more time as consumer-shopper, chauffeur, family counselor, social arranger, and hostess as we move up the class structure, and in child care. Since child care does not lend itself easily to mechanization (Strasser 1982), it fails to appear in the list of ways that technology liberates women. Children remain women's responsibility, including arranging for child care, such as is available. Women also spend more time and energy striving to meet new, exacting household care standards. "Easy-care" fabrics and changed norms and habits bring demands for clean clothes daily or even more often, and frequent changes of towels and linens. Special wash cycles and anti-grease and anti-static products add complexity to mechanical processes. Windows, floors, and walls are to be shining and spotless. Meals become more elaborate as does entertaining, a class-oriented phenomenon (Bose 1979, Cowan 1976, Oakley 1975, Vanek 1974). Finally, household labor is subject to the time schedules of others, schedules that are not necessarily coordinated with each other. Weekly paychecks determine when shopping will be done; husbands' working hours and children's school schedules determine those of housewives. An expanded consumer-shopper role makes the housewife subject to "changes in the distribution network and expansion of services [that] demand physical mobility. . . . The centralization of shopping centers and services may make distribution more efficient, but at the expense of the housewife's time" (Weinbaum & Bridges 1976, pp. 92–93). If the woman has a paid job, she must perform her household tasks around that schedule as well.

A technologized household within an increasingly technologized society thus has liberated women to perform new kinds of household labor and to become dependent on the new technology. It can limit women's choices and enable the political economy to strengthen its control over women's household labor.

It is no mystery why, on balance, household technology operates to control women's domestic labor more than liberating women from it. Technology, as part of the sociopolitical order that produced it, serves that social order and its prevailing ideology. As we have seen, women's unpaid labor in the home is a key prop supporting the capitalist-patriarchal political order. Technology logically serves this end. But how technology performs this role and promotes this end needs further explanation.

The linkage of women's domestic labor, technology, and the political economy has an important history. In a movement that covered especially the first three decades of the twentieth century, home economists proposed to apply scientific management principles to the housewife and dignity to household labor, and also to enable the middle class housewife to cope with an increasingly servantless society. Not only was the housewife to become a good household manager through using efficient new methods, she would also have at her disposal new appliances and products to enhance the ease and efficiency of her work. The corporate sector, newly geared up and organized for expanded mass production and distribution, found in the household a virtually untapped and ready market. The domestic science movement and corporate enterprise became willing allies in "selling Mrs. Consumer" (Cowan 1976, Ehrenreich & English 1979, Nyhart 1982, Strasser

1982). The effects were something other than the home economists had envisioned. Household labor remained low-status work; housewives were less managers than their own maids-of-all-work. Though less burdensome, household tasks proliferated to fill up the time allotted, the corporate sector obligingly taking charge with an endless array of goods and services. The penetration of the household was effected; the age of consumerism grew and flourished (Ehrenreich & English 1979, Ewen 1976). In streamlined, spotless kitchens, housewives were servants to husband and children in a strengthened patriarchal family.

Today, the ideology has shifted: The message is that technology not only lightens housework, it so eases the task as to almost do away with it. Women are still housewives (heterosexual and middle class norms persist), but some of them also "work," the terms "working wives" and "working mothers" reminding us of women's true vocations (and that somehow wives and mothers aren't working). Although the growing numbers of single-person households have been recognized as a market, housewives remain the main marketing focus for household goods and services. How has technology continued to play a role in reinforcing the gender division of labor and the control of women's household labor?

Technology helps the corporate economy to appropriate the housewife's time. New products and processes demand that the housewife educate herself about them, shop for them and comparison shop, and experiment with them, whether microwave ovens, convenience foods, or cleaning aids. Although some products are labor-saving, many are not, such as those adding an extra step in laundering, or making a quality addition to cooking. Others, such as decorating aids and some polishing products, provide make-work for the housewife who supposedly has time on her hands.

Technology helps to underpin the continued existence of an isolated nuclear family structure. The more individual households there are, the more household appliances and products are needed. In a household that is a traditional nuclear family, household technology improves the maintenance of the labor force by the housewife. Through the mediation of this personal wife-mother-servant, the washer-dryer cleans clothes for husband and family members, the refrigerator preserves their food, the stove cooks their meals, the car transports them to and from work, school, and play.

The use-value of women's domestic labor is thereby stressed, that love, not money, is the reward for her personalized service to her family. The individualized, privatized nature of her work becomes a plus that is to bring job satisfaction and work autonomy. In thus supporting precapitalist and preindustrial elements of women's domestic labor, technology as used in the individuated family masks and strengthens the very real dependencies that are created. There is dependency on the technology itself. More important is a resulting economic dependency for the woman within the patriarchal family and on the economy. She becomes dependent on her husband if he is sole or main breadwinner and thus providing the technology (on which he is also dependent); the entire family is tied further into the economy in order to obtain these technological "necessities." Far from domestic labor's being outside the capitalist economy, which had never been the case (see, for example, Fee 1976), domestic labor and thus the housewife, through increased use of and dependency on technology, become more closely linked into the exchange relations of capitalism. As more married women move into the labor force to maintain the family's standard of living, and other women continue to work for pay to maintain themselves and their households, the need for more household technology grows and the ties with capitalist exchange relations are further reinforced. Technology, in providing material advantage, helps to mask a strengthened patriarchal authority and economic dependency that obtain both for an unemployed housewife and for women partially and fully in the labor force.

MYTH AND REALITY

If the liberatory effects of household technology are outweighed by its controlling ones, why does the idea persist that household technology liberates women?[9] Several of the arguments advanced above suggest reasons why, either implicitly or explicitly.

American society, grown affluent in part through its technological know-how, is built on a strong faith in the virtues of technology. Although increasingly questioned as of late, the faith permeates a sizable portion of the American value system, particularly in the halls of economic and political power (see Bush this volume, Rothschild 1981a). The faith was almost unchallenged—Henry Adams notwithstanding—in the early decades of this century when the marriage between the domestic science movement and the corporate economy began the serious work of technologizing the American home. The promoters of household technology no less than its consumers were imbued with the technological faith. Despite growing cracks in the faith today—motivated by malfunctioning appliances, power outages, and expense, as much as by pollution and nuclear weaponry—technology for the household on balance is considered useful and a good. Many would not give up their "goodies," even while criticizing technological society.

And with some reason. The reality is that household labor is far easier with modern technology, in view especially of the indoor plumbing, central heating, refrigeration, electricity, and major appliances that are found today in most U.S. households. The American woman outdoes her sisters a good part of the world over, even in much of the industrialized West where adequate plumbing, central heating, and kitchen appliances are less widespread than in the United States. In industrialized socialist societies, women are liberated to work for pay and then to shoulder the full burdens of housework without modern conveniences (Scott 1974). And in most of the world, women still haul every drop of water their families use, often over considerable distances (Boulding 1976).

Material conditions for American women working in the home are relatively favorable in another way. In the marketplace, working conditions, even for the middle level and professional employee, have become increasingly mechanized, regimented, and proletarianized (Braverman 1974). Workers experience alienation; skills are degraded or lost; automation eliminates jobs, and the need for the workers performing them. Despite the growing controls exercised by the political economy over the woman performing domestic labor at home, she retains some measure of autonomy and ability to organize her time (Oakley 1975). She is not subject to the same routinization and regimentation as the wage worker. Nor is her job threatened with elimination or displacement. Performing her work alone, she still has a variety of tasks and sometimes new ones to learn. Some craft elements remain as she takes a job through from start to finish. Satisfaction can come from successful job completion and from appreciation of her work by family members. More time available for children can bring fulfilling rewards. Thus, the precapitalist and preindustrial character of women's domestic labor carries within it values that the housewife understandably would want to preserve. Why can't the juxtaposition of technology and preindustrial work habits and values bring her the best of both worlds?

The paradox is that exercising and preserving these values under a capitalist-patriarchal system occurs at the expense of strengthening that system's control over her work and herself. The political order manipulates those values and the material conditions that support them, transforming the whole into an ideology to serve its ends. The housewife isolated in the home performing services happily and with ease for household members is a receptive market for household technology. From the reality that technology eases household burdens and that there are satisfactions in pleasing those you love, it is a small step to maintain convincingly that technology can virtually eliminate housework (therefore, why should anyone help her?) and that serving others without pay is women's highest calling. Perpetuating the traditional nuclear family as the norm and the household as women's preferred and major job—because it is so easy and satisfying—also reinforces women's marginality in the labor force, thus further serving the political economy.

The values of nurturance, caring, job satisfaction, and personal over monetary rewards are not false values; nor is household technology an unmitigated evil. But, when these values and the uses of technology are manipulated to reinforce the gender division of labor, they act to control women's domestic labor and women. To maintain that household technology liberates women serves the political order. Over a century ago, John Stuart Mill understood that rather than "a forced slave" men desire "a willing one" (1971, p. 30).

PROMISE AND THREAT

A favorable material position for the American housewife, made possible in part by technology, can, however, provide a precondition for liberation. It was no accident that the initial thrust of the current feminist movement began in the 1960s among relatively affluent white middle-class women who appeared almost as stereotypes of happy suburban housewives in the traditional nuclear family. Called the "problem that has no name," Betty Friedan's (1963) description of the malaise and unease of the suburban housewife struck in them an instant and responsive chord. As they whipped up instant brownies and self-polished their kitchen floors, these women discovered they were not alone in missing the satisfactions and rewards advertised. Victims of the "feminine mystique," they discovered they were being manipulated by a consumer-oriented society in which they were second-class citizens and lacked economic and political power to effect change. Technology and an affluent society (for them) had done their work too well. Comfort plus the make-work provided to fill their time helped to prime them for a raised consciousness when the spark was struck. Political organization followed with the formation of the National Organization for Women in 1966 and a reformist program for social and political change.

Technology, more indirectly, was an impetus for the so-called radical wing of the women's movement that arose mostly on college campuses in the late sixties. Raised in affluent homes usually by non-employed mothers, and then experiencing civil rights, anti-poverty, and anti-war protest, the young feminists were among a generation that questioned and for a time rejected their lives of privilege, including many of its material comforts. From these feminists came not only fundamental challenges to a patriarchal structure and ideology and to economic exploitation, but also challenges to heterosexual bias and to inequities of race, class, and age, as they affect and oppress women (see Evans 1979).

Technology, and more particularly household technology, did not explicitly cause feminism to arise when it did. But the middle class nuclear family, and women's position within that family which technology helped to create and sustain, provided an important precondition for the changed consciousness among the women of privilege who were to initiate the feminist movement. There are lessons and models for the 1980s.

Despite heightened concerns, feminism is still strongly white and middle class, although less so than a decade ago. In an increasingly technologized society in which households, too, are more technologized, this apparent limitation can also be a strength. As earlier, the material reality can help to provide a new level of consciousness and new strategies for change, this time bringing technological analysis more clearly to bear.

As in this chapter (and others in this volume), analyses can be developed that demonstrate how technology can be a manipulative means to oppress and control women. Women, however, need not be urged to reject the technology that, for example, can make the difference between the single mother's being able to cope effectively with job, housework, and children, or not. Rather, the emphasis can be on developing ways to use such technology—selectively, collectively—that put women in greater control.[10] Nor should analyses and proposals for uses of household technology imply to poor and working class women that middle-class comforts—effective plumbing and heating, washer-dryers, freezers, and dishwashers—are unnecessary frills. To advocate as well that the privileged individually give up their comforts does not directly solve anyone else's problems.

More constructively, those with skills and access to resources can move into the design, building, and marketing not only of household technology, but of housing itself, as well as the design generally of urban systems. Empowering women, particularly those less privileged, to improve and create their own built-environments can be an important step for women to gain technological control of those environments (see, for example, Sprague). A central objective must turn on exploring ways that technology can be developed and used to break down the gender division of labor in the home, rather than leaving it untouched or reinforcing it. Recently, interest has been revived in the concept of socializing housework by bringing it into the public sphere (Hayden 1981).

The most dramatic technological innovation of this decade, the microcomputer, and its application to home use, promises a more privatized home environment. As presently developing, the home computer also reinforces the gender division of labor: mother using it for recipes and household accounts, children—boys more than girls—using it for games and perhaps some learning, and dad using it as an adult toy and possibly for professional work. Futurist projections for the computerized household replicate a traditional nuclear family that reflects class and race divisions as well (Rothschild 1980). The dystopian picture drawn by Kurt Vonnegut (1952) thirty years ago of a future computerized America that is elitist, classist, and sexist, may be coming closer to reality than we realize and should give feminists pause. Heightened consciousness motivating serious feminist technological analysis is in order.

Feminist analysis of household technology and the future of women must also take into account the so-called New Right. The New Right's bitter opposition to the Equal Rights Amendment and to women's reproductive rights, along with its support of a conservative political economy, demonstrates clearly how preserving the patriarchal family is linked to preserving advanced industrial capitalism. The linkage demonstrates how the gender division of labor is socially constructed to support political ideology.

When the New Right preempts the family and its caring and nurturant values, casting the family in a traditional but outmoded model, it implies that other household arrangements and having choices among them are not only "anti-family," but anti-American. And when feminist analysis criticizes the role that technology has played in reinforcing the very image of the family that the New Right champions, that criticism appears as an attack on the family. Feminist analysis, in developing a critique and an environment for women's control over technology, must consciously take on the challenge that the New Right poses.

I have argued in this chapter that technology, as integral to a capitalist-patriarchal political order, has not liberated women from their housewife role. It has helped the political order to reinforce the gender division of labor and to control women's domestic labor and women. But because household technology has eased domestic labor and brought comfort and convenience especially to the more privileged classes, it has helped to provide a precondition for liberation, especially among those classes. The task of feminist analysis in the 1980s is to discover how technology designed for the home, within an increasingly automated and corporatized society, can be fashioned to benefit all women and come under their control.

NOTES

1. For an earlier treatment of the thesis of this chapter, see Rothschild 1981b.
2. See Drucker (1967) and "Why *Machina ex Dea*" in this volume.
3. Thus, patriarchy is not confined to capitalist society exclusively. Despite claims to the contrary, so-called socialist societies practice a hierarchic gender division of labor which helps to sustain their systems.
4. I am indebted to the work of a number of feminist theorists in developing this socialist feminist analysis, but particularly to that of Zillah Eisenstein and Iris Young. Young's use of the term *gender* as opposed to *sexual* division of labor to underscore that this division is socially constructed and her insight into the way the gender division of labor underpins capitalism have strongly influenced my theoretical analysis that follows.
5. Rayna Rapp makes an important distinction between *household* and *family*: a *household* being a "locus of shared activities" in which people "enter into relations of production,

reproduction, and consumption with one another," and a *family* being an ideological concept through which "normative recruitment to those relations" is made. See Rapp (1978) and Rapp, Ross, and Bridenthal (1979, pp. 176–79).

6. This model has worked less well for poor and working class families, white or black, because males do not earn enough to sustain the household. Although less able to provide financially, such males, too, have been viewed traditionally as having authority as head of household.
7. See also Cowan (1983).
8. For these and other comparative statistics of women's labor force participation, see U.S. Bureau of the Census (1981, p. 388).
9. For a critical analysis of the liberatory effects of technology, see Goode (1970).
10. See, for example, Jan Zimmerman (1979), who argues that women ignore technology at their peril. Unless women educate themselves and take charge, others will control technology and women. See also *Future, Technology and Woman* (1981).

REFERENCES

Abbott, Edith. 1918. *Women in industry: A study in American economic history*. New York: D. Appleton.

Baxandall, Rosalyn; Ewen, Elizabeth; and Gordon, Linda. 1976. The working class has two sexes. *Monthly Review* 28 (July-Aug.):1–9.

Bose, Christine, 1979. Technology and changes in the division of labor in the American home. *Women's Studies International Quarterly* 2:295–304.

Boulding, Elise. 1976. *The underside of history: A view of women through time*. Boulder, Colo.: Westview Press.

Braverman, Harry. 1974. *Labor and monopoly capital: The degradation of work in the twentieth century*. New York: Monthly Review Press.

Cowan, Ruth Schwartz. 1976. The "industrial revolution" in the home: Household technology and social change in the 20th century. *Technology and Culture* 17 (January):1–23.

Cowan, Ruth Schwartz. 1983. *More work for mother: The ironies of household technology from the open hearth to the microwave*. New York: Basic Books.

Drucker, Peter F. 1967. Technology and society in the twentieth century. *Technology in Western civilization*, v. II, ed. Melvin Kranzberg and Carroll W. Pursell, Jr. New York: Oxford University Press: 22–33.

Ehrenreich, Barbara; and English, Deirdre. 1979. *For her own good: 150 years of the experts' advice to women*. Garden City, N.Y.: Anchor Press/Doubleday.

Eisenstein, Zillah, ed. 1979. *Capitalist patriarchy and the case for socialist feminism*. New York: Monthly Review Press.

Evans, Sara. 1979. *Personal politics: The roots of women's liberation in the civil rights movement and the New Left*. New York: Alfred A. Knopf.

Ewen, Stuart. 1976. *Captains of consciousness*. New York: McGraw-Hill.

Fee, Terry. 1976. Domestic labor: An analysis of housework and its relations to the production process. *The Review of Radical Political Economics* 8 (Spring):1–8.

Friedan, Betty. 1963. *The feminine mystique*. New York: W. W. Norton.

Future, Technology and Woman. 1981. Proceedings of the conference (March). San Diego, CA: San Diego State University.

Gendron, Bernard. 1977. *Technology and the human condition*. New York: St. Martin's Press.

Glazer-Malbin, Nona. 1976. Housework. *Signs* 1 (Summer):905–22.

Goode, William S. 1970. *World revolution and family patterns*. New York: Free Press.

Hartmann, Heidi. 1974. Capitalism and women's work in the home. Ph.D. thesis, Yale University.

Hartmann, Heidi. 1976. Capitalism, patriarchy, and job segregation by sex. *Women and the workplace: the implications of occupational segregation*, ed. Martha Blaxall and Barbara Regan. Chicago: University of Chicago Press: 137–69.

Hayden, Dolores. 1981. *The grand domestic revolution*. Cambridge, Mass.: MIT Press.

Kessler-Harris, Alice. 1976. Women, work, and the social order. *Liberating women's history*, ed. Berenice Carroll. Urbana: University of Illinois Press: 330–43.

Kessler-Harris, Alice. 1981. *Women have always worked: A historical overview*. Old Westbury, N.Y.: The Feminist Press; and New York: McGraw-Hill.

Lopata, Helena Z. 1971. *Occupation housewife*. New York: Oxford University Press.

Mill, John Stuart. 1971. *On the subjection of women*. New York: Fawcett. (orig. publ. 1869).

Noble, David F. 1977. *America by design: Science, technology, and the rise of corporate capitalism*. New York: Alfred A. Knopf.

Nyhart, Lynn. 1982. Introducing "Scientific Management" into the home: Efficiency and the home economics movement, 1900–1920. Presented at annual meeting of the Society for the History of Technology, Philadelphia, October.

Oakley, Ann. 1975. *Woman's work: The housewife, past and present*. New York: Pantheon.

Oppenheimer, Valerie Kincade. 1970. *The female labor force in the United States: Demographic and economic factors governing its growth and changing composition*. Berkeley, Calif: Population Monograph Series, No. 5.

Rapp, Rayna. 1978. Family and class in contemporary America: Notes toward an understanding of ideology. *Science & Society* 42 (Fall):278–300.

Rapp, Rayna; Ross, Ellen; and Bridenthal, Renate. 1979. Examining family history. *Feminist Studies* 5 (Spring):174–200.

Rothschild, Joan. 1980. Sexism and/in the future. *Alternative Futures* 3 (Summer):54–61.

Rothschild, Joan A. 1981a. A feminist perspective on technology and the future. *Women's Studies International Quarterly* 4:65–74.

Rothschild, Joan. 1981b. Technology, "women's work" and the social control of women. *Women, power and political systems*, ed. Margherita Rendel, London: Croom Helm: 160–83.

Sacks, Karen. 1974. Engels revisited: Women, the organization of production, and private property. *Woman, culture, and society*, ed. Michelle Zimbalist Rosaldo and Louise Lamphere. Stanford, Calif.: Stanford University Press: 207–22.

Scott, Hilda. 1974. *Does socialism liberate women*? Boston: Beacon Press.

Sokoloff, Natalie. 1980. *Between money and love: The dialectics of women's home and market work*. New York: Praeger.

Sprague, Joan Forrester, Executive Director. Women's Institute for Housing and Economic Development, Inc. Boston, MA.

Strasser, Susan. 1982. *Never done: A history of American housework*. New York: Pantheon.

Thrall, Charles A. 1982. The conservative use of modern household technology. *Technology and Culture* 23 (April):175–94.

U.S. Bureau of the Census. 1981. *Statistical abstract of the United States*.

Vanek, Joann. 1974. Time spent in housework. *Scientific American* 231 (November):116–20.

Vanek, Joann. 1978. Household technology and social status: Rising living standards and status and residence differences in housework. *Technology and Culture* 19 (July):361–75.

Vonnegut, Kurt, Jr. 1952. *Player piano*. New York: Dell Publishing.

Weinbaum, Batya; and Bridges, Amy. 1976. The other side of the paycheck: monopoly capital and the structure of consumption. *Monthly Review* 28 (July–Aug.):88–103.

Welter, Barbara. 1966. The cult of true womanhood, 1820–1860. *American Quarterly* 18 (Summer):151–74.

Young, Iris. 1981. Beyond the unhappy marriage: A critique of the dual systems theory. *Women and revolution*, ed. Lydia Sargent. Boston: South End Press: 43–69.

Zaretsky, Eli. 1976. *Capitalism, the family, & personal life*. New York: Harper & Row.

Zimmerman, Jan. 1979. Women's need for high technology. *Conference proceedings: Women and technology: Deciding what's appropriate*. Missoula, Montana: Women's Resource Center, April.

PART II
TECHNOLOGY AND VALUES: DEA AND DEUS RECONSIDERED

Introduction

A recurrent and important theme in the philosophy of science and technology is the relationship of scientific and technological activity to nature and, thus, the relationship of human beings to nature. Cast in a man-nature framework, however, these discussions have ignored the strong and traditional identification of woman with nature and, thus, a significant range of dualistic thought embedded in the philosophy and value assumptions of Western culture. The chapters in this section speak to the meaning and implications of such dualisms for the development and outlook of Western science and technology.

Tracing the transformation of attitudes toward the earth and nature during the Scientific Revolution, Carolyn Merchant's chapter shows how the controlling imagery was transformed from that of reverence to one of domination. Linking woman and nature, ancient and medieval imagery that depicted a nurturing mother earth acted as a sanction to forbid its invasion for mining or similar use. But, as a mechanistic worldview advanced to underpin mechanical and scientific invention and the developing commercial interests, the organic framework was undermined. Conquest and domination replaced the female principle as the controlling imagery, as mastery and exploitation of nature emerged and prevailed.

In the next chapter, Ynestra King joins woman and nature and ecological perspectives to delineate the theory and movement of ecofeminism. Based on principles found in both feminism and ecology, ecofeminism links ecological harmony and integration with the natural environment with a feminist identification of woman and nature. The hierarchy that is projected onto nature, manifested in both social domination and domination of nature, is reflected in the view of woman as Other and in her domination and subjugation. Stressing a connectedness with nature and seeking an end to all hierarchies, ecofeminism has developed a culture and politics of nonviolent resistance to all forms of destruction of nature. Militarism and its arsenal of nuclear and other weaponry thus become a prime ecofeminist target. To illustrate, King describes such actions against the military by ecofeminist groups alone and in concert with other antimilitary, antiwar movements.

Taking a psychological approach, Evelyn Keller in the next chapter explores gender dualism as it is manifested in science and scientific inquiry. The prevailing scientific approach to knowledge that is male in character, suppressing the intuitive and holistic, reflects gender ideology that is rooted in part in psychological factors of personality development. Rejecting the intuitive identification of woman and nature she finds in ecofeminism, Keller employs object-relations theory to explain how males and females are conditioned to observe the world and its phenomena in different ways. Using the case example of biologist Barbara McClintock's holistic approach to her subject, Keller demonstrates the thesis that gender ideology in support of scientific ideology helps to explain not only why women and men scientists approach their work differently, but also why the numbers of women scientists remain small.

From divergent viewpoints, these feminist perspectives on female-male dualisms as they affect science and technology challenge us to rethink prevailing beliefs about the interplay of science, technology, and nature. Feminist critiques in particular push us to examine some of the hidden values and assumptions that underpin abstract rationalist and instrumentalist approaches to the philosophy of science and technology.

6

*Mining the Earth's Womb**

Carolyn Merchant

The domination of the earth through technology and the corresponding rise of the image of the world as *Machina ex Deo* were features of the Scientific Revolution of the sixteenth and seventeenth centuries. During this period, the two ideas of mechanism and the domination of nature came to be core concepts and controlling images of our modern world. An organically oriented mentality prevalent from ancient times to the Renaissance, in which the female principle played a significant positive role, was gradually undermined and replaced by a technological mindset that used female principles in an exploitative manner. As Western culture became increasingly mechanized during the 1600s, a female nurturing earth and virgin earth spirit were subdued by the machine.

The change in controlling imagery was directly related to changes in human attitudes and behavior toward the earth. Whereas the older nurturing earth image can be viewed as a cultural constraint restricting the types of socially and morally sanctioned human actions allowable with respect to the earth, the new images of mastery and domination functioned as cultural sanctions for the denudation of nature. Society needed these new images as it continued the processes of commercialism and industrialization, which depended on activities directly altering the earth—mining, drainage, deforestation, and assarting (grubbing up stumps to clear fields). The new activities utilized new technologies—lift and force pumps, cranes, windmills, geared wheels, flap valves, chains, pistons, treadmills, under- and overshot watermills, fulling mills, flywheels, bellows, excavators, bucket chains, rollers, geared and wheeled bridges, cranks, elaborate block and tackle systems, worm, spur, crown, and lantern gears, cams and eccentrics, ratchets, wrenches, presses, and screws in magnificent variation and combination.

These technological and commercial changes did not take place quickly; they developed gradually over the ancient and medieval eras, as did the accompanying environmental deterioration. Slowly, over many centuries,

---

* Adapted from chaps. 1 and 7 in *The Death of nature: Women, ecology, and the Scientific Revolution* by Carolyn Merchant.

early Mediterranean and Greek civilization had mined and quarried the mountainsides, altered the forested landscape, and overgrazed the hills. Nevertheless, technologies were low level, people considered themselves parts of a finite cosmos, and animism and fertility cults that treated nature as sacred were numerous. Roman civilization was more pragmatic, secular, and commercial and its environmental impact more intense. Yet Roman writers such as Ovid, Seneca, Pliny, and the Stoic philosophers openly deplored mining as an abuse of their mother, the earth. With the disintegration of feudalism and the expansion of Europeans into new worlds and markets, commercial society began to have an accelerated impact on the natural environment. By the sixteenth and seventeenth centuries, the tension between technological development in the world of action and the controlling organic images in the world of the mind had become too great. The old structures were incompatible with the new activities.

Both the nurturing and domination metaphors had existed in philosophy, religion, and literature—the idea of dominion over the earth in Greek philosophy and Christian religion; that of the nurturing earth, in Greek and other pagan philosophies. But, as the economy became modernized and the Scientific Revolution proceeded, the dominion metaphor spread beyond the religious sphere and assumed ascendancy in the social and political spheres as well. These two competing images and their normative associations can be found in sixteenth-century literature, art, philosophy, and science.

The image of the earth as a living organism and nurturing mother had served as a cultural constraint restricting the actions of human beings. One does not readily slay a mother, dig into her entrails for gold, or mutilate her body, although commercial mining would soon require that. As long as the earth was considered to be alive and sensitive, it could be considered a breach of human ethical behavior to carry out destructive acts against it. For most traditional cultures, minerals and metals ripened in the uterus of the Earth Mother, mines were compared to her vagina, and metallurgy was the human hastening of the birth of the living metal in the artificial womb of the furnace—an abortion of the metals' natural growth cycle before its time. Miners offered propitiation to the deities of the soil and subterranean world, performed ceremonial sacrifices, and observed strict cleanliness, sexual abstinence, and fasting before violating the sacredness of the living earth by sinking a mine. Smiths assumed an awesome responsibility in precipitating the metal's birth through smelting, fusing, and beating it with hammer and anvil; they were often accorded the status of shaman in tribal rituals and their tools were thought to hold special powers (Eliade 1962, pp. 53–70, 79–96).

The Renaissance image of the nurturing earth still carried with it subtle ethical controls and restraints. Such imagery found in a culture's literature can play a normative role within the culture. Controlling images operate as ethical restraints or as ethical sanctions—as subtle "oughts" or "ought-nots." Thus, as the descriptive metaphors and images of nature change, a behavioral restraint can be changed into a sanction. Such a change in the image and description of nature was occurring during the course of the Scientific Revolution.

It is important to recognize the normative import of descriptive statements about nature. Contemporary philosophers of language have critically reassessed the earlier positivist distinction between the "is" of science and the "ought" of society, arguing that descriptions and norms are not opposed to one another by linguistic separation into separate "is" and "ought" statements, but are contained within each other. Descriptive statements about the world can presuppose the normative; they are then ethic-laden. A statement's normative function lies in the use itself as description. The norms may be tacit assumptions hidden within the descriptions in such a way as to act as invisible restraints or moral ought-nots. The writer or culture may not be conscious of the ethical import yet may act in accordance with its dictates. The hidden norms may become conscious or explicit when an alternative or contradiction presents itself. Because language contains a culture within itself, when language changes, a culture is also changing in important ways. By examining changes in descriptions of nature, we can then perceive something of the changes in cultural values. To be aware of the interconnectedness of descriptive and normative statements is to be able to evaluate changes in the latter by observing changes in the former (Cavell 1971, pp. 148, 165).

Not only did the image of nature as nurturing mother contain ethical implications but the organic framework itself, as a conceptual system, also carried with it an associated value system. Contemporary philosophers have argued that a given normative theory is linked with certain conceptual frameworks and not with others. The framework contains within itself certain dimensions of structural and normative variation, while denying others belonging to an alternative or rival framework (Taylor 1973).

We cannot accept a framework of explantion and yet reject its associated value judgments, because the connections to the values associated with the structure are not fortuitous. New commercial and technological innovations, however, can upset and undermine an established conceptual structure. New human and social needs can threaten associated normative constraints, thereby demanding new ones.

While the organic framework was for many centuries sufficiently integrative to override commercial development and technological innovation, the acceleration of such changes throughout Western Europe during the sixteenth and seventeenth centuries began to undermine the organic unity of the cosmos and society. Because the needs and purposes of society as a whole were changing with the commercial revolution, the values associated with the organic view of nature were no longer applicable; hence, the plausibility of the conceptual framework itself was slowly, but continuously, being threatened.

THE GEOCOSM: THE EARTH AS A NURTURING MOTHER

Not only was nature in a generalized sense seen as female, but also the earth, or geocosm, was universally viewed as a nurturing mother—sensitive, alive, and responsive to human action. The changes in imagery and attitudes relating to the earth were of enormous significance as the mechanization of nature proceeded. The nurturing earth would lose its function as a normative restraint as it changed to a dead, inanimate, physical system.

The macrocosm theory likened the cosmos to the human body, soul, and spirit with male and female reproductive components. Similarly, the geocosm theory compared the earth to the living human body, with breath, blood, sweat, and elimination systems.

For the Stoics, who flourished in Athens during the third century B.C., after the death of Aristotle, and in Rome through the first century A.D., the world itself was an intelligent organism; God and matter were synonymous. Matter was dynamic, composed of two forces: expansion and condensation—the former directed outward, the latter inward. The tension between them was the inherent force generating all substances, properties, and living forms in the cosmos and the geocosm.

Zeno of Citium (ca. 304 B.C.) and M. Tullius Cicero (106–43 B.C.) held that the world reasons, has sensation, and generates living rational beings: "The world is a living and wise being, since it produces living and wise beings" (Cicero 1775, p. 96). Every part of the universe and the earth was created for the benefit and support of another part. The earth generated and gave stability to plants, plants supported animals, and animals in turn served human beings; conversely, human skill helped to preserve these organisms. The Universe itself was created for the sake of rational beings—gods and men—but God's foresight insured the safety and preservation of all things. Humankind was given hands to transform the earth's resources and dominion over them: timber was to be used for houses and ships, soil for crops, iron for plows, and gold and silver for ornaments. Each part and imperfection existed for the sake and ultimate perfection of the whole.

The living character of the world organism meant not only that the stars and planets were alive, but that the earth too was pervaded by a force giving life and motion to the living beings on it. Lucius Seneca (4 B.C.–A.D. 65), a Roman Stoic, stated that the earth's breath nourished both the growths on its surface and the heavenly bodies above by its daily exhalations:

> How could she nourish all the different roots that sink into the soil in one place and another, had she not an abundant supply of the breath of life? . . . all these [heavenly bodies] draw their nourishment from materials of earth . . . and are sustained . . . by nothing else than the breath of the earth. . . . Now the earth would be unable to nourish so many bodies . . . unless it were full of breath, which it exhales from every part of it day and night (Seneca 1910, p. 244).

The earth's springs were akin to the human blood system; its other various fluids were likened to the mucus, saliva, sweat, and other forms of lubrication in the human body, the earth being organized " . . . much after the plan of our bodies, in which there are both veins and arteries, the former blood vessels, the latter air vessels. . . . So exactly alike is the resemblance to our bodies in nature's formation of the earth, that our ancestors have spoken of veins (= springs) of water." Just as the human body contained blood, marrow, mucus, saliva, tears, and lubricating fluids, so in the earth there were varius fluids. Liquids that turned hard became metals, such as gold and silver, other fluids turned into stones, bitumens, and veins of sulfur. Like the human body, the earth gave forth sweat: "There is often a gathering of thin, scattered moisture like dew, which from many points flows into one spot. The dowsers call it *sweat*, because a kind of drop is either squeezed out by the pressure of the ground or raised by the heat" (Seneca 1910, pp. 126–27).

Leonardo da Vinci (1452–1519) elaborated the Greek analogy between the waters of the earth and the ebb and flow of human blood through the veins and heart:

> The water runs from the rivers to the sea and from the sea to the rivers, always making the same circuit. The water is thrust from the utmost depth of the sea to the high summits of the mountains, where, finding the veins cut, it precipitates itself and returns to the sea below, mounts once more by the branching veins and then falls back, thus going and coming between high and low, sometimes inside, sometimes outside. It acts like the blood of animals which is always moving, starting from the sea of the heart and mounting to the summit of the head (Cornford 1937, p. 330).

The earth's venous system was filled with metals and minerals. Its veins, veinlets, seams, and canals coursed through the entire earth, particularly in the mountains. Its humors flowed from the veinlets into the larger veins. The earth, like the human, even had its own elimination system. The tendency for both to break wind caused earthquakes in the case of the former and another type of quake in the latter:

> The material cause of earthquakes . . . is no doubt great abundance of wind, or store of gross and dry vapors, and spirits, fast shut up, and as a man would

> say, emprisoned in the caves, and dungeons of the earth; which wind, or vapors, seeking to be set at liberty, and to get them home to their natural lodgings, in a great fume, violently rush out, and as it were, break prison, which forcible eruption, and strong breath, causeth an earthquake (Gabriel Harvey quoted in Kendrick 1974, p. 542, spelling modernized).

Its bowels were full of channels, fire chambers, glory holes, and fissures through which fire and heat were emitted, some in the form of fiery volcanic exhalations, others as hot water springs. The most commonly used analogy, however, was between the female's reproductive and nurturing capacity and the mother earth's ability to give birth to stones and metals within its womb through its marriage with the sum.

In his *De Rerum Natura* of 1565, the Italian philosopher Bernardino Telesio referred to the marriage of the two great male and female powers: "We can see that the sky and the earth are not merely large parts of the world universe, but are of primary—even principal rank. . . . They are like mother and father to all the others" (Telesio 1967, p. 308). The earth and the sun served as mother and father to the whole of creation: all things are "made of earth by the sun and that in the constitution of all things the earth and the sun enter respectively as mother and father." According to Giordano Bruno (1548–1600), every human being was "a citizen and servant of the world, a child of Father Sun and Mother Earth" (Bruno 1964, p. 72).

A widely held alchemical belief was the growth of the baser metals into gold in womblike matrices in the earth. The appearance of silver in lead ores or gold in silvery assays was evidence that this transformation was underway. Just as the child grew in the warmth of the female womb, so the growth of metals was fostered through the agency of heat, some places within the earth's crust being hotter and therefore hastening the maturation process. "Given to gold, silver, and the other metals [was] the vegetative powers whereby they could also reproduce themselves. For, since it was impossible for God to make anything that was not perfect, he gave to all created things, with their being, the power of multiplication." The sun acting on the earth nurtured not only the plants and animals but also "the metals, the broken sulfuric, bituminous, or nitrogenous rocks; . . . as well as the plants and animals—if these are not made of earth by the sun, one cannot imagine of what else or by what other agent they could be made" (Telesio 1967, p. 309).

The earth's womb was the matrix or mother not only of metals but also of living things. Paracelsus compared the earth to a female whose womb nurtured all life.

> Woman is like the earth and all the elements and in this sense she may be considered a matrix; she is the tree which grows in the earth and the child is

> like the fruit born of the tree. . . . Woman is the image of the tree. Just as the earth, its fruits, and the elements are created for the sake of the tree and in order to sustain it, so the members of woman, all her qualities, and her whole nature exist for the sake of her matrix, her womb. . . .
>
> And yet woman in her own way is also a field of the earth and not at all different from it. She replaces it, so to speak; she is the field and the garden mold in which the child is sown and planted (Paracelsus 1951, p. 25).

The earth in the Paracelsian philosophy was the mother or matrix giving birth to plants, animals, and men.

The image of the earth as a nurse, which had appeared in the ancient world in Plato's *Timaeus* and the *Emerald Tablet* of Hermes Trismegistus, was a popular Renaissance metaphor. According to sixteenth-century alchemist Basil Valentine, all things grew in the womb of the earth, which was alive, and vital, and the nurse of all life:

> The quickening power of the earth produces all things that grow forth from it, and he who says that the earth has no life makes a statement flatly contradicted by facts. What is dead cannot produce life and growth, seeing that it is devoid of the quickening spirit. . . . This spirit is the life and soul that dwell in the earth, and are nourished by heavenly and sidereal influences. . . . This spirit is itself fed by the stars and is thereby rendered capable of imparting nutriment to all things that grow and of nursing them as a mother does her child while it is yet in the womb. . . . If the earth were deserted by this spirit it would be dead (Valentine 1974, p. 333).

In general, the Renaissance view was that all things were permeated by life, there being no adequate method by which to designate the inanimate from the animate. It was difficult to differentiate between living and nonliving things because of the resemblance in structures. Like plants and animals, minerals and gems were filled with small pores, tubelets, cavities, and streaks through which they seemed to nourish themselves. Crystalline salts were compared to plant forms, but criteria by which to differentiate the living from the nonliving could not successfully be formulated. This was due not only to the vitalistic framework of the period but to striking similarities between them. Minerals were thought to possess a lesser degree of the vegetative soul, because they had the capacity for medicinal action and often took the form of various parts of plants. By virtue of the vegetative soul, minerals and stones grew in the human body, in animal bodies, within trees, in the air and water, and on the earth's surface in the open country (Adams 1938, pp. 102–36).

Popular Renaissance literature was filled with hundreds of images associating nature, matter, and the earth with the female sex. The earth was alive and considered to be a beneficent, receptive, nurturing female. For most writers, there was a mingling of traditions based on ancient sources. In general, the pervasive animism of nature created a relationship of immediacy with the human being. An I-thou relationship in which nature was considered to be a person-writ-large was sufficiently prevalent that the ancient tendency to treat it as another human still existed. Such vitalistic imagery was thus so widely accepted by the Renaissance mind that it could effectively function as a restraining ethic.

In much the same way, the cultural belief-systems of many American Indian tribes had for centuries subtly guided group behavior toward nature. Smohalla of the Columbia Basin Tribes voiced the Indian objections to European attitudes in the mid-1800s:

> You ask me to plow the ground! Shall I take a knife and tear my mother's breast? Then when I die she will not take me to her bosom to rest.
>
> You ask me to dig for stone! Shall I dig under her skin for her bones? Then when I die I cannot enter her body to be born again.
>
> You ask me to cut grass and make hay and sell it, and be rich like white men! But how dare I cut off my mother's hair? (quoted in McLuhan 1971, p. 56).

In the 1960s, the Native American became a symbol in the ecology movement's search for alternatives to Western exploitative attitudes. The Indian animistic belief-system and reverence for the earth as a mother were contrasted with the Judeo-Christian heritage of dominion over nature and with capitalist practices resulting in the "tragedy of the commons" (exploitation of resources available for any person's or nation's use). But as will be seen, European culture was more complex and varied than this judgment allows. It ignores the Renaissance philosophy of the nurturing earth as well as those philosophies and social movements resistant to mainstream economic change.

NORMATIVE CONSTRAINTS AGAINST THE MINING OF MOTHER EARTH

If sixteenth-century descriptive statements and imagery can function as an ethical constraint and if the earth was widely viewed as a nurturing mother, did such imagery actually function as a norm against improper use of the earth? Evidence that this was indeed the case can be drawn from theories of the origins of metals and the debates about mining prevalent during the sixteenth century.

What ethical ideas were held by ancient and early modern writers on the extraction of the metals from the bowels of the living earth? The Roman compiler Pliny (A.D. 23–79), in his *Natural History*, had specifically warned against mining the depth of Mother Earth, speculating that earthquakes were an expression of her indignation at being violated in this manner:

> We trace out all the veins of the earth, and yet . . . are astonished that it should occasionally cleave asunder or tremble: as though, forsooth, these signs could be any other than expressions of the indignation felt by our sacred parent! We penetrate into her entrails, and seek for treasures . . . as though each spot we tread upon were not sufficiently bounteous and fertile for us! (Pliny 1858, vol. 6, pp. 68–69)

He went on to argue that the earth had concealed from view that which she did not wish to be disturbed, that her resources might not be exhausted by human avarice:

> For it is upon her surface, in fact, that she has presented us with these substances, equally with the cereals, bounteous and ever ready, as she is, in supplying us with all things for our benefit! It is what is concealed from our view, what is sunk far beneath her surface, objects, in fact, of no rapid formation, that urge us to our ruin, that send us to the very depth of hell. . . . when will be the end of thus exhausting the earth, and to what point will avarice finally penetrate! (Pliny 1858, vol. 6, p. 69)

Here, then, is a striking example of the restraining force of the beneficent mother image—the living earth in her wisdom has ordained against the mining of metals by concealing them in the depths of her womb.

While mining gold led to avarice, extracting iron was the source of human cruelty in the form of war, murder, and robbery. Its use should be limited to agriculture and those activities that contributed to the "honors of more civilized life":

> For by the aid of iron we lay open the ground, we plant trees, we prepare our vineyard trees, and we force our vines each year to resume their youthful state, by cutting away their decayed branches. It is by the aid of iron that we construct houses, cleave rocks, and perform so many other useful offices of life. But it is with iron also that wars, murders, and robberies are effected, . . . not only hand to hand, but . . . by the aid of missiles and winged weapons, now launched from engines, now hurled by the human arm, and now furnished with feathery wings. Let us therefore acquit nature of a charge that here belongs to man himself (Pliny 1858, vol. 6, p. 205).

In past history, Pliny stated, there had been instances in which laws were passed to prohibit the retention of weapons and to ensure that iron was used solely for innocent purposes, such as the cultivation of fields.

In the *Metamorphoses* (A.D. 7), the Roman poet Ovid wrote of the violence done to the earth during the age of iron, when evil was let loose in the form of trickery, slyness, plotting, swindling, and violence, as men dug into the earth's entrails for iron and gold:

> The rich earth
> Was asked for more; they dug into her vitals,
> Pried out the wealth a kinder lord had hidden
> In stygian shadow, all that precious metal,
> The root of evil. They found the guilt of iron,
> And gold, more guilty still. And War came forth.
> (Ovid 1955, 1. 137–43)

The violation of Mother Earth resulted in new forms of monsters, born of the blood of her slaughter:

> Jove struck them down
> With thunderbolts, and the bulk of those huge bodies
> Lay on the earth, and bled, and Mother earth,
> Made pregnant by that blood, brought forth new bodies,
> And gave them, to recall her older offspring,
> The forms of men. And this new stock was also
> Contemptuous of gods, and murder-hungry
> And violent. You would know they were sons of blood.
> (Ovid 1955, 1. 155–62)

Seneca also deplored the activity of mining, although, unlike Pliny and Ovid, he did not consider it a new vice, but one that had been handed down from ancient times. "What necessity caused man, whose head points to the stars, to stoop, below, burying him in mines and plunging him in the very bowels of innermost earth to root up gold?" Not only did mining remove the earth's treasures, but it created "a sight to make [the] hair stand on end—huge rivers and vast reservoirs of sluggish waters." The defiling of the earth's waters was even then a noteworthy consequence of the quest for metals (Seneca 1910, p. 207–08).

These ancient strictures against mining were still operative during the early years of the commercial revolution when mining activities, which had lapsed after the fall of Rome, were once again revived. Ultimately, such constraints would have to be defeated by proponents of the new mercantilist philosophy.

An allegorical tale, reputedly sent to Paul Schneevogel, a professor at Leipzig about 1490–1495, expressed opposition to mining encroachments into the farmlands of Lichtenstat in Saxony, Germany, an area where the new mining activities were developing rapidly. In the following allegorical vision of an old hermit of Lichtenstat, Mother Earth is dressed in a tattered green robe and seated on the right hand of Jupiter who is represented in a court case by "glib-tongued Mercury" who charges a miner with matricide. Testimony is presented by several of nature's deities:

> Bacchus complained that his vines were uprooted and fed to the flames and his most sacred places desecrated. Ceres stated that her fields were devastated; Pluto that the blows of the miners resound like thunder through the depths of the earth, so that he could hardly reside in his own kingdom; the Naiad, that the subterranean waters were diverted and her fountains dried up; Charon that the volume of the underground waters had been so diminished that he was unable to float his boat on Acheron and carry the souls across to Pluto's realm, and the Fauns protested that the charcoal burners had destroyed whole forests to obtain fuel to smelt the miner's ores (Adams 1938, p. 172).

In his defense, the miner argued that the earth was not a real mother, but a wicked stepmother who hides and conceals the metals in her inner parts instead of making them available for human use.

In the old hermit's tale, we have a fascinating example of the relationship between images and values. The older view of nature as a kindly mother is challenged by the growing interests of the mining industry in Saxony, Bohemia, and the Harz Mountains, regions of newly found prosperity. The miner, representing these newer commercial activities, transforms the image of the nurturing mother into that of a stepmother who wickedly conceals her bounty from the deserving and needy children.

Henry Cornelius Agrippa's polemic *The Vanity of Arts and Sciences* (1530) reiterated some of the moral strictures against mining found in the ancient treatises, quoting the passage from Ovid portraying miners digging into the bowels of the earth in order to extract gold and iron. "These men," he declared, "have made the very ground more hurtful and pestiferous, by how much they are more rash and venturous than they that hazard themselves in the deep to dive for pearls." Mining thus despoiled the earth's surface, infecting it, as it were, with an epidemic disease (Agrippa 1694, pp. 81–82).

If mining were to be freed of such strictures and sanctioned as a commercial activity, the ancient arguments would have to be refuted. This task was taken up by Georg Agricola (1494–1555), who wrote the first "modern" treatise on mining. His *De Re Metallica* ("On Metals," 1556) marshaled the arguments of the detractors of mining in order to refute them and thereby promote the activity itself.

According to Agricola, people who argued against the mining of the earth for metals did so on the basis that nature herself did not wish to be discovered what she herself had concealed:

> The earth does not conceal and remove from our eyes those things which are useful and necessary to mankind, but, on the contrary, like a beneficent and kindly mother she yields in large abundance from her bounty and brings into the light of day the herbs, vegetables, grains, and fruits, and trees. The minerals, on the other hand, she buries far beneath in the depth of the ground, therefore they should not be sought (Agricola 1950, pp. 6–7).

This argument, taken directly from Pliny, reveals the normative force of the image of the earth as a nurturing mother.

A second argument of the detractors, reminiscent of Seneca and Agrippa, and based on Renaissance "ecological" concerns was the disruption of the natural environment and the pollutive effects of mining.

> But, besides this, the strongest argument of the detractors [of mining] is that the fields are devastated by mining operations, for which reason formerly Italians were warned by law that no one should dig the earth for metals and so injure their very fertile fields, their vineyards, and their olive groves. Also they argue that the woods and groves are cut down, for there is need of wood for timbers, machines, and the smelting of metals. And when the woods and groves are felled, then are exterminated the beasts and birds, many of which furnish a pleasant and agreeable food for man. Further, when the ores are washed, the water which has been used poisons the brooks and streams, and either destroys the fish or drives them away. Therefore the inhabitants of these regions, on account of the devastation of their fields, woods, groves, brooks, and rivers, find great difficulty in procuring the necessaries of life, and by reason of the destruction of the timber they are forced to greater expense in erecting buildings. Thus it is said, it is clear to all that there is greater detriment from mining than the value of the metals which the mining produces (Agricola 1950, p. 8).

Agricola may have been alluding to laws passed by the Florentines between 1420 and 1485, preventing people from dumping lime into rivers upstream from the city for the purpose of "poisoning or catching fish," as it caused severe problems for those living downstream. The laws were enacted both to preserve the trout, "a truly noble and impressive fish" and to provide Florence with "a copious and abundant supply of such fish" (Trexler 1974, p. 463).

Such ecological consciousness, however, suffered because of the failure of law enforcement, as well as because of the continuing progress of mining activities. Agricola, in his response to the detractors of mining, pointed out the congruences in the need to catch fish and to construct metal tools for the well-being of the human race. His effort can be interpreted as an attempt to liberate the activity of mining from the constraints imposed by the organic framework and the nurturing earth image, so that new values could sanction and hasten its development.

To the argument that the woods were cut down and the price of timber therefore raised, Agricola responded that most mines occurred in unproductive, gloomy areas. Where the trees were removed from more productive sites, fertile fields could be created, the profits from which would reimburse the local inhabitants for their losses in timber supplies. Where the birds and animals had been destroyed by mining operations, the profits could be used to purchase "birds without number" and "edible beasts and fish elsewhere" and refurbish the area (Agricola 1950, p. 17).

The vices associated with the metals—anger, cruelty, discord, passion for power, avarice, and lust—should be attributed instead to human conduct: "It is not the metals which are to be blamed, but the evil passions of men which become inflamed and ignited; or it is due to the blind and impious desires of their minds." Agricola's arguments are a conscious attempt to separate the older normative constraints from the image of the metals themselves so that new values can then surround them (Agricola 1950, p. 16).

Edmund Spenser's treatment of Mother Earth in the *Faerie Queene* (1595) was representative of the concurrent conflict of attitudes about mining the earth. Spenser entered fully into the sixteenth-century debates about the wisdom of mining, the two greatest sins against the earth being, according to him, avarice and lust. The arguments associating mining with avarice had appeared in the ancient texts of Pliny, Ovid, and Seneca, while during Spenser's lifetime the sermons of Johannes Mathesius, entitled *Beregpostilla, oder Sarepta* (1578), inveighed against the moral consequences of human greed for the wealth created by mining for metals (Kendrick 1974, pp. 548–53).

In Spenser's poem, Guyon presents the arguments against mining taken from Ovid and Agricola, while the description of Mammon's forge is drawn from the illustrations to the *De Re Metallica*. Gold and silver pollute the spirit and debase human values just as the mining operation itself pollutes the "purest streams" of the earth's womb:

> Then gan a cursed hand the quiet wombe
> Of his great Grandmother with steele to wound,
> And the hid treasures in her sacred tombe
> With Sacrilege to dig. Therein he found
> Fountaines of gold and silver to abound,
> Of which the matter of his huge desire
> And pompous pride eftsoones he did compound.
>
> (Spenser 1758, Bk II, Canto 7, verse 17)

The earth in Spenser's poem is passive and docile, allowing all manner of assault, violence, ill-treatment, rape by lust, and despoilment by greed. No longer a nurturer, she indiscriminately, as in Ovid's verse, supplies flesh to all life and lacking in judgment brings forth monsters and evil creatures. Her offspring fall and bite her in their own death throes. The new mining activities have altered the earth from a bountiful mother to a passive receptor of human rape (Kendrick 1974).

John Milton's *Paradise Lost* (1667) continues the Ovidian image, as Mammon leads "bands of pioneers with Spade and Pickaxe" in the wounding of the living female earth:

. . . By him first
Men also, and by his suggestion taught,
Ransack'd the Center, and with impious hands
Rifl 'd the bowels of their mother Earth
For Treasures better hid. Soon had his crew
Op'nd into the Hill a spacious wound
And dig'd out ribs of Gold.
(Milton 1975, Bk I, 11. 684–90)

Not only did mining encourage the mortal sin of avarice, it was compared by Spenser to the second great sin, human lust. Digging into the matrices and pockets of earth for metals was like mining the female flesh for pleasure. The sixteenth- and seventeenth-century imagination perceived a direct correlation between mining and digging into the nooks and crannies of a woman's body. Both mining and sex represent for Spenser the return to animality and earthly slime. In the *Faerie Queene*, lust is the basest of all human sins. The spilling of human blood, in the rush to rape the earth of her gold, taints and muddies the once fertile fields (Kendrick 1974).

The sonnets of the poet and divine John Donne (1573–1631) also played up the popular identity of mining with human lust. The poem "Love's Alchemie" begins with the sexual image, "Some that have deeper digged loves Myne than I,/say where his centrique happiness doth lie" (Donne 1957, p. 35). The Platonic lover, searching for the ideal or "centrique" experience of love, begins by digging for it within the female flesh, an act as debasing to the human being as the mining of metals is to the female earth. Happiness is not to be obtained by avarice for gold and silver, nor can the alchemical elixir be produced from base metals. Nor does ideal love result from an ascent up the hierarchical ladder from base sexual love to the love of poetry, music, and art to the highest Platonic love of the good, virtue, and God. The same equation appears in Elegie XVIII, "Love's Progress":

Search every sphaere
And firmament, our Cupid is not there;
He's an infernal god and under ground,
With Pluto dwells, where gold and fire abound:
Men to such Gods, their sacrificing Coles,
Did not in Altars lay, but pits and holes,
Although we see Celestial bodies move
Above the earth, the earth we Till and love:
So we her ayres contemplate, words and heart
And Virtues; but we love the Centrique part.
(Donne 1957, p. 104, 11. 27–36)

Lust and love of the body do not lead to the celestial love of higher ideals; rather, physical love is associated with the pits and holes of the female body, just as the love of gold depends on the mining of Pluto's caverns within the female earth, "the earth we till and love." Love of the sexual "centrique" part of the female will not lead to the aery spiritual love of virtue. The fatal association of monetary revenue with human avarice, lust, and the female mine is driven home again in the last lines of the poem:

> Rich Nature hath in women wisely made
> Two purses, and their mouths aversely laid:
> They then, which to the lower tribute owe,
> That way which that Exchequer looks, must go.

Avarice and greed after money corrupted the soul, just as lust after female flesh corrupted the body.

The comparison of the female mine with the new American sources of gold, silver, and precious metals appears again in Elegie XIX, "Going to Bed." Here, however, Donne turns the image upside down and uses it to extoll the virtues of the mistress.

> License my roaving hands, and let them go,
> Before, behind, between, above, below.
> O my America! my new-found-land,
> My kingdome, safeliest when with one man man'd
> My Myne of precious stones, My Emperie,
> How blest am I in this discovering thee!
> (Donne 1957, p. 107, 11. 25–30)

In these lines, the comparison functions as a sanction—the search for precious gems and metals, like the sexual exploration of nature or the female, can benefit a kingdom or a man.

Moral restraints were thus clearly affiliated with the Renaissance image of the female earth and were strengthened by associations with greed, avarice, and lust. But the analogies were double-edged. If the new values connected with mining were positive, and mining was viewed as a means to improve the human condition, as they were by Agricola, then the comparison could be turned upside down. Sanctioning mining sanctioned the rape or technological exploration of the earth. The organic framework, in which the Mother-Earth image was a moral restraint against mining, was literally being undermined by the new commercial activity.

In the seventeenth century, Francis Bacon carried the new ethic a step further through metaphors that compared miners and smiths to scientists and technologists penetrating nature and shaping her on the anvil. Bacon's new man of science must not think that the "inquisition of nature is in any part interdicted or forbidden." Nature must be "bound into service" and made a "slave," put "in constraint" and "molded" by the mechanical arts. The "searchers and spies of nature" are to discover her plots and secrets (Bacon 1870, vol. 4, pp. 20, 287, 294).

This method, so readily applicable when nature is denoted by the female gender, degraded and made possible the exploitation of the natural environment. Nature's womb harbored secrets that through technology could be wrested from her grasp for use in the improvement of the human condition:

> There is therefore much ground for hoping that there are still laid up in the womb of nature many secrets of excellent use having no affinity or parallelism with anything that is now known . . . only by the method which we are now treating can they be speedily and suddenly and simultaneously presented and anticipated (quoted in Marsak 1964, p. 45).

The final step was to recover and sanction man's dominion over nature. Due to the Fall from the Garden of Eden (caused by the temptation of a woman), the human race lost its "dominion over creation." Before the Fall, there was no need for power or dominion, because Adam and Eve had been made sovereign over all other creatures. In this state of dominion, mankind was "like unto God." While some, accepting God's punishment, had obeyed the medieval strictures against searching too deeply into God's secrets, Bacon turned the constraints into sanctions. Only by "digging further and further into the mine of natural knowledge" could mankind recover that lost dominion. In this way, "the narrow limits of man's dominion over the universe" could be stretched "to their promised bounds" (Bacon 1870, vol. 4, p. 247, vol. 3, pp. 217, 219; Bacon 1964, p. 62).

Although a female's inquisitiveness may have caused man's fall from his god-given dominion, the relentless interrogation of another female, nature, could be used to regain it. As he argued in *The Masculine Birth of Time*, "I am come in very truth leading to you nature with all her children to bind her to your service and make her your slave." "We have no right," he asserted, "to expect nature to come to us." Instead, "Nature must be taken by the forelock, being bald behind." Delay and subtle argument "permit one only to clutch at nature, never to lay hold of her and capture her" (Bacon 1964, pp. 62, 129, 130).

Nature existed in three states—at liberty, in error, or in bondage:

> She is either free and follows her ordinary course of development as in the heavens, in the animal and vegetable creation, and in the general array of the universe; or she is driven out of her ordinary course by the perverseness, insolence, and forwardness of matter and violence of impediments, as in the case of monsters; or lastly, she is put in constraint, molded, and made as it were new by art and the hand of man; as in things artificial (Bacon 1870, vol. 4, p. 294).

The first instance was the view of nature as immanent self-development, the nature naturing herself of the Aristotelians. This was the organic view of nature as a living, growing, self-actualizing being. The second state was necessary to explain the malfunctions and monstrosities that frequently appeared and that could not have been caused by God or another higher power acting on his instruction. Since monstrosities could not be explained by the action of form or spirit, they had to be the result of matter acting perversely. Matter in Plato's *Timaeus* was recalcitrant and had to be forcefully shaped by the demiurge. Bacon frequently described matter in female imagery, as a "common harlot." "Matter is not devoid of an appetite and inclination to dissolve the world and fall back into the old chaos." It therefore must be "restrained and kept in order by the prevailing concord of things." "The vexations of art are certainly as the bonds and handcuffs of Proteus, which betray the ultimate struggles and efforts of matter" (Bacon 1870, vol. 4, pp. 320, 325, 257).

The third instance was the case of art (technē)—man operating on nature to create something new and artificial. Here, "nature takes orders from man and works under his authority." Miners and smiths should become the model for the new class of natural philosophers who would interrogate and alter nature. They had developed the two most important methods of wresting nature's secrets from her, "the one searching into the bowels of nature, the other shaping nature as on an anvil." "Why should we not divide natural philosophy into two parts, the mine and the furnace?" For "the truth of nature lies hid in certain deep mines and caves," within the earth's bosom. Bacon, like some of the practically minded alchemists, would "advise the studious to sell their books and build furnaces" and, "forsaking Minerva and the Muses as barren virgins, to rely upon Vulcan" (Bacon 1870, vol. 4, pp. 343, 287, 343, 393).

The new method of interrogation was not through abstract notions, but through the instruction of the understanding "that it may in very truth dissect nature." The instruments of the mind supply suggestions, those of the hand give motion and aid the work. "By art and the hand of man," nature can then be "forced out of her natural state and squeezed and molded." In this way, "human knowledge and human power meet as one" (Bacon 1870, vol. 4, pp. 246, 29, 247).

Here, in bold sexual imagery, is the key feature of the modern experimental method—constraint of nature in the laboratory, dissection by hand and mind, and the penetration of hidden secrets—language still used today in praising a scientist's "hard facts," "penetrating mind," or the "thrust of his argument." The constraints against mining the earth have been turned into sanctions in language that legitimates the exploitation and "rape" of nature for human good.

Scientific method, combined with mechanical technology, would create a "new organon," a new system of investigation, that unified knowledge with material power. The technological discoveries of printing, gunpowder, and the magnet in the fields of learning, warfare, and navigation "help us to think about the secrets still locked in nature's bosom." "They do not, like the old, merely exert a gentle guidance over nature's course; they have the power to conquer and subdue her, to shake her to her foundations." Under the mechanical arts, "nature betrays her secrets more fully . . . than when in enjoyment of her natural liberty" (Bacon 1964, pp. 96, 93, 99).

Mechanics, which gave man power over nature, consisted in motion; that is, in "the uniting or disuniting of natural bodies." Most useful were the arts that altered the materials of things—"agriculture, cookery, chemistry, dying, the manufacture of glass, enamel, sugar, gunpowder, artificial fires, paper, and the like." But in performing these operations, one was constrained to operate within the chain of causal connections; nature could "not be commanded except by being obeyed." Only by the study, interpretation, and observation of nature could these possibilities be uncovered; only by acting as the interpreter of nature could knowledge be turned into power. Of the three grades of human ambition, the most wholesome and noble was "to endeavor to establish and extend the power and dominion of the human race itself over the universe." In this way, "the human race [could] recover that right over nature which belongs to it by divine bequest" (Bacon 1870, Vol. 4, pp. 294, 257, 32, 114, 115).

By the close of the seventeenth century, a new science of mechanics in combination with the Baconian ideal of technological mastery over Nature had helped to create the modern worldview. The core of female principles that had for centuries subtly guided human behavior toward the earth had given way to a new ethic of exploitation. The nurturing earth mother was subdued by science and technology.

REFERENCES

Adams, Frank D. 1938. *The birth and development of the geological sciences*. New York: Dover.

Agricola, Georg. 1950. *De re metallica*, 1556. trans. Herbert C. Hoover and Lou H. Hoover. New York: Dover.

Agrippa, Henry C. 1694. *The vanity of arts and sciences*. London. (Orig. publ. in Latin, 1530.)

Bacon, Francis. 1870. *Works*, ed. James Spedding, Robert L. Ellis, Douglas D. Heath. 14 vols. London: Longmans Green.

Bacon, Francis. 1964. *The philosophy of Francis Bacon*, ed. and trans. Benjamin Farrington. Liverpool, England: Liverpool University Press.

Bruno, Giordano. 1964. *The expulsion of the triumphant beast*, 1584, ed. and trans. Arthur D. Imerti. New Brunswick, N.J.: Rutgers University Press.

Cavell, Stanley. 1971. Must we mean what we say? *Philosophy and linguistics*, ed. Colin Lyas. London: Macmillan: 131–65.
Cicero, M. Tullius. 1775. *Of the nature of the gods*, ed. T. Francklin. London.
Cornford, Francis M. 1937. *Plato's cosmology*. New York: Liberal Arts Press.
Donne, John. 1957. *Poems of John Donne*, ed. Herbert Grierson. London: Oxford University Press.
Eliade, Mircea. 1962. *The forge and the crucible*, trans. Stephan Corrin. New York: Harper & Row.
Kendrick, Walter M. 1974. Earth of flesh, flesh of earth: Mother Earth in the *Faerie Queene*. *Renaissance Quarterly* 27:33–48.
Marsak, Leonard M., ed. 1964. *The rise of modern science in relation to society*. London: Collier-Macmillan.
McLuhan, T. C. 1971. *Touch the earth*. New York: Simon and Schuster.
Milton, John. 1975. *Paradise lost*, 1667, ed., Scott Elledge. New York: W. W. Norton.
Ovid, Publius. 1955. *Metamorphoses*, A.D. 7, trans. Rolfe Humphries. Bloomington: Indiana University Press.
Paracelsus, Theophrastus. 1951. *Selected Writings*, ed. J. Jacobi. Princeton, N.J.: Princeton University Press.
Pliny. 1858. *Natural history*, ca. A.D. 23–79, trans. J. Bostock and H. T. Riley. London: Bohn.
Seneca, Lucius. 1910. *Physical science in the time of Nero; being a translation of the Quaestiones naturales of Seneca*, ca. A.D. 65, trans. John Clarke. London: Macmillan.
Spenser, Edmund. 1758. *The Faerie Queen*, 1590–95, ed. John Upton, 2 vols. London. Vol. 1.
Taylor, Charles. 1973. Neutrality in political science. *The philosophy of social explanation*, ed. Alan Ryan. London: Oxford: 139–70.
Telesio, Bernardino. 1967. *De rerum natura iuxta propia principia*, 1587 (first published 1565). *Renaissance Philosophy* ed. and trans. Arturo B. Fallico and Herman Shapiro. New York: Modern Library.
Trexler, Richard. 1974. Measures against water pollution in fifteenth-century Florence. *Viator* 5:455–67.
Valentine, Basil. 1974. *The practica, with twelve keys*, 1678. In *The hermetic museum restored and enlarged*, trans. Arthur E. Waite. New York: Samuel Weiser.

7

Toward an Ecological Feminism and a Feminist Ecology

Ynestra King

> [Woman] became the embodiment of the biological function, the image of nature, the subjugation of which constituted that civilization's title to fame. For millennia men dreamed of acquiring absolute mastery over nature, of converting the cosmos into one immense hunting ground. It was to this that the idea of man was geared in a male-dominated society. This was the significance of reason, his proudest boast.
>
> —Horkheimer and Adorno 1972, p. 248.

All human beings are natural beings. That may seem like an obvious statement, yet we live in a culture which is founded on repudiation and domination of nature. This has a special significance for women because, in patriarchal thought, women are believed to be closer to nature than men. That gives women a particular stake in ending the domination of nature—in healing the alienation between human and nonhuman nature. That is the ultimate goal of the ecology movement, but the ecology movement is not necessarily feminist. For the most part, ecologists, with their concern for nonhuman nature, have yet to understand that they have a particular stake in ending the domination of women because a central reason for woman's oppression is her association with the despised nature they are so concerned about. The hatred of women and the hatred of nature are intimately connected and mutually reinforcing. Starting with this premise, this chapter explores why feminism and ecology need each other and suggests the very beginnings of a theory of ecological feminism—ecofeminism.

What is ecology? Ecological science concerns itself with the interrelationships of all forms of life. It aims to harmonize nature, human and nonhuman. It is an integrative science in an age of fragmentation and specialization of knowledge. It is also a critical science, which grounds and necessitates a critique of our existing society. It is a reconstructive science in that it suggests directions for reconstructing human society in harmony with the natural environment.

Ecologists are asking the pressing questions of how we might survive on the planet and develop systems of food and energy production, architecture, and ways of life which will allow human beings to fulfill our material needs and live in harmony with nonhuman nature. This work has led to a social critique by biologists and an exploration of biology and ecology by social thinkers. The perspective that self-consciously attempts to integrate both biological and social aspects of the relationship between human beings and their environment is known as "social ecology." This perspective, developed primarily by Murray Bookchin (1982), has embodied the anarchist critique which links domination and hierarchy in human society to the despoliation of nonhuman nature.[1] While this analysis is useful, social ecology without feminism is incomplete.

Feminism grounds this critique of domination by identifying the prototype of other forms of domination, that of man over woman. Potentially, feminism, creates a concrete global community of interests among particularly life-oriented peoples of the world: women. Feminist analysis supplies theory, program, and process without which the radical potential of social ecology remains blunted. The theory and movement known as ecofeminism pushes social ecology to understand the necessary connections between ecology and feminism so that social ecology can reach its own avowed goal of creating a free and ecological way of life.

What are these connections? Social ecology challenges the dualistic belief that nature and culture are separate and opposed. Ecofeminism finds misogyny at the root of that opposition. Ecofeminist principles are based on the following beliefs:

1. The building of Western industrial civilization in opposition to nature interacts dialectically with and reinforces the subjugation of women because women are believed to be closer to nature in this culture against nature.

2. Life on earth is an interconnected web, not a hierarchy. There is not a natural hierarchy, but a multitiered human hierarchy projected onto nature and then used to justify social domination. Therefore ecofeminist movement politics and culture must show the connections between all forms of domination, including the domination of nonhuman nature, and be itself anti-hierarchical.

3. A healthy, balanced ecosystem, including human and nonhuman inhabitants, must maintain diversity. Ecologically, environmental simplification is as significant a problem as environmental pollution. Biological simplification, i.e., wiping out of whole species, corresponds to reducing human diversity into faceless workers, or to the homogenization of taste and culture

through mass consumer markets. Social life and natural life are literally simplified to the inorganic for the convenience of market society. Therefore, we need a decentralized global movement founded on common interests but celebrating diversity and opposing all forms of domination and violence. Potentially, ecofeminism is such a movement.

4. The survival of the species necessitates a renewed understanding of our relationship to nature, of our own bodily nature and nonhuman nature around us; it necessitates a challenging of the nature-culture dualism and a corresponding radical restructuring of human society according to feminist and ecological principles.

> When we speak of transformation we speak more accurately out of the vision of a process which will leave neither surfaces nor depths unchanged, which enters society at the most essential level of the subjugation of women and nature by men. . . . (Rich 1979, p. 248).

The ecology movement, in theory and practice, attempts to speak for nature, the "other" which has no voice and is not conceived of subjectively in our civilization. Feminism represents the refusal of the original "other" in patriarchal human society to remain silent or to be the "other" any longer. Its challenge of social domination extends beyond sex to social domination of all kinds because the domination of sex, race, class, and nature are mutually reinforcing. Women are the "others" in human society who have been silent in public, and who now speak through the feminist movement.

WOMEN, NATURE, AND CULTURE: THE ECOFEMINIST POSITION

In the process of building Western industrial civilization, nature became something to be dominated, overcome, made to serve the needs of men. She was stripped of her magical powers and properties as these beliefs were relegated to the trashbin of superstition. Nature was reduced to "natural resources" to be exploited by human beings to fulfill human needs and purposes which were defined in opposition to nature (see Merchant 1980).[2] A dualistic Christianity had become ascendant with the earlier demise of old Goddess religions, paganism, and animistic belief systems (Reuther 1975). With the disenchantment of nature came the conditions for unchecked scientific exploration and technological exploitation (Merchant 1980). We bear the consequences today of beliefs in unlimited control over nature and in science's ability to solve any problem, as nuclear power plants are built without provisions for waste disposal, or satellites sent into space without provision for retrieval.

In this way, nature became "other," something essentially different from the dominant to be objectified and thus subordinated. Women, who are identified with nature, have been similarly objectified and subordinated in patriarchal society. Women and nature, in this sense, are the original "others." Simone de Beauvoir (1968) has clarified this connection. For de Beauvoir, "transcendence" is the work of culture, it is the work of men. It is the process of overcoming immanence, a process of culture-building which is opposed to nature and which is based on the increasing domination of nature. It is enterprise. Immanence, symbolized by woman, is that which calls man back, that which reminds man of what he wants to forget. It is his own links to nature that he must forget and overcome to achieve manhood and transcendence:

> Man seeks in woman the Other as Nature and as his fellow being. But we know what ambivalent feelings Nature inspires in man. He exploits her, but she crushes him, he is born of her and dies in her; she is the source of his being and the realm that he subjugates to his will; Nature is a vein of gross material in which the soul is imprisoned, and she is the supreme reality; she is contingence and Idea, the finite and the whole; she is what opposes the Spirit, and the Spirit itself. Now ally, now enemy, she appears as the dark chaos from whence life wells up, as this life itself, and as the over-yonder toward which life tends. Woman sums up Nature as Mother, Wife, and Idea; these forms now mingle and now conflict, and each of them wears a double visage (de Beauvoir 1968, p. 144).

For de Beauvoir, patriarchal civilization is almost the denial of men's mortality—of which women and nature are incessant reminders. Women's powers of procreation are distinguished from the powers of creation, the accomplishments through the vehicles of culture by which men achieve immortality. And yet, this transcendence over women and nature can never be total. Hence, the ambivalence, the lack of self without other, the dependence of the self on the other both materially and emotionally. Thus develops a love-hate fetishization of women's bodies, which finds its ultimate manifestation in the sadomasochistic, pornographic displays of women as objects to be subdued, humiliated, and raped—the visual enactment of these fears and desires.[3]

An important contribution of de Beauvoir's work is to show that men seek to dominate women and nature for reasons which are not simply economic. They do so as well for psychological reasons which involve a denial of a part of themselves, as do other male culture-making activities. The process begins with beating the tenderness and empathy out of small boys and directing their natural human curiosity and joy in affecting the world around them into arrogant attitudes and destructive paths.

For men raised in woman-hating cultures, the fact that they are born of women and dependent upon nonhuman nature for existence is frightening. The process of objectification, of the making of women and nature into "others" to be appropriated and dominated, is based on a profound forgetting by men. They forget that they are born of women, dependent on women in their early helpless years, and dependent on nonhuman nature all their lives, which allows first for objectification and then for domination. "The loss of memory is a transcendental condition for science. All objectification is a forgetting" (Horkheimer & Adorno 1972, p. 230).

But the denied part of men is never fully obliterated. The memory remains in the knowledge of mortality and the fear of women's power. A basic fragility of gender identity therefore exists that surfaces when received truths about women and men are challenged and the sexes depart from the "natural" roles. Opposition to the not-very-radical U.S. Equal Rights Amendment can be partially explained on these grounds. More threatening are homosexuality and the gay liberation movement because they name a more radical truth—that sexual orientation is not indelible, nor is it naturally heterosexual. Lesbianism, particularly, which suggests that women, who possess this bottled up, repudiated primordial power, can be self-sufficient, reminds men that they may not be needed. Men are forced into remembering their own need for women to enable them to support and mediate the construction of their private reality and their public civilization. Again, there is the need to repress memory and suppress women.

The recognition of the connections between woman and nature or of women's bridge-like position poses three possible directions for feminism. One direction is the integration of women into the world of culture and production by severing the woman/nature connection. Writes anthropologist Sherry Ortner, "Ultimately both men and women can and must be equally involved in projects of creativity and transcendence. Only then will women be seen as aligned with culture, in culture's ongoing dialectic with nature" (1974, p. 87). This position does not necessarily question nature/culture dualism itself, and it is the position taken by most socialist-feminists (see King 1981) and by de Beauvoir and Ortner despite their insights into the connections between women and nature. They seek the severance of the woman/nature connection as a condition of women's liberation. Other feminists have built on the woman/nature connection by reinforcing this connection: woman and nature, the spiritual and intuitive versus men and the culture of patriarchal rationality.[4] This position also does not necessarily question nature/culture dualism itself or recognize that women's ecological sensitivity and life orientation is a socialized perspective which could be socialized right out of us depending on our day-to-day lives. There is no reason to believe that women placed in positions of patriarchal power will act any differently from men or that we can bring about feminist revolution without a conscious understanding of history and a challenge to economic and political power structures.

Ecofeminism suggests a third direction: that feminism recognize that although the nature/culture opposition is a product of culture, we can, nonetheless, *consciously choose* not to sever the woman nature connections by joining male culture. Rather, we can use it as a vantage point for creating a different kind of culture and politics that would integrate intuitive/spiritual and rational forms of knowledge, embracing both science and magic insofar as they enable us to transform the nature/culture distinction itself and to envision and create a free, ecological society.

ECOFEMINISM AND THE INTERSECTIONS OF FEMINISM AND ECOLOGY

The implications of a culture based on the devaluation of life-giving (both biological and social) and the celebration of life-taking are profound for ecology and for women. This fact about our culture links the theories and the politics of the ecology and the feminist movements. Adrienne Rich has written,

> We have been perceived for too many centuries as pure Nature, exploited and raped like the earth and the solar system; small wonder if we now long to become Culture: pure spirit, mind. Yet it is precisely this culture and its political institutions which have split us off from itself. In so doing it has also split itself off from life, becoming the death culture of quantification, abstraction, and the will to power which has reached its most refined destructiveness in this century. It is this culture and politics of abstraction which women are talking of changing, of bringing into accountability in human terms (1976, p. 285).

The way to ground a feminist critique of "this culture and politics of abstraction" is with a self-conscious ecological perspective that we apply to all theories and strategies, in the way that we are learning to apply race and class factors to every phase of feminist analysis.

Similarly, ecology requires a feminist perspective. Without a thorough feminist analysis of social domination that reveals the interconnected roots of misogyny and a hatred of nature, ecology remains an abstraction: it is incomplete. If male ecological scientists and social ecologists fail to deal with misogyny, the deepest manifestation of nature-hating in their own lives, they are not living the ecological lives or creating the ecological society they claim.

The goals of harmonizing humanity and nonhuman nature, at both the experiential and theoretical levels, cannot be attained without the radical vision and understanding available from feminism. The ecofeminist perspective thus affects our technology. Including everything from the digging stick to nuclear bombs, technology signifies the tools that human beings use to interact with nature. The twin concerns of ecofeminism with human liberation and with our relationship to nonhuman nature open the way to developing a set of technological ethics required for decision making about technology.

Ecofeminism also contributes an understanding of the connections between the domination of persons and the domination of nonhuman nature. Ecological science tells us that there is no hierarchy in nature itself, but rather a hierarchy in human society. Building on this unmasking of the ideology of natural hierarchy of persons, ecofeminism uses its ecological perspective to develop the position that there is no hierarchy in nature: among persons, between persons and the rest of the natural world, or among the many forms of nonhuman nature. We live on the earth with millions of species, only one of which is the human species. Yet, the human species, in its patriarchal form, is the only species which holds a conscious belief that it is entitled to dominion over the other species, and the planet. Paradoxically, the human species is utterly dependent on nonhuman nature. We could not live without the rest of nature: it could live without us.

Ecofeminism draws on another basic principle of ecological science, unity in diversity, and develops it politically. Diversity in nature is necessary, and enriching. One of the major effects of industrial technology—capitalist or socialist—is environmental simplification. Many species are being simply wiped out, never to be seen on the earth again. In human society, commodity capitalism is intentionally simplifying human community and culture so that the same products can be marketed anywhere to anyone. The prospect is for all of us to be alike, with identical needs and desires, around the globe: Coca Cola in China, blue jeans in Russia, and American rock music virtually everywhere. Few peoples of the earth have not had their lives touched and changed to some degree by the technology of industrialization. Ecofeminism as a social movement resists this social simplification through supporting the rich diversity of women the world over, and finding a oneness in that diversity. Politically, ecofeminism opposes the ways that differences can separate women from each other through the oppressions of class, privilege, sexuality, race, and nationality.

The special message of ecofeminism is that, when women suffer through both social domination and the domination of nature, most of life on this planet suffers and is threatened as well. For the brutalization and oppression of women is connected with the hatred of nature and with other forms of domination, and with threatened ecological catastrophe. It is significant that feminism and ecology as social movements have emerged now as nature's revolt against domination plays itself out in human history and nonhuman nature at the same time. As we face slow environmental poisoning and the resulting environmental simplification, or the possible unleashing of our nuclear arsenals, we can hope that the prospect of the extinction of life on the planet will provide a universal impetus to social change. Ecofeminism supports utopian visions of harmonious, diverse, decentralized communities, using only those technologies based on ecological principles, as the only practical solution for the continuation of life on earth.

Visions and politics are joined as an ecofeminist culture and politic begin to emerge. Central to this development is ecofeminist praxis: taking direct action to effect changes that are immediate and personal as well as long term and structural. Direct actions include learning holistic health and alternate ecological technologies, living in communities which explore old and new forms of spirituality that celebrate all life as diverse expressions of nature, considering the ecological consequences of our lifestyles and personal habits, and participating in creative public forms of resistance. This sometimes involves engaging in nonviolent civil disobedience to physically stop the machines which are arrayed against life.

TOWARD AN ECOFEMINIST PRAXIS: FEMINIST ANTIMILITARISM

Theory never converts simply or easily into practice; in fact, theory often lags behind practice, attempting to articulate the understanding behind things people are already doing. Praxis is the unity of thought and action, or theory and practice. Many of the women who founded the feminist antimilitarist movement in Europe and the United States share the ecofeminist perspective I have articulated. I believe that the movement as I will briefly describe it here grows out of such an understanding. For the last three years, I have been personally involved in the feminist antimilitarist movement, so the following is a firsthand account of this example of ecofeminist praxis.

The connections between violence against women, a militarized culture, and the development and deployment of nuclear weapons have long been evident to pacifist feminists (Deming 1974). Ecofeminists like myself, whose concerns with all of life stem from an understanding of the connections between misogyny and the destruction of nature, began to see militarism and the death-courting weapons industry as the most immediate threat to continued life on the planet, while the ecological effects of other modern technologies pose a more long term threat. In this manner, militarism has become a central issue for most ecofeminists. Along with this development, many of us accepted the analysis of violence made by pacifist feminists and, therefore, began to see nonviolent direct action and resistance as the basis of our political practice.

The ecofeminist analysis of militarism is concerned with the militarization of culture and the economic priorities reflected by our enormous "defense" budgets and dwindling social services budgets. Together, these pose threats to our freedom and threaten our lives, even if there is no war and none of the nuclear weapons are ever used. We have tried to make clear the particular ways that women suffer from war-making—as spoils to victorious armies, as refugees, as disabled and older women and single mothers who are dependent on dwindling social services. We connect the fear of nuclear annihilation with women's fear of male violence in our everyday lives. The level of weaponry as well as the militaristic economic priorities are products of patriarchal culture that speaks violence at every level. For ecofeminists, military technology reflects a pervasive cultural political situation. It is connected with rape, genocide, and imperialism; with starvation and homelessness; the poisoning of the environment; and the fearful lives of the world's peoples—especially those of women. Military and state power hierarchies join and reinforce each other through military technology.

Particularly as shaped by ecofeminism, the feminist antimilitarist movement in the United States and Europe is a movement against a monstrously destructive technology and set of power relationships embodied in militarism.

Actions have been organized at the Pentagon in the United States and at military installations in Europe. The Women's Pentagon Action was conceived at an ecofeminist conference I initiated and organized with several other women in spring 1980.[5] It has taken place at the Pentagon twice so far, on November 16 and 17, 1980, and November 15 and 16, 1981. It included about 2,000 women the first year, and more than twice that the second. We took care to make the actions reflect all of our politics. Intentionally, there were no speakers, no leaders; the action sought to emphasize the connections between the military issue and other ecofeminist issues. The action was planned in four stages, reflecting the depth and range of the emotions felt and the interconnection of issues, and culminating in direct resistance. A Unity Statement, describing the group's origins and concerns was drafted collectively. In the first stage, "mourning," we walked among the graves at Arlington National Cemetery and placed tombstones symbolically for all the victims of war and other forms of violence against women, beginning with a marker for "the unknown woman." The second stage was "rage," a venting of our anger. Next, the group circled the Pentagon, reaching all the way around, and singing for the stage of "empowerment." The final stage, "defiance," included a civil disobedience action in which women blocked entrances and were arrested in an act of nonviolent direct resistance. The choice to commit civil disobedience was made individually, without pressure from the group.[6]

The themes of the Women's Pentagon Action have carried over into other actions our group has participated in, including those organized by others. At the June 12–14, 1982, disarmament demonstrations in New York City, the group's march contingent proclaimed the theme: "A feminist world is a nuclear free zone," the slogan hanging beneath a huge globe held aloft. Other banners told of visions for a feminist future and members wore bibs that read "War is manmade," "Stop the violence in our lives," and "Disarm the patriarchy." There have been similar actions, drawing inspiration from the original Women's Pentagon Actions elsewhere in the United States and in Europe. In California, the Bohemian Club—a male-only playground for corporate, government, and military elite—was the site of a demonstration by women who surrounded the club in protest (Starhawk 1982, p. 168). In England, on December 12, 1982, 30,000 women surrounded a U.S. military installation, weaving into the fence baby clothes, scarves, and other objects which meant something to them. At one point, spontaneously, the word "FREEDOM" rose from the lips of the women and was heard round and round the base. Three thousand women nonviolently blocked the entrances to the base on December 13 (see Fisher 1983).

The politics being created by these actions draw on women's culture: embodying what is best in women's life-oriented socialization, building on women's differences, organizing antihierarchically in small groups in visually and emotionally imaginative ways, and seeking an integration of issues. These actions exemplify ecofeminism. While technocratic experts (including feminists) argue the merits and demerits of weapons systems, ecofeminism approaches the disarmament issue on an intimate and moral level. Ecofeminism holds that a personalized, decentralized, life-affirming culture and politics of direct action are crucially needed to stop the arms race and transform the world's priorities. Because such weaponry does not exist apart from a contempt for women and all of life, the issue of disarmament and threat of nuclear war is a feminist issue. It is the ultimate human issue and the ultimate ecological issue. And so ecology, feminism, and liberation for all of nature, including ourselves, are joined.

NOTES

1. I am indebted to Bookchin for my own theoretical understanding of social ecology which is basic to this chapter.

2. Merchant interprets the Scientific Revolution as the death of nature, and argues that it had a particularly detrimental effect on women.
3. See Susan Griffin (1981) for a full development of the relationship between nature-hating, woman-hating, and pornography.
4. Many such feminists call themselves ecofeminists. Some of them cite Susan Griffin's *Woman and Nature* (1978) as the source of their understanding of the deep connections between women and nature, and their politics. *Woman and Nature* is an inspirational poetic work with political implications. It explores the terrain of our deepest naturalness, but I do not read it as a delineation of a set of politics. To use Griffin's work in this way is to make it into something it was not intended to be. In personal conversation and in her more politically explicit works such as *Pornography and Silence* (1981), Griffin is antidualistic, struggling to bridge the false oppositions of nature and culture, passion and reason. Both science and poetry are deeply intuitive processes. Another work often cited by ecofeminists is Mary Daly's *Gyn/ecology* (1978). Daly, a theologian/philosopher, is also an inspirational thinker, but she is a genuinely dualistic thinker, reversing the "truths" of patriarchal theology. While I have learned a great deal from Daly, my perspective differs from hers in that I believe that any truly ecological politics including ecological feminism must be ultimately anti-dualistic.
5. "Women and Life on Earth: Ecofeminism in the 80s," Amherst, Mass., March 21–23, 1980. Each of my sister founders of Women and Life on Earth contributed to the theory of ecofeminism I have articulated here, and gave me faith in the political potential of an ecofeminist movement. All of them would probably disagree with parts of this chapter. Nonetheless, I thank Christine Di Stefano, Deborah Gaventa, Anna Gyorgy, Amy Hines, Sue Hoffman, Carol Iverson, Grace Paley, Christina Rawley, Nancy Jack Todd, and Celeste Wesson.
6. See Ynestra King (1983) for my personal account and evaluation of the action.

REFERENCES

Bookchin, Murray. 1982. *The ecology of freedom: The emergence and dissolution of hierarchy.* Palo Alto: Cheshire Books.

Daly, Mary. 1978. *Gyn/ecology: The metaethics of radical feminism.* Boston: Beacon Press.

de Beauvoir, Simone. 1968. *The second sex.* New York: Modern Library, Random House.

Deming, Barbara. 1974. *We cannot live without our lives.* New York: Grossman.

Fisher, Berenice. 1983. Women ignite English movement. *Womanews* (February).

Griffin, Susan. 1978. *Woman and nature: The roaring inside her.* New York: Harper & Row.

Griffin, Susan. 1981. *Pornography and silence: Culture's revenge against nature.* New York: Harper & Row.

Horkheimer, Max; and Adorno, Theodor W. 1972. *Dialectic of enlightenment.* New York: Seabury Press.

King, Ynestra. 1981. Feminism and the revolt of nature. *Heresies* 13 (Fall):12–16.

King, Ynestra. 1983. All is connectedness: Scenes from the Women's Pentagon Action USA. *Keeping the peace: A women's peace handbook 1.* ed. Lynne Johnes. London: The Women's Press.

Merchant, Carolyn. 1980. *The death of nature: Women, ecology, and the Scientific Revolution.* New York: Harper & Row.

Ortner, Sherry B. 1974. Is female to male as nature is to culture? *Woman, culture and society.* eds. Michelle Zimbalist Rosaldo and Louise Lamphere. Stanford, Calif.: Stanford University Press: 67–87.

Reuther, Rosemary. 1975. *New woman/new earth: Sexist ideologies and human liberation*. New York: Seabury Press.
Rich, Adrienne. 1976. *Of woman born*. New York: W. W. Norton.
Rich, Adrienne. 1979. *On lies, secrets, and silence: Selected prose*. New York: W. W. Norton.
Starhawk, 1982. *Dreaming the dark: Magic, sex and politics*. Boston: Beacon Press.

8
Women, Science, and Popular Mythology

Evelyn Fox Keller

INTRODUCTION

During the 1960s (a period sometimes referred to as the post-Sputnik era), the United States witnessed a major campaign to develop scientific talent. Stimulated by the growing concern for "lost" talent, a now familiar but at the time shocking fact emerged into public consciousness: The proportion of women in American science, while never high, had declined steadily since the 1920s and was then, in the mid 60s, only half of what it had been 40 years earlier. What was shocking about this fact was that it jarred our confidence in the progressive unfolding of egalitarian ideals. It brought to the fore a contradiction that we had been living with for many years: On the one hand, children were educated according to the ostensible principle of sexual equality; and, on the other hand, a dramatic opposition prevailed between what were seen as appropriate roles for adult men and women.

In the years that followed, the subject of women in science has received a great deal of attention. Data has been collected, reported, and analyzed by numerous individuals, government agencies, and special committees of professional societies; research and promotional efforts have been supported by the National Science Foundation and the National Institute of Education; and affirmative action programs have been instituted across the nation. Throughout this period, the reasons for the low representation of women in science, particularly in the upper echelons of the scientific community, were discussed and analyzed in numerous articles (Keller 1974, Kistiakowsky 1980, Rossi 1966, White 1970). In my own article, after enumerating the various impediments confronting a woman in science, I suggested that perhaps the single most powerful inhibitor was the widespread belief in the intrinsic masculinity of scientific thought (Keller 1974).

Today, after a decade of consciousness raising, active recruiting, and affirmative action, it is appropriate to ask: How much has changed? The answer depends on the focus of one's analysis, but a number of authors have concluded that change has been disappointingly slow. In 1975, Betty Vetter (1975) wrote:

> Women scientists . . . have not achieved parity of opportunity despite the forces of affirmative action. The gains in the participation of women in the U.S. scientific enterprise are pitifully small, and the obstacles still standing in the path of those who wish to enter and participate fully in that enterprise always have been and still are enormous (p. 713).

In a more recent review of women in physics, Vera Kistiakowsky (1980) writes:

> In summary, the predominant impression gained from looking at the statistics is that there has not been very much change since the beginning of the century, or since the 1971 American Physical Society study (p. 35).

She notes, however, along with other authors, certain potentially important exceptions: The percentage of Ph.D.'s awarded to women has increased (finally exceeding what it was in 1920) and is still increasing; a few more women are on the faculties of the major research institutions; some overall increase in the proportion of women at the assistant professor level can be seen. On all levels, however, the numbers are still very small. Perhaps of greatest importance are changes in cultural attitudes we have witnessed over the past decade. The general acceptance of women in traditionally male roles has increased significantly, and the message that science is a man's field has become dramatically muted. No doubt, the growth in the number of women in undergraduate scientific and technological courses of study reflects these changes, suggesting the possibility of our seeing a greater proportion of women scientists in the future.

There are several reasons, however, to suspect the survival of deep cultural forces which continue to alienate women from science. Not only has the employment profile of women in the scientific professions remained essentially unchanged, but the number of women entering these professions is still relatively small. At the Massachusetts Institute of Technology (M.I.T.), for example, where the increase in the number of women students has been truly dramatic, the proportion today is still only about 19 percent. When compared with the success of some other traditionally male institutions in recruiting women students (e.g., Princeton, where 38 percent of the present student body is female), the growth at M.I.T. seems somewhat less impressive. But more worrisome yet are certain indications that the popular mythology of the masculinity of the scientific male mind continues to persist.

While in many circles it has become decidedly unchic to suggest that women should not be physicists, mathematicians, engineers, etc., in other circles, indeed the very circles one might least expect to hear such things, that is precisely what is being suggested. There is a growing voice among contemporary feminists reasserting the age-old dichotomy between women and science on the one hand, and the affinity between women and nature on the other. At its most extreme, we hear from certain radical French feminists that: "The will to theory is the most pernicious of male activities" (Marks and De Courtivron 1979, p. xi). Tentatively, a number of feminist theorists in the United States are asking such questions as: Is objectivity a code word for domination? or, Is objectivity something feminists want? At the same time, and in something of the same spirit, women's close kinship with nature is being acknowledged and embraced in the birth of a new movement—Ecofeminism.[1] Underlying the convergence of ecology and feminism that this movement advocates is the equation between woman and nature. The ravages of nature for which science and technology are held responsible become, under this equation, ravages against women (see, e.g., Griffin 1978). In opposition to the coercive and manipulative relation that male science and technology have traditionally maintained to nature is offered a more sympathetic, intuitive, respectful, and loving relation—one that recognizes the interconnectedness of all things. It is argued that women, as kin to nature, are especially privileged to provide such a relation—that their expertise and concerns as mothers and nurturers both can be and historically has been brought to bear on environmental issues. In short, conservation and ecology are claimed as feminist concerns.

My point here is that, although it may now be muted in many circles, the mythology which has for so long divided women from science is hardly dead. It even seems to be undergoing a kind of renaissance. While liberals attempt to escape the belief system which identifies science as male and nature as female, the very same beliefs are being re-embraced by a number of feminists. Such a resurgence suggests deeper roots to these beliefs than might otherwise have been thought. It is my purpose to examine those roots, as well as to explore their implications for women and science, both now and in the future.

In order to do so, however, the mythology itself needs to be elaborated. Its ingredients are contained in a set of familiar claims expressing the kind of polarities which have long been noted as organizers of our language, our perceptions, and our reality. Far from being unrelated, these claims tend to cluster together with a revealing coherence and are, therefore, worth examining in toto. A sample set might read as follows:

1. Science is impersonal, women are personal; science deals with things, women with people;
2. "The basic feminine sense of self is connected to the world, the basic masculine sense of self is separate" (Chodorow 1978, p. 169). Relatedly,

it is claimed that objectivity requires a total removal of the self from the object of study;

3. "There are two ways of knowing: The male way of knowing in its highest development is objective, analytical, scientific investigation. The female way of knowing in the completest [sic] sense is the mother's intuitive knowledge of her baby" (Guntrip 1969, p. 261);
4. Science is reason, unalloyed by feeling. "Feeling is the female element while thinking is a male element" (Guntrip 1969, p. 261; see Mitroff 1974 for an extensive refutation of this claim);
5. Science is "hard" and toughminded; women are "soft" and sentimental;
6. Scientists are cold and asexual; women are erotic (see, e.g., the studies of Liam Hudson 1966, 1968 for documentation of the prevalence of this view);
7. The scientific mind is male, nature is female; the aim of science is the domination of nature;
8. Science seeks power, women seek harmony.

The endurance of belief in these claims obliges us to ask a number of questions: What do they derive from? What accounts for their endurance? and how do they affect women, science, and the relation between the two? My strategy in trying to answer these questions will be to examine the psychological basis of such beliefs, and then consider the bearing of these beliefs on a single illustrative example of women in science. But first, a few general remarks may help to orient the discussion that follows and explain the relevance of a psychological perspective.

POPULAR MYTHOLOGY ABOUT WOMEN AND SCIENCE[2]

These claims, taken together, constitute a mythology. I say this not to imply that they are not true (they may or may not be) but, rather, to remove them from the realm of irreducible fact and to locate them in the realm of social construct. Insofar as they are widely held, they take on an ideological function, in the sense that Geertz uses this term—they become "maps of problematic social reality and matrices for the creation of collective conscience" (Geertz 1973). As such, they cannot be regarded as either simply true or simply false but, rather, by their very nature, they bear a degree of contingent truth. To the extent that both science and gender are socially constructed, culturally shared myths about these inevitably (at least in part) both reflect and shape the realities we observe. Such myths need not be either universal or unique to be functional—they may, and indeed do, coexist alongside other myths about science[3] (and even about women). The multiplicity of popularly held images, in fact, may be crucial to supporting the diversity observed within science. But no alternative myths are available to effectively neutralize the impact of the central mythology under consideration here. Not only has that mythology helped guarantee that most scientists are men but, more important, as I will also argue, it has influenced our very definitions of science and helped to promote a particularly narrow, and perhaps even distorted conception of objectivity.

In this last claim, I make certain assumptions about the nature of the scientific enterprise and about objectivity which should be made explicit. One such assumption is that science is a more pluralistic enterprise than is suggested by this mythology or, for that matter, than is suggested by the conception dominant within any particular discipline at a particular time. Furthermore, it is this pluralist potential which allows for the influence of cultural forces. Much philosophical and historical analysis has undermined the view of science as impelled entirely by its own logical and internal dynamics, and the work of Hanson (1958) and Kuhn (1962) are crucial here. Kuhn's *The Structure of Scientific Revolutions* (1962) led to a spate of inquiries into the influence of social and political forces on the development of scientific theories. Far from implying a total relativity, or a denigration of science (as some have interpreted it), I take this effort to be consistent with an acceptance of the essential goals of science.

The essential goal of theory in general I take to be to represent our experience of the world in as comprehensive and inclusive a way as possible; in that effort we seek a maximal intersubjectivity. Our search for truth is objective insofar as it strives for a characterization of our experience which transcends local, parochial vantage points, which transcends the expression of particular needs and fears, and which accordingly supports consensual agreement. As such, objectivity can be understood as a quintessentially human goal, even if it is a goal which can never quite be achieved. One crucial, though by no means the only, function it serves is of enabling us to be master or mistress in our own house (or world)—a function we should not confuse, though we sometimes do, with domination. And even if, by virtue of our historical experience, we have no noun to express mastery in the feminine, we ought nevertheless be able to recognize the universality of that impulse.

Science may well have given us the most fully developed expression we have seen of what could almost be called a "drive" for objectivity, but it is crucial to distinguish between the objective effort and the objectivist illusion (or what Piaget calls the realist illusion). Piaget (1972) offers a way to do this:

> Objectivity consists in so fully realizing the countless intrusions of the self in everyday thought and the countless illusions which result—illusions of sense, language, point of view, value, etc.—that the preliminary step to every judgement

> is the effort to exclude the intrusive self. Realism, on the contrary, consists in ignoring the existence of self and thence regarding one's own perspective as immediately objective and absolute. Realism is thus anthropocentric illusion, finality—in short, all those illusions which teem in the history of science (p. 34).

What Piaget's distinction enables us to recognize is that, in despairing of the most simple-minded fulfillment of the goal of objectivity, namely, the objective realist's dream of providing an error-free description of the world "out there"—indeed, in despairing of *any* fulfillment of the goal of objectivity—we do not need to give up on objectivity as a process. The very use of the word as a noun is here (and in Piaget's quote as well) misleading; it is, in fact, a kind of trap, though one which our language constantly invites us into. It suggests the existence of a subjectless form of knowledge. Properly speaking, "objective" ought to be an adverb, rather than an adjective, and "objectivity" a shorthand for an ongoing process rather than a state or condition that has or ever can be reached. Acknowledging the unobtainability of the realist's dream—a dream which Piaget calls "anthropocentric illusion"—thus, need not diminish our commitment to objectivity, understood now as process, but, on the contrary, may enable us to reaffirm that commitment more fully than ever.

This, I suggest, we can do by extending the critiques of Hanson (1958) and Kuhn (1962), and those who have followed them, to include an inquiry into the influence of affective forces on scientific thought—to ask: What is the meaning of the realist, or objectivist, dream? What kinds of fantasies, fears, or wishes does it express? In short, what are the personal dimensions of the claims that science makes to impersonality?

In asking these questions, I find myself faced with a certain irony. Though I began this discussion with an explicitly feminist concern, my intention was to shift the inquiry to more general issues. It is all too likely, however, that the last questions I pose will, notwithstanding my own intent, nonetheless be perceived as yet (and simply) another aspect of my feminist concern. This point is elegantly, if somewhat facetiously, expressed by Mary Ellman (1968). In her introduction to *Thinking About Women*, she responds to the accusation that "women always get personal" by suggesting: "I'd say, men always get impersonal. If you hurt their feelings, they make Boyle's Law out of it" (p. xiii). My intention, however, is to introduce into the realm of theoretical discourse what has been traditionally—as part of the very same mythology I am attempting to analyze—merely a "woman's question."

What I am suggesting is that it is the personal, affective basis of the scientific impulse which lends coherence to the illusions and myths that pervade our thinking about science—which lend coherence to what I call its objectivist distortions, to the perception of scientific thought as masculine, and to its confusion with power and domination. As I will now try to show, an exploration of this affective basis provides important keys to our understanding of the roots, dynamics, and endurance of these myths and illusions.

PSYCHOLOGICAL ORIGINS

One way to get at the emotional substructure of this mythology is to look at the developmental matrix out of which we form our ideas about gender, about objectivity, about mastery, and about love. For this, I have found that branch of psychoanalytic theory known as object relations theory to be particularly useful. Object relations theory is an attempt to account for personality development in terms of both innate drives and actual relations with other objects (by which psychoanalysts mean subjects). In this way, it is considerably more amenable than traditional psychoanalytic theory to an integration of external cultural and internal psychological forces. At the same time, by focusing on the earliest levels of development, it permits an integration of our understanding of cognitive, affective, and gender development. What emerges is a development model which, notwithstanding the controversial nature of psychoanalytic thought, provides an explanation of the origin and entrenchment of an identification between impersonal, objective, and masculine, given the parenting and cultural arrangements in which we grow.[4]

According to psychoanalytic theory, and a good deal of psychological theory, we do not begin life with any sense of ourselves as autonomous agents, either male or female, interacting with a world apart from ourselves. Rather, that sense is built up over time, in a process which is profoundly influenced by our experience in the world and by our expectations of those around us. As infants, we live in an amorphous, psychologically undifferentiated state of symbiotic unity with the person who takes primary care of us—almost universally our mothers. Out of this state, our sense of self, of reality, and of gender must be forged. In the process, we acquire the capacity for both objective thought and psychic autonomy, i.e., for cognitive and emotional independence. Developmentally, and operationally, these two capacities work in concert. Both rest on a capacity for distinguishing subject from object. Both grow out of that very difficult and often painful process of sorting out self from other, of separation and individuation from the mother—the first and most ambiguously other. And both retain the tell-tale marks of their early developmental setting. Because of the context out of which these capacities are acquired, both objectivity and psychological autonomy remain subject to the influence of unresolved conflicts about that early separation. The way we characterize, define, and aspire to both objectivity and autonomy remains profoundly colored by, on the one hand, our anxieties about being alone, and on the other hand, our anxieties about yielding up to the primitive temptations of going back, of giving up our hard won status of separateness and selfhood. These anxieties can, and do, work to inhibit or exaggerate the move toward independence, be it cognitive or emotional.

The development of a gender identity feeds into this process in complex ways—ways that can be, and, for us, generally are different for the two sexes.

> Although children of both sexes must learn equally to distinguish self from other, and have essentially the same needs for autonomy, to the extent that boys rest their very sexual identity on an opposition to what is both experienced and defined as feminine, the development of their gender identity is likely to accentuate the process of separation. As boys, they must undergo a two fold "dis-identification from mother" (Greenson 1968)—first for the establishment of a self identity, and second for the consolidation of a male gender identity. Further impetus is added to this process by the external cultural pressure on the young boy to establish as stereotypic masculinity, now culturally as well as privately connoting independence and autonomy. The cultural definitions of masculine as that which can never appear feminine, and of autonomy as that which can never be realized, conspire to reinforce the child's earliest associations of female with the pleasures and dangers of merging, and male with both the comfort and loneliness of separateness. The boy's internal anxiety about self and gender is here echoed by the cultural anxiety; together they can lead to postures of exaggerated and rigidified autonomy and masculinity which can—indeed which may be designed to—defend against that anxiety and the longing which generates it (Keller 1978, pp. 425–26).

In this way, the very act of separating subject from object, objectivity itself, comes to be associated with masculinity. Under the combination of psychological and cultural pressures, that association can, and often does, lend both objectivity and masculinity to defensive overstatement.

The connections between this process and our myths about science work, as myths always do, through stereotypes—which is not to diminish their importance, for stereotypic images work in powerfully formative ways. One of the ways they work is by selection. Bernice Eiduson (1973) has commented on this. In summarizing the literature on the psychology of scientists, she observes:

> Scientists as a group seem to be caught up in the same stereotypes that the public holds about them, and, in fact, the researchers seem to have been drawn into science by some of the same fantasies and stereotypes (p. 15).

According to the model I have just described, the picture of science as autonomous, as objectivist, and as masculine—whether or not it is accurate—

would inevitably be particularly appealing to those for whom such a picture is emotionally both gratifying and functional. That such self-selection does in fact take place, seems to be confirmed by the psychological literature on personality characteristics of scientists (Eiduson 1962, McClelland 1962, Roe 1956). In turn, it is not hard to see how such selection could lead to a perpetuation and entrenchment of that picture—above and beyond its purely scientific justification.

What I have described here is a network of interactions between cultural values, gender development, and our (stereotypic) beliefs about science—a system which has, incidentally, a host of secondary consequences. For example, it allows for science to derive extra prestige from whatever masculinist biases exist in the culture, and simultaneously for what we call masculine to derive prestige from the value we place on science. In the process, what is called feminine—be it a branch of knowledge, a way of thinking, or woman herself—becomes devalued by the cultural value placed on science. These cultural values in turn feed back on the developmental process which, of course, never occurs in a vacuum. Children grow into, and aspire toward, gender identities that are defined by the culture. Thus a self-perpetuating and self-reinforcing system is maintained; and, while it is not immutable, the difficulty in dislodging it has to be understood in terms of all its facets.

It is beyond the scope of this chapter to try to situate this process in its social and historical context, as a full understanding of its dynamics ultimately requires.[5] The predominantly psychological perspective employed here is necessarily incomplete; nevertheless, it does provide an account which is sufficiently coherent and complete in its own terms to warrant our asking: what implications follow from it? It seems to me that this account can be read in two very different ways—one fairly pessimistic, and the other optimistic.

The pessimistic reading is that the breach which separates women from science is very deep, and its mending might require more of a change in social arrangements than many people would accept. It would seem particularly unhopeful to the extent that the burden of change is seen as falling entirely on women. Of course, that is not to say that, in a liberal climate, we won't see more women scientists than we have in the past but it does suggest: a) that they would remain a minority, and b) that they would tend to be self-selected by the same mechanism that I argue has in the past helped select male scientists. In that way, women in science could reproduce the two-culture split we are already so familiar with, possibly even a sharpened version of that split.

Alternatively, to the extent that science is itself malleable—in its self-conception and its ideological commitments—a more optimistic reading is possible. To the extent that the vision of science as objectivist, autonomous, and masculine relaxes its hold, among scientists and nonscientists alike, we might envisage a professional climate not only more sympathetic to women, but more sympathetic to all those whose values (often described as humanistic) are at variance with this vision (see, e.g., Fee 1981). But such a suggestion immediately raises a question about what kinds of changes are actually imagined. What would it mean for science to change its self-conception and ideological commitments, and still be considered science?[6]

I suggest that the best way to answer this question is by looking more closely than we are accustomed at the range of activities to which the name science has actually been put. Science is not a monolithic structure, either intellectually or emotionally, despite its own stereotypes. Rather, one sees at work a constant interplay between contrasting themes, with the evolution of science reflecting a certain selection of dominant themes. In part, this selection is influenced by ideological issues and, in part, by the discoveries scientists make. Science is neither simply created nor simply discovered. It is both. The process by which internal and external factors interact in the development of science is what we understand least well; at the same time, it is that process that most critically needs to be explored, and, indeed, is the principal focus of much contemporary history of science. The way in which mythology functions in this development is through its participation in the process by which dominant themes are selected. But still, however dominant reigning "paradigms" may be, minor themes continue to be played, and sometimes even heard. Part of what Kuhn calls a "Scientific Revolution" is the emergence of what had been a minor theme as a major theme. The process by which such transformations take place is, of course, enormously complex, but a brief look at one such transformation which may now be occurring in biology might serve as an informative illustration.

IMPLICATIONS FOR SCIENCE: A CASE STUDY

The central persona of this illustration is Barbara McClintock, long known as one of America's most eminent cytogeneticists. McClintock's career and her contributions to biology are the subject of a full-length book (Keller 1983), but certain features of that story can be briefly told here. These serve to exemplify the diversity of styles and themes in scientific research, and can simultaneously provide an occasion for considering the relevance (or irrelevance) of gender and gender stereotypes on styles of scientific thought.

Many years ago, Barbara McClintock embarked on a course of experiments which led her to an interpretation of genetic function and organization which at the time seemed too remote from the mainstream of biological thought for most biologists to comprehend, let alone accept. From a series of detailed microscopic and genetic analyses of mutable loci on the chromosomes of the maize plant, she concluded that the genetic complement of maize is characterized by a degree of inherent instability. Certain genetic elements are capable of autonomous (i.e., not externally induced) transposition from one site in the chromosomal complement to another. Furthermore, this transposition plays a crucial role in the control of gene action and the regulation of developmental processes. In her first paper on this subject, McClintock (1951) suggested:

> The numerous phenotypic expressions attributable to changes at one locus need not be related, in each case, to changes in the genic components at the locus, but rather to changes in the mechanism of association and interaction of a number of individual chromosome components with which the factor or factors at the locus are associated. According to this view, *it is organized nuclear systems that function as units at any one time in development* (p. 34; emphasis added).

Today, thirty years later, transposition has become a well accepted phenomenon in molecular biology, and interest in its role in regulation and development is growing. Increasingly, many of those biologists who are most directly involved in these discoveries are beginning to suspect far more global mechanisms of genetic control than had earlier been assumed. Accordingly, a number of themes belonging to what might be called an organismic perspective, which had been muted for the three intervening decades, are now beginning to be heard.

For several reasons, the case of Barbara McClintock seems a particularly good one through which to try to address the question of whether female scientists, by virtue of being women, might introduce different styles and perspectives into scientific thought. Not only is McClintock a woman, but she is one whose rejection of gender stereotypes appears to be total. And even by the most conventional standards, she is an eminently toughminded, meticulous, rigorous, and "objective" scientist. At the same time, it also needs to be said that, in important ways, her posture as a scientist is strikingly unconventional. In both style of research and theoretical position, she resides outside of what has been, for the last thirty years, the dominant tradition in genetics. Certain elements of her methodological approach and even of the thrust of her theoretical conclusions might suggest to some the presence of a feminine style; and, although I will mainly argue against this interpretation, it is, nevertheless, useful to explore the temptation to so regard them.

The main conclusion which I believe emerges from a series of interviews I have conducted with Barbara McClintock[7] is that, while there clearly are aspects of her relation to her work which offer alternatives to the dominant mythology about science, these echo themes which are *not* alien to the scientific enterprise. Rather, they are subthemes with a long tradition, even if at times they may seem almost entirely submerged. In some ways, these themes may seem especially compatible with female psychology (as we understand that to be), but they are by no means exclusive to it. In the end, I would argue that they are not only familiar in the thought of many male scientists, but are consonant with and perhaps even essential to the scientific enterprise as a whole.

Some examples might serve to elucidate these points. One of the predominant themes which emerged in these interviews was the importance of "letting the material speak to you," of being able to "let the material tell you what to do." Her chief criticism of the way science is normally done lies in the lack of respect for the system and the corresponding lack of awareness of one's own "tacit assumptions." She feels that much of the work is done because one wants to impose an answer on the system; too many researchers have the answer ready, and know what they want the material to tell them. Anything else it tells them, they don't recognize as there, or they think it's a mistake and throw it out. "If you'd only just let the material tell you!" But to be able to hear what the material has to tell you (the material, in her case, is the corn plant), one must have a "feeling for the organism." By this she means understanding how it grows, understanding its parts, understanding when something is going wrong with it. A plant, she explains, is not just a piece of plastic but, rather, is something which grows, which is constantly being affected by the environment, constantly showing attributes of its growth. In order to properly interpret what you see, it is necessary to "know" every individual plant. That requires watching the plant from the very beginning, for no two are exactly alike. Each one is different and you have to know that difference.

A "feeling for the organism" must follow the scientist into the laboratory, through all of his or her work. In McClintock's microscopic studies of *neurospora* chromosomes (so small that others had been unable to identify them), she found that the more she worked with the chromosomes, the "bigger and bigger" they got, until finally, "I wasn't outside, I was down there—I was part of the system." As "part of the system," even the internal parts of the chromosomes became visible. "I actually felt as if I were down there and these were my friends."

Much of this material suggests a kind of respect and attention—almost nurturant—that some people would see as the privilege of women. This last quote in particular seems to vividly illustrate a notion that the radical French feminist, Hélène Cixous, calls "super-seeing" in which (she quotes Clarise Lispector here), "My eyes ended up no longer distinguishing themselves from the thing seen" (1979). For Cixous, "super-seeing" is a peculiarly feminine capacity.

Yet, McClintock employs it, along with her capacity for respect, attentiveness, and her feeling for the organism, as a scientist. Nor, as a scientist, is she unique. To some extent, these traits are familiar characteristics of the naturalist tradition; others we think of as the marks of all truly creative scientists — even of the creative imagination in general. Ralph Waldo Emerson wrote: "I become a transparent eyeball; I am nothing; I see all." Clearly, it would be a mistake to think of these traits as being unavailable to male scientists. McClintock herself was trained and encouraged by men, and influenced by many (male) thinkers (some, e.g., the geneticist Richard B. Goldschmidt, with a somewhat similar bent) before her. It may be, however, that she was able to exploit certain modes of scientific thought more fully and more visibly than others — particularly in an age when they were becoming less visible—by virtue of being a woman and an outsider. That is, as a woman, she may have been freer to transcend the constraints that a commitment to the masculinity of the scientific mind imposes—she could be clearer about the place of what we call "feminine" virtues in scientific work than much of the rhetoric permits. In that case, it would be the corresponding failure of many male scientists to acknowledge and encourage the development of these traits that might reflect the presence of what could be called a masculinist bias in science.

Barbara McClintock is not an ecofeminist. She would be the first to reject the notion of a feminist science. At the same time, it has also to be said that not only would ecofeminists find her style of research sympathetic, they would find her vision of cellular organization even more so. In fact, the consonance between McClintock's theories of genetic organization and her approach to her subject of investigation are striking; they suggest a contradiction to the view that the psychology of research is irrelevant to the logic or the substance of scientific discovery. Here, an investigation premised on attention to the individual, on a "feeling for the organism," on "forgetting yourself," and "letting the material tell you what to do" resulted in discoveries which, in turn, led her to a picture of the cell as radically divergent from the dominant picture of molecular biology as was her methodological style. During the decades when the cell was becoming a relatively straightforward chemical machine to most biologists, to McClintock it was opening up in complexity. In lieu of the linear hierarchy described by the central dogma of molecular biology, in which the DNA encodes and transmits all instructions for the unfolding of a living cell, her research yielded a view of the DNA in delicate interaction with the cellular environment—an organismic view. In this view, one cannot consider the genome as such (i.e., the DNA) as being all important—far more important is the "overall organism." As she sees it, "The genome makes the necessary products according to a program that reacts to signals [coming] from elsewhere. . . . It will function only in respect to the environment in which it is found." In McClintock's work, the program encoded by the DNA is itself subject to change. No longer is a master control to be found in a single component of the cell; rather, control resides in the complex interactions of the entire system.

Interaction is a key word here, and a favorite one for ecological advocates — male and female alike. It is also a crucial word in the long and complex history of organismic thought in biology. If that history has been less than successful, at least a partial explanation for that fact may be found in the ideological commitments which predispose scientists to favor "master control" over interactionist theories. Today, transposition has become a well accepted phenomenon, but the larger implications which McClintock saw in this work remain far from general acceptance. Biology finds itself at a philosophical crossroad; we cannot yet say which route it will take.

CONCLUSION

In the view of science presented here, change depends less on the introduction of a specifically female culture into science than on the rethinking of sexual polarities and the abandonment of a sexual division of intellectual labor altogether. If McClintock's approach to science offers us a different model from the one we are most familiar with, it would be a mistake to yield to the temptation of interpreting that difference as a simple reflection of gender difference. Given the conditions that have historically prevailed for the entrance of women into science, it is generally not possible to regard women scientists as exemplars of a female culture. By necessity, their acculturation has almost always had to be anomalous. Nevertheless, by virtue of the fact that they have not been socialized as men, and have in general been forced to occupy positions peripheral to the dominant scientific culture, their perspectives and contributions to science often bear the marks of their peripheral status. As such, they can help illuminate the forces that shape the dominant culture, and, together with their male counterparts on the periphery, help point the way to a less gender-bound science. What is unusual about McClintock's approach to science must be understood not in terms of a commitment (on her part) to gender ideologies in any form, or to any notion of a feminine science, but precisely in her rejection of gender ideologies altogether, in her commitment to a life of the mind in which "the matter of gender drops away."

The question of whether gender will drop away from conceptions of science in the future, or whether we are doomed to play out ancient polarities between science and women, and possibly within science, remains finally something we can at this point only guess about. Barbara McClintock worked as a scientist in an age in which the gender mythology I have elaborated here retained a strong hold on our thinking—within science as well as without. Now we are in an age of transition in which sex role ideology is relaxing its grip (at least in most circles) and in which women are becoming more visible in the scientific world. As a consequence, it is possible that sexual polarities are also disappearing from scientific thought.

However, more likely, the introduction of more women into science is not by itself sufficient to bring about such change. Scientific ideology is not, after all, *solely* determined by gender ideology. Rather, both ideologies have deep roots in the entire economic and political context in which science has evolved. If the conception of objectivity traditional to science is a parochial one, influenced by a particular ideology about gender, it is one which has also served our particular political and economic history exquisitely well. The suspicion that "the subject-object split legitimizes the logic of domination" (Fee 1981) is not unfounded, and even though the precise nature of the relation between objectivism and domination is an issue that remains in need of further examination, we have learned a great deal from recent scholarship (Rose & Rose 1980) about the interdependency of science and politics. If women are in a privileged position to bring the epistemological critique that is equally necessary for the liberation of science and the liberation of society, it is both because we have been especially vulnerable—viewed as passive, natural objects—to the logic of domination, and because our status as inhabitants of a different (a female) culture provides us with an invaluable perspective—the view from the periphery. But a feminist and psychological critique is only a beginning. Ultimately, it must work hand in hand with other social analyses of science in order to arrive at an understanding of the ways in which science has traditionally both reflected and contributed to the social and political structures we wish to change.

NOTES

1. The first large meeting of this movement, "Women and Life on Earth: Ecofeminism in the 80's," convened at the University of Massachusetts, Amherst, March 21–23, 1980.
2. Key pieces of the argument that follows have been presented elsewhere (e.g., Keller 1982). I repeat them here, first, for the sake of completeness, and second, on behalf of readers unfamiliar with this literature.
3. There is, for example, also the image of the scientist engaged in a mystical search for truth, seeking transcendence rather than power, impassioned, in love with his subject. It might be noted, however, that this mythology tends to be reserved for the "great" or unusually creative scientist; and, despite popular accounts, it is more likely to be the normal than the revolutionary scientist who determines the character of science—indeed, who determines what can be accepted as revolutionary rather than, say, "crackpot."
4. This model has been elaborated in greater detail in Keller (1978).
5. A more comprehensive analysis is attempted in my forthcoming book, *Reflections on Gender and Science*.
6. The vision of a different science is a familiar theme. In the 60s, the plea for a science based

on a more erotic relation to reality achieved a good deal of popularity from the writings of Norman O. Brown and Herbert Marcuse, and now, in the 80s, the cry for a different, more loving, more life-respecting science is taken up again by the ecofeminists. There is little question however that such a vision is as romantic now as it was in the 60s. Perhaps where I most seriously depart from these visionaries is in my conception of science and of how it works.

7. These interviews were conducted between September 1978 and February 1979. McClintock quotes not otherwise cited refer to these interviews.

REFERENCES

Chodorow, Nancy. 1978. *The reproduction of mothering: Psychoanalysis and the sociology of gender*. Berkeley: Univ. of California Press.

Cixous, Hélène. 1979. Poetry is/and (the) political. The Second Sex Conference, New York University, September 27–29.

Eiduson, Bernice. 1962. *Scientists: Their psychological world*. New York: Russell Sage Foundation.

Eiduson, Bernice. 1973. *Science as a career choice*. New York: Russell Sage Foundation.

Ellman, Mary. 1968. *Thinking about women*. New York: Harcourt Brace Jovanovich, Inc.

Fee, Elizabeth. 1981. Is feminism a threat to scientific objectivity? *International Journal of Women's Studies* 4, no. 4:378–92.

Geertz, Clifford. 1973. *The interpretation of cultures*. New York: Basic Books.

Greenson, Ralph. 1968. Disidentifying from mother: Its special importance for the boy. *Explorations in psychoanalysis*. New York: International Univ. Press.

Griffin, Susan. 1978. *Woman and nature: The roaring inside her*. New York: Harper & Row.

Guntrip, Harry. 1969. *Schizoid phenomena, object-relations, and the self*. New York: International University Press.

Hanson, Norwood R. 1958. *Patterns of discovery*. Cambridge, Eng: Cambridge Univ. Press.

Hudson, Liam. 1966. *Contrary imaginations*. New York: Schocken Books.

Hudson, Liam. 1968. *Frames of mind*. London: Methuen.

Keller, Evelyn Fox. 1974. Women in science: An analysis of a social problem. *Harvard Magazine*, October:14–19.

Keller, Evelyn Fox. 1978. Gender and science. *Psychoanalysis and Contemporary Thought*. 1:409–33.

Keller, Evelyn Fox. 1982. Feminism and science. *Signs* 7(3) (Spring):589–602.

Keller, Evelyn Fox. 1983. *A feeling for the organism: The life and work of Barbara McClintock*. San Francisco: W. H. Freeman.

Keller, Evelyn Fox. *Reflections on gender and science*. New York: Longman. (forthcoming)

Kistiakowsky, Vera. 1980. Women in physics: Unnecessary, injurious and out of place? *Physics Today*. February:32–40.

Kuhn, Thomas S. 1962. *The structure of scientific revolutions*. Chicago: Univ. of Chicago Press.

Marks, Elaine; and De Courtivron, Isobel. 1979. *New French feminisms*. Amherst: University of Massachusetts Press.

McClelland, David. 1962. On the dynamics of creative physical scientists. *The ecology of human intelligence*, ed. L. Hudson. London: Penguin.

McClintock, Barbara. 1951. Chromosome organization and genic expression. *Cold Spring Harbor Symposium for Quantitative Biology*. Cold Spring Harbor, New York:13–47.

Mitroff, Ian. 1974. *The subjective side of science: An inquiry into the psychology of the Apollo moon scientists*. Amsterdam: Elsevier.

Piaget, Jean. 1972. *Child's conception of the world*. Totowa, N.J.: Littlefield, Adams.

Roe, Ann. 1956. *The psychology of occupations*. New York: Wiley.

Rose, Hilary; and Rose, Steven. 1980. *Ideology of/in the natural sciences*. Cambridge, Mass.: Schenkman.

Rossi, Alice. 1966. Women in science: Why so few? *Science* 148:1196–1202.

Vetter, Betty. 1975. Women in the natural sciences. *Signs: Journal of Women in Culture and Society* 1:713–20.

White, Martha. 1970. Psychological and social barriers to women in science. *Science* 170: 413–16.

PART III
FEMINIST PERSPECTIVES FOR A TECHNOLOGICAL AGE

Introduction

Many of the issues of concern to feminist analysis in a technological age have been suggested by earlier articles in this volume: the status of women as workers, the effects of computers and other advanced technologies on our lives, and the values that underpin the theory and practice of science and technology. Feminist perspectives are called for not only because women have been left out of most analyses, but also because certain issues and questions affecting women and men, and our entire ecology, have not been framed at all or have been given scant attention. In this final section, the authors turn to some of these issues and questions, showing the impact of feminist values to move inquiry into new directions.

Chapter 9, by Corlann Bush, speaks to technology assessment. Starting from three common views of technology as tool, threat, or triumph, Bush reveals them as myths that feminist analysis must unthink. We must free our minds in order to rethink new social and technological relationships for assessing technology and framing public policy. Bush calls for an equity analysis of technology that would focus on risks and benefits within technology's contexts. These include the developmental, the user, the environmental, and cultural contexts. In part, setting a framework for the essays that follow, Bush demonstrates how a feminist equity analysis of technology underscores the need for collective, rather than individual, solutions and the need to frame such solutions.

Sally Gearhart in chapter 10 offers the view that we may be beyond such solutions. Applying an epistemological and values critique, Gearhart discusses the development and use of technology that is peculiar to the human species. Using their particular kind of intelligence, human beings have chosen to develop a technology that reflects and perpetuates their alienation from the rest of nature and the ravaging of that nature. The point has been reached that all life on earth, including human life, may well be destroyed. Since the process, grounded as it is in human knowledge and approaches to knowledge, appears irreversible, Gearhart offers her "modest proposal." To save the natural world of which we are a part, Gearhart proposes that the destroyers self-destruct.

The changes in the ways that human beings could procreate in the future and the special consequences for women concern Jalna Hanmer in chapter 11. Moving from established technologies such as artificial insemination and in vitro fertilization to more futuristic technologies such as cloning, parthenogenesis, and the artificial placenta, Hanmer discusses the social and political as well as scientific and technological forces at work, and the ethical and legal issues that are raised. As women struggle for reproductive control, only artificial insemination offers them that possibility. When the experimenters become the ethicists as well, as in the case of Edwards and Steptoe and in vitro fertilization, for which increased financial and governmental supports have been made available, women become the ones controlled. Genetic manipulation of the embryo would alter, and cloning would eliminate, women's genetic contribution to the fetus, while development of the artificial placenta, allowing full gestation outside the womb, would eliminate women's role in reproduction entirely. Women and men then change places, the male becoming the creator with a continuous experience of reproductive consciousness.

In contrast, Marge Piercy's Mattapoisett, described by Patrocinio Schweickart in chapter 12, is a rare example of artificial reproduction existing in an egalitarian society, women having voluntarily given up their power over reproduction. In Schweickart's chapter, future possibilities for science and technology are explored through feminist utopian fiction. Drawing on two antitechnology visions, by Dorothy Bryant and Sally Gearhart, and two projections of advanced technological societies, by Marge Piercy and Ursula Le Guin, Schweickart shows that, despite strong differences in the kinds of technology projected, the commonalities of these authors are striking. Each society portrayed rejects violence, is built on ecological principles, and recognizes the relationship between patriarchy and the domination principle in science and technology. Citing de Beauvoir (as did King earlier), Schweickart finds the authors agreed that the domination of women and the domination of nature serve as models for each other. Thus, the four utopias are joined at the level of feminist values. For Gearhart and Bryant, science and technology cannot be defined apart from the logic of domination and, thus, their utopias reject modern technology. For Le Guin and Piercy, projecting scientifically and technologically advanced societies, values can be so transformed that technology is no longer a tool of power.

In thus suggesting new frameworks for technology assessment and policymaking, in questioning fundamentally the mindset of our technology, in raising crucial issues about trends in human reproduction, and in projecting future scientific and technological possibilities, the authors in Part III describe feminist values and their possible impact for technological society. These values call for a balance of nature; an end to social domination, whether of sex, race, or class; the breakdown of hierarchies; and a society based on principles of equity—values that feminists seek to implement for technological scholarship and technology itself.

9

Women and the Assessment of Technology: to Think, to Be; to Unthink, to Free

Corlann Gee Bush

Everything is what it is, what it isn't, and its direct opposite. That technique, so skillfully executed might help account for the compelling irrationality . . . *double double think is very easy to deal with if we just realize that we have only to double double unthink it.*

—Dworkin 1974, p. 63.

Although Andrea Dworkin is here analyzing Pauline Reage's literary style in the *Story of O*, her realization that we can "double double unthink" the mind fetters by which patriarchal thought binds women is an especially useful one. For those of us who want to challenge and change female victimization, it is a compelling concept.

SOMETHING ELSE AGAIN

The great strength of the women's movement has always been its twin abilities to unthink the sources of oppression and to use this analysis to create a new and synthesizing vision. Assertiveness is, for example, something else again: a special, learned behavior that does more than merely combine attributes of passivity and aggressiveness. Assertiveness is an unthinking and a transcendence of those common, control-oriented behaviors.[1]

Similarly, in their books *Against Our Will* and *Rape: The Power of Consciousness*, Susan Brownmiller (1974) and Susan Griffin (1979) unthink rape as a crime of passion and rethink it as a crime of violence, insights which led to the establishment of rape crisis and victim advocacy services. But a good feminist shelter home-crisis service is something else again: it is a place where women are responsible for the safety and security of other women, where women teach self-defense and self-esteem to each other. In like manner, women's spirituality is something else again. Indebted both to Mary Daly for unthinking Christianity in *Beyond God the Father* (1973) and *The Church and the Second Sex* (1968) and to witchcraft for rethinking ritual, women's spirituality is more than a synthesis of those insights, it is a transformation of them.

In other words, feminist scholarship and feminist activism proceed not through a sterile, planar dialectic of thesis, antithesis, synthesis, but through a dynamic process of unthinking, rethinking, energizing, and transforming. At its best, feminism creates new life forms out of experiences as common as seawater and insights as electrifying as lightning.

The purpose of this chapter is to suggest that a feminist analysis of technology would be, like assertiveness, something else again. I will raise some of the questions that feminist technology studies should seek to ask, and I will attempt to answer them. Further, I hope to show how scholars, educators, and activists can work together toward a transformation of technological change in our society.

The endeavor is timely not least because books such as this, journal issues, articles, and conferences are increasingly devoting time and energy to the subject or because technologically related political issues such as the antinuclear movement and genetic engineering consume larger and larger amounts of both our news space and our consciousness. The most important reason why feminists must unthink and rethink women's relationship to technology is that the *tech-fix* (Weinberg 1966, p. 6) and the public policies on which it is based are no longer working. The tech-fix is the belief that technology can be used to solve all types of problems, even social ones. Belief in progress and the tech-fix has long been used to rationalize inequity: it is only a matter of time until technology extends material benefits to all citizens, regardless of race, sex, class, religion, or nationality.

> Technology has expanded our productive capacity so greatly that even though our distribution is still inefficient, and unfair by Marxian precepts, there is more than enough to go around. Technology has provided a "fix"—greatly expanded production of goods—which enables our capitalistic society to achieve many of the aims of the Marxist social engineer without going through the social revolution Marx viewed as inevitable. Technology has converted the seemingly intractable social problem of *widespread* poverty into a relatively tractable one (Weinberg 1966, p. 7).

While Weinberg himself advocates cooperation among social *and* technical engineers in order to make a "better society, and thereby, a better life, for all of us who are part of society" (Weinberg 1966, p. 10), less conscientious philosophers and politicians have seen in the tech-fix a justification for laissez-faire economics and discriminatory public policy. Despite its claim to the contrary, the tech-fix has not worked well for most women or for people of color; recent analyses of the feminization of poverty, for example, indicate that jobs, which have always provided men with access to material goods, do not get women out of poverty.

> Social welfare programs based on the old male model of poverty do not consider the special nature of women's poverty. One fact that is little understood and rarely reflected in public welfare policy is that women in poverty are almost invariably productive workers, participating fully in both the paid and the unpaid work force. The inequities of present public policies molded by the traditional economic role of women cannot continue. Locked into poverty by capricious programs designed by and for male policymakers . . . women who are young and poor today are destined to grow old and poor as the years pass. Society cannot continue persisting with the male model of a job automatically lifting a family out of poverty . . . (McKee 1982, p. 36).

As this example illustrates, the traditional social policies for dealing with inequity—*get a job*—and traditional technological solutions—*produce more efficiently*—have not worked to make a better society for women. Therefore, it is essential that women begin the unthinking of these traditions and the rethinking of new relationships between social and technical engineering.

UNTHINKING TECH-MYTHS

In her poem, "To An Old House in America," Adrienne Rich describes the attitude that women should take toward the task of unthinking public policy in regard to technology: "I do not want to simplify/Or: I would simplify/ By naming the complexity/It has been made o'er simple all along" (Rich 1975, p. 240). Partly because it is in their best interest to do so and partly because they truly see nothing else, most politicians and technocrats paint the canvas of popular opinion about technology with the broadest possible brushstrokes, rendering it, in pure type, as TOOL, as THREAT, or as TRIUMPH.[2] From each of these assumptions proceed argument, legislation, public policy, and, ironically, powerlessness. In order to develop a feminist critique of technology, we must analyze these assumptions and unthink them, making them simpler by naming their complexity.

The belief that technology represents the triumph of human intelligence is one of America's most cherished cultural myths; it is also the easiest to understand, analyze, and disprove. Unfortunately, to discuss it is to resort to cliches: "There's nothing wrong that a little good old American ingenuity can't fix"; "That's progress"; or "Progress is our most important product." From such articles of faith in technology stemmed Manifest Destiny, the mechanization of agriculture, the urbanization of rural and nomadic cultures, the concept of the twentieth as the "American Century," and every World's Fair since 1893. That such faith seems naive to a generation that lives with the arms race, acid rain, hazardous waste, and near disasters at nuclear power plants is not to diminish one *byte* either Western culture's faith in the tech-fix or its belief that technological change equals material progress. And, indeed, like all generalizations, this myth is true—at least partially. Technology *has* decreased hardships and suffering while raising standards of health, living, and literacy throughout the industrialized world.

But, not without problems, as nay-sayers are so quick to point out. Those who perceive technology as the ultimate threat to life on the planet look upon it as an iatrogenic disease, one created, like nausea in chemotherapy patients, by the very techniques with which we treat the disease. In this view, toxic wastes, pollution, urban sprawl, increasing rates of skin cancer, even tasteless tomatoes are all problems created through our desire to control nature through technology. Characterized by their desire to go cold turkey on the addiction to the tech-fix, contemporary critics of technology participate in a myriad of activities and organizations (Zero Population Growth, Friends of the Earth, Sierra Club, the Greenpeace Foundation) and advocate a variety of goals (peace, arms limitation, appropriate technology, etc.). And, once again, their technology-as-threat generalization is true, or at least as true as its opposite number: in truth, no one, until Rachael Carson (1955), paid much attention to the effects of technology on the natural world it tried to control; indeed, technology has created problems as it has set out to solve others.

Fortunately, the inadequacy of such polarized thinking is obvious: technology is neither wholly good nor wholly bad. "It has both positive and negative effects, and it usually has the two *at the same time and in virtue of each other*" (Mesthene 1970, p. 26). Every innovation has both positive and negative consequences that pulse through the social fabric like waves through water.

Much harder to unthink is the notion that technologies are merely tools: neither good nor bad but neutral, moral only to the extent that their user is moral. This, of course, is the old saw "guns don't kill people, people kill people" writ large enough to include not only guns and nuclear weapons but also cars, televisions, and computer games. And there is truth here, too. Any given person can use any given gun at any given time either to kill another person for revenge or to shoot a grouse for supper. The gun is the tool through which the shooter accomplishes his or her objectives. However, just as morality is a collective concept, so too are guns. As a class of objects, they comprise a technology that is designed for killing in a way that ice picks, hammers, even knives—all tools that have on occasion been used as weapons—are not. To believe that technologies are neutral tools subject only to the motives and morals of the user is to miss completely their collective significance. Tools and technologies have what I can only describe as *valence*, a bias or "charge" analagous to that of atoms that have lost or gained electrons through ionization. A particular technological system, even an individual tool, has a tendency to interact in similar situations in identifiable and predictable ways. In other words, particular tools or technologies tend to be favored in certain situations, tend to perform in a predictable manner in these situations, and tend to bend other interactions to them. Valence tends to seek out or fit in with certain social norms and to ignore or disturb others.

Jacques Ellul (1964) seems to be identifying something like valence when he describes "the specific weight" with which technique is endowed:

> It is not a kind of neutral matter, with no direction, quality, or structure. It is a power endowed with its own peculiar force. It refracts in its own specific sense the wills which make use of it and the ends proposed for it. Indeed, independently of the objectives that man pretends to assign to any given technical means, that means always conceals in itself a finality which cannot be evaded (pp. 140–41).

While this seems to be overstating the case a bit—valence is not the atom, only one of its attributes—tools and techniques do have tendencies to pull or push behavior in definable ways. Guns, for example, are valenced to violence; the presence of a gun in a given situation raises the level of violence by its presence alone. Television, on the other hand, is valenced to individuation; despite the fact that any number of people may be present in the same room at the same time, there will not be much conversation because the presence of the TV itself pulls against interaction and pushes toward isolation. Similarily, automobiles and microwave ovens are individuating technologies while trains and campfires are accretionary ones.

Unthinking tech-myths and understanding valence also require greater clarity of definition (Winner 1977, pp. 10–12). Several terms, especially *tool*, *technique*, and *technology*, are often used interchangeably when, in fact, they describe related but distinguishable phenomena. *Tools* are the implements, gadgets, machines, appliances, and instruments themselves. A hammer is, for example, a tool as is a spoon or an automatic washing machine. *Techniques* are the skills, methods, procedures, and processes that people perform in order to use tools. Carpentry is, therefore, a technique that utilizes hammers, baking is a technique that uses spoons, and laundering a technique that employs washing machines. *Technology* refers to the organized systems of interactions that utilize tools and involve techniques for the performance of tasks and the accomplishment of objectives. Hammers and carpentry are some of the tools and techniques of architectural or building technology. Spoons and baking, washing machines and laundering are some of the tools and techniques of domestic or household technology.

A feminist critique of the public policy debate over technology should, thus, unthink the tripartite myth that sees technology in simple categories as tool, triumph, or threat. In unthinking it, we can simplify it by naming its complexity:

- A tool is not a simple isolated thing but is a member of a class of objects designed for specific purposes.
- Any given use of tools, techniques, or technologies can have both beneficial and detrimental effects at the same time.
- Both use and effect are expressions of a valence or propensity for tools to function in certain ways in certain settings.
- Polarizing the rhetoric about technology enables advocates of particular points of view to gain adherents and power while doing nothing to empower citizens to understand, discuss, and control technology on their own.

"Making it o'er simple all along" has proven an excellent technique for maintaining social control. The assertion that technology is beneficial lulls people into believing that there is nothing wrong that can't be fixed, so they do nothing. Likewise, the technophobia that sees technology as evil frightens people into passivity and they do nothing. The argument that technology is value-free either focuses on the human factor in technology in order to obscure its valence or else concentrates on the autonomy of technology in order to obscure its human control. In all cases, the result is that people feel they can do nothing. In addition, by encouraging people to argue with and blame each other, rhetoric wars draw public attention away from more important questions such as who is making technological decisions?, on what basis?, what will the effects be?

CONTEXT, CONTEXT, WHITHER ART THOU, CONTEXT?

In unthinking the power dynamics of technological decision making, a feminist critique needs to pay special attention to the social messages whispered in women's ears since birth: mother to daughter, "Don't touch that, you'll get dirty"; father to daughter, "Don't worry your pretty little head about it"; teacher to young girl, "It doesn't matter if you can't do math"; woman to woman, "Boy, a man must have designed this."

Each of these statements is talking about a CONTEXT in which technological decisions are made, technical information is conveyed, and technological innovations are adopted. That such social learning is characterized by sex role stereotyping should come as no surprise. What may be surprising is not the depths of women's ignorance—after all, women have, by and large, been encouraged to be ignorant—but the extent to which men in general, inventors, technocrats, even scholars, all share an amazing ignorance about the contexts in which technology operates. There are four:

1. *The design or developmental context* which includes all the decisions, materials, personnel, processes, and systems necessary to create tools and techniques from raw materials.
2. *The user context* which includes all the motivations, intentions, advantages, and adjustments called into play by the use of particular techniques or tools.
3. *The environmental context* that describes nonspecific physical surroundings in which a technology or tool is developed and used.
4. *The cultural context* which includes all the norms, values, myths, aspirations, laws, and interactions of the society of which the tool or technique is a part.

Of these, much more is known about the design or developmental context of technology than about the other three put together. Western culture's collective lack of knowledge about all but the developmental context of technology springs in part from what Langdon Winner calls technological orthodoxy: a "philosophy of sorts" that has seldom been "subject to the light of critical scrutiny" (Winner 1979, p. 75). Standard tenets of technological orthodoxy include:

- That men know best what they themselves have made.
- That the things men make are under their firm control.
- That technologies are neutral: they are simply tools that can be used one way or another; the benefit or harm they bring depends on how men use them (Winner 1979, p. 76).

If one accepts these assumptions, then there is very little to do except study processes of design and invent ever-newer gadgets. The user and environmental contexts become obscured if not invisible, an invisibility further confirmed by the fact that, since the Industrial Revolution, men have been inventors and designers while women have been users and consumers of technology. By and large, men have created, women have accommodated.

The sex role division of labor that characterizes Western societies has ensured that boys and girls have been brought up with different expectations, experiences, and training, a pattern that has undergone remarkably little change since the nineteenth century.

> Games for girls were carefully differentiated from boys' amusement. A girl might play with a hoop or swing gently, but the "ruder and more daring gymnastics of boys" were outlawed. Competitive play was also anathema: A "little girl

> should never be ambitious to swing higher than her companions." Children's board games afforded another insidious method of inculcating masculinity and femininity. On a boys' game board the player moved in an upward spiral, past temptations, obstacles, and reverses until the winner reached a pinnacle of propriety and prestige. A girls' playful enactment of her course in life moved via a circular ever-inward path to the "mansion of happiness," a pastel tableau of mother and child. The dice of popular culture were loaded for both sexes and weighted with domesticity for little women. The doctrine of (separate) spheres was thereby insinuated in the personality of the child early in life and even during the course of play (Ryan 1979, p. 92).

It is difficult to invent a better mousetrap if you're taught to be afraid of mice; it is impossible to dream of becoming an engineer if you're never allowed to get dirty.

As compared to women, men do, indeed, know a great deal about what they would call the "design interface" of technology; they know more about how machines work; they discovered the properties of elements and the principles of science. They know math, they develop cost-benefit-risk analyses; they discover, invent, engineer, manufacture, and sell. Collectively, men know almost everything there is to know about the design and development of tools, techniques, and systems; but they understand far less about how their technologies are used—in part because there is less money in understanding than in designing, in part because the burden of adjusting to technological change falls more heavily on women. What is worse, however, is that most men do not know that they do not know anything about women and the user context.

> From the preliminary conceptualization to the final marketing of a product, most decision making about technology is done by men who design, usually subconsciously, a model of the physical world in which they would like to live, using material artifacts which meet the needs of the people—men—they best know. The result [is] technological development based on particular sets of male conditioning, values, and roles. . . (Zimmerman 1981, p. 2).

Ironically, until very recently, most women did not realize that they possessed information of any great significance. With all the cultural attention focused on the activity in the developmental context, it was hard to see beyond the glare of the spotlights into the living rooms and kitchens and laundries where women were working and living out the answers to dozens of unverbalized questions: How am I spending my time here?; How is my work different from what I remember my mother doing?; Am I really better off?; Why does everything seem so out of control? Rephrased, these are the questions that will comprise a feminist assessment of technology: How have women's roles changed as a result of modern technology?; Has women's status in society kept pace with the standard of living?; Do women today have more opportunities or merely more expectations?; What is the relationship of material possessions to personal freedom?

Think for a moment about washing machines. Almost every family in the United States has access to one; across the country, women spend thousands of hours each day in sorting, washing, drying, folding, and ironing clothes. The automatic washing machine has freed women from the pain and toil described so well by Agnes Smedley (1973) in *Daughter of Earth*. But as washing technology has changed, so too has clothing (it gets dirtier faster) and wardrobes (we own more clothes) and even standards of cleanliness (clothes must be whiter than white), children change clothes more often, there are more clothes to wash. Joann Vanek (1974, p. 118), in her work on time spent in housework, asserts that women spent as much time in household related tasks in 1966 as they did in 1926.

More has changed, however, than just standards of cleanliness. Doing laundry used to be a collective enterprise. When I was a child in the late 1940s and early 1950s, my mother and grandmother washed the family's clothes together. My grandmother owned a semi-automatic machine but she lived 45 miles away; my mother had hot water, a large sink, and five children. Every Sunday, we would dump the dirty clothes in a big wicker basket and drive to my grandmother's house where all the womenfolk would spend the afternoon in the basement, talking and laughing as we worked. By evening, the wicker basket would again be full, but this time with neatly folded, clean smelling piles of socks, sheets, towels, and underwear that would have to last us a week. Crisply ironed dresses and slacks, on hangers, waited to be hung, first on those little hooks over the side doors of the car, then in our closets at home.

Nostalgic as these memories are, doing laundry was not romantic. It was exhausting, repetitious work, and neither my mother nor I would trade in our own automatic washers to go back to it (Armitage 1982, pp. 3–6). Yet, during my childhood, laundry was a communal activity, an occasion for gossip, friendship, and bonding. Laundering was hard work, and everyone in the family and in the society knew it and respected us as laborers. Further, having laundry and a day on which to do it was an organizing principle (Monday, washday; Tuesday, iron; Wednesday. . .) around which women allocated their time and resources. And, finally, there was closure, a sense of completion and accomplishment impossible to achieve today when my sister washes, dries, folds, and irons her family's clothes everyday or when I wash only because I have nothing to wear.

Admittedly, this homey digression into soap opera (One Woman's Wash) is a far cry from the design specification and cost-benefit analyses men use to describe and understand the developmental context of washing machines, but it is equally valid for it describes the user context in the user's terms.

Analyzing the user context of technological change is a process of collecting thousands and thousands of such stories and rethinking them into an understanding of the effects of technological change on women's lives.[3] From unthinking the developmental context such and rethinking the user context, it is only a short step to studying the environmental and cultural contexts of technological change. Of these, our knowledge of the environmental context is the better developed, partly because we have given it more serious attention but mostly because environmental studies has been a legitimate career option for men.

While concern about the effects of technology on the natural environment is an idea that can be traced back to de Crevecoeur (1968 [1782]) and James Fenimore Cooper (1832), Rachael Carson (1955, 1961, 1962) is the person most responsible for our current level of ecological awareness and for the scientific rather than aesthetic basis on which it rests. As we learn more about the fragile reciprocity within ecosystems, we begin to unthink the arrogance of our assumption that we are separate from and superior to nature. In an ecosystem, it is never possible to do only *one* thing; for every action there are chain reactions of causes and effects. The continued survival of the world depends upon developing more precise models of the environment so we can predict and prevent actual catastrophe without being immobilized by the risking of it.

Perhaps no one could have foreseen that the aerosol sprays we used to apply everything from paint to anti-perspirant would degrade the earth's ozone layer, but no one seems to have asked. That drums for burying toxic waste would eventually corrode and leak seems so obvious that millions ought to have been able to predict the risk, yet no one seems to have had the desire or the clout to deal with the problem of hazardous waste before it became a crisis. In pursuit of progress, we have been content to ignore the ecological consequences of our technological decisions because, until it was pointed out to us, we did not realize that there *was* an environmental context surrounding the tools we use.

The environmental impact analysis (EIA) has become the most popular means by which governments and industries attempt to predict and assess the ecological impact of technological change. While most EIAs are long, tedious, and nonconfrontive, the idea behind them and much of the work that has gone into them is sound. In her articles on appropriate technology, Judy Smith (1978, 1981) from the Women and Technology Project in Missoula, Montana, has suggested that sex-role impact reports could be used to improve our understanding of the cultural context of technology in much the same way that the EIA has improved our knowledge of the environmental context.

And we do need something, for we know next to nothing about the interactions of culture and technology, having always seen these as separate phenomena. Most people welcome technological change because it is *material*, believing that it makes things better, but it doesn't make them different. They resist social change because it is *social* and personal; it is seen as making things different . . . and worse. The realization that technological change stimulates social change is not one that most people welcome.

Feminists need to unthink this cultural blindness. Because women are idealized as culture carriers, as havens of serenity in a heartless world (Lasch 1977), women are supposed to remain passive while the rest of the culture is allowed, even encouraged, to move rapidly ahead. Women are like the handles of a slingshot whose relatively motionless support enables the elastic and shot to build up energy and to accelerate past them at incredible speeds. The culture measures its progress by women's stasis. When women do try to move, when they try to make changes rather than accommodations, they are accused of selfishness, of me-ness, of weakening the family, of being disloyal to civilization (Rich 1979, pp. 275–310).

However, it is crucial that feminists continue to unthink and rethink the cultural contexts of technology for a reason more significant than our systematic exclusion from it: it is dangerous not to. Technology always enters into the present culture, accepting and exacerbating the existing norms and values. In a society characterized by a sex-role division of labor, any tool or technique—it has valence, remember—will have dramatically different effects on men than on women.

Two examples will serve to illustrate this point. Prior to the acquisition of horses between the late sixteenth and mid-seventeenth centuries, women and dogs were the beasts of burden for Native American tribes on the Great Plains. Mobility was limited by both the topography and the speed at which people and dogs could walk. Physical labor was women's province in Plains culture, but since wealth in those societies was determined by how many dogs a person "owned" and since women owned the dogs, the status of women in pre-equestrian tribes was relatively high—they owned what men considered wealth (Roe 1955, p. 29). Women were central to the economic and social life of their tribes in more than the ownership of dogs. They controlled the technology of travel and food: they were responsible for the foraging, gathering, and preserving of food for the tribe and, in many cases, determined the time and routes of tribal migration. They had access to important women's societies and played a central part in religious and community celebrations (Liberty 1982, p. 14).

Women's roles in Plains Indian societies changed profoundly and rapidly as horses were acquired and domesticated. In less than two centuries—for some tribes in less than a generation—a new culture evolved. The most immediate changes were technological and economic; horses became the technology for transportation and they were owned by men. Women could still own dogs, but this was no longer the measure of wealth it had been.

With their "currency" debased, women's status slipped further as important economic, social, and religious roles were reassigned to men. As the buffalo became a major source of food and shelter, the value of women's foraging activities decreased. Hunting ranges were expanded, causing more frequent moves with women doing more of the packing up and less of the deciding about when and where to go. As each tribe's hunting range increased, competition for land intensified; and warfare, raiding, and their concomitants for women—rape and slavery—also increased.

Of course, not all the effects were negative. Technologies are substitutes for human labor: horses made women's work easier and more effective. Also, several tribes, including the Blackfeet, allowed a woman to retain ownership of her own horse and saddle. However, a woman was seldom allowed to trade or raid for horses, and her rights to her husband's herd usually ended with his death.

Thus, for Native American women, the horse was a mixed blessing. It eased their burdens and made transportation easier. But it also added new tasks and responsibilites without adding authority over those tasks or increasing autonomy. The opposite was true for men; the horse provided few new tasks and responsibilities—men had always been responsible for hunting, defense, and warfare—but it did enhance these traditional roles, giving men more decision-making authority, more autonomy, and more access to status. Paradoxically, while a woman's absolute status was greatly improved by the changes from dog to horse culture, her status relative to men actually declined. In this manner, horses changed the nature of Native American culture on the high plains, but women and men were affected in profoundly different ways.

A similar phenomenon occurred at the end of the horse farming era in the Palouse region of Idaho and Washington in the United States. During the 1920s, it was common for a farmer to employ 15 to 25 hired men and to use 25 to 44 horses to harvest his crops; farmers and their hands worked back-breaking, twenty-hour days. On the other hand, women also worked long days during harvest, cooking five meals a day for as many as forty people. During the year, women were responsible for a family's food, nutrition, health, safety, and sanitation. Women's work had economic value. Performing their traditional roles as wives, mothers, and homemakers, women were economically crucial to the survival of the labor intensive family farm (Bush 1982). Unfortunately, in the same manner that the horse made a Plains Indian woman's work easier even as it lowered her status relative to men, so too did the conversion from horses to diesel power and electricity ease the farm wife's hardships while it decreased the economic significance of her labor. In both cases, technological innovation had profoundly different consequences for men's and women's work. In both cases, the innovation was coded or valenced in such a way that it loaded the status of men's roles while eroding status for women.

TECHNOLOGY AND EQUITY

Technology is, therefore, an equity issue. Technology has everything to do with who benefits and who suffers, whose opportunities increase and whose decrease, who creates and who accommodates. If women are to transform or "re-valence" technology, we must develop ways to assess the equity implications of technological development and develop strategies for changing social relationships as well as mechanical techniques. To do this, we must have a definition of technology that will allow us to focus on such questions of equity.

Not surprisingly, there are no such empowering definitions in the existing literature. Equity has not been a major concern of either technophobes or technophiles. In fact, most definitions of technology fall short on several counts. The most commonly accessible definitions, those in dictionaries, tell us little: Webster's "the science of the industrial arts" and "science used in a practical way," and the American Heritage Dictionary's "the application of science, especially to industrial and commerical objectives" and "the entire body of methods, and materials used to achieve such objectives" are definitions so abstract as to be meaningless. Other attempts clarify function but lose the crucial connection to science, as in James Burke's (1980, p. 23) "the sum total of all the objects and systems used to produce goods and perform services."

Better definitions connect technology to other categories of human behavior and to human motivation:

> A form of cultural activity devoted to the production or transformation of material objects, or the creation or procedural systems, in order to expand the realm of practical human possibility (Hannay & McGinn 1980, p. 27).

On rare occasions, definitions do raise equity questions as in John McDermott's attempt:

> Technology, in its concrete, empirical meaning, refers fundamentally to systems of rationalized control over large groups of men, events, and machines by small groups of technically skilled men operating through organizational hierarchy (McDermott 1969, p. 29).

However, this definition is really defining *technocracy* rather than *technology*. More often, there are romantic definitions that enmesh us in cotton candy:

> [Technology's task] is to employ the earth's resources and energy income in such a way as to support all humanity while also enabling all people to enjoy the whole earth, all its historical artifacts and its beautiful places without any man enjoying life around earth at the cost of another (Fuller 1969, p. 348).

While no one could argue with such ideals, Buckminster Fuller leaves us where the boon and bane theorists leave us—confounded by double-think. It is impossible to ask tough questions of such a definition or to examine closely why technology does not now support all humanity equally.

More distressing is the tendency of scholars to use the generic "he/man" to represent all of humanity. For example, "without one man interfering with the other, without any man enjoying life around the earth at the cost of another" is a statement that completely disregards the fact that, around the earth, men enjoy their lives at *women's* cost. Similarly, statements such as "because of the autonomy of technique, man cannot choose his means any more than his ends" (Ellul 1964, p. 40) and "the roots of the machine's genealogical tree is in the brain of this conceptual man . . . after all it was he who made the machine" (Usher 1954, p. 22) grossly mislead us because they obscure the historical and contemporary roles that women have played in technological development.[4] Worse, they reinforce the most disabling myth of all, the assumption that men and women are affected similarly by and benefit equally from technological change.

Therefore, because of the oversimplification of some definitions and the exclusion of women from others, feminists need to rethink a definition of technology that both includes women and facilitates an equity analysis. Such a definition might be:

> Technology is a form of human cultural activity that applies the principles of science and mechanics to the solution of problems. It includes the resources, tools, processes, personnel, and systems developed to perform tasks and create immediate particular, and personal and/or competitive advantages in a given ecological, economic, and social context (Bush in *Taking hold of technology* 1981, p. 1).

The chief virtue of this definition is its consideration of advantage; people accept and adopt technology to the extent that they see advantage for themselves and, in competitive situations, disadvantage for others. Thus, an equity analysis of an innovation should focus on benefits and risks within the contexts in which the technology operates. An equity analysis of a technology would examine the following:

The Developmental Context
- the principles of science and mechanics applied by the tool or technique
- the resources, tools, processes, and systems employed to develop it
- the tasks to be performed and the specific problems to be solved

The User Context	• the current tool, technique, or system that will be displaced by its use • the interplay of this innovation with others that are currently in use • the immediate personal advantage and competitive advantage created by the use of technology • the second and third level consequences for individuals
The Environmental Context	• the ecological impact of accepting the technology versus the impact of continuing current techniques
The Cultural Context	• the impact on sex roles • the social system affected • the organization of communities • the economic system involved and the distribution of goods within this system

A specific example will serve to illustrate how an equity analysis might be approached. Refrigeration was "invented" in the 1840s in Apalachicola, Florida, by John Gorrie as a by-product of his work on a cure for malaria (Burke 1980, p. 238). Gorrie's invention was a freezing machine that used a steam-driven piston to compress air in a cylinder that was surrounded by salt water. (As the piston advances, it compresses air in the cylinder; as the piston retracts, the air expands.) An expanding gas draws heat from its surroundings; after several strokes of the piston, the gas has extracted all the heat available from the surrounding brine. If a flow of continuously cold air is then pumped out of the cylinder into the surrounding air, the result is air conditioning; if the air is continuously allowed to cool the brine solution, the brine itself will draw heat from water, causing it to freeze and make ice. If the gas (air) or brine is allowed to circulate in a closed system, heat will be drawn from the surrounding air or matter (food), causing refrigeration.

The Developmental Context

Thus, refrigeration applies the laws of science (specifically the properties of gases) and the principles of mechanics (thermodynamics and compression) to perform the tasks of making ice, preserving and freezing food, and cooling air. Refrigeration also solves the problems of retarding food spoilage and coping with heat waves, thereby creating personal advantage. The resources and tools used include a gas, a solution, a source of energy, and a piston-driven compressor.

The developmental context is enormously complex and interconnected; however, a general analysis would include all the supply, manufacture, and distribution systems for the refrigeration units themselves—everything from the engineers who design the appliances, to the factory workers who make, inspect, and pack them, to the truckers who transport them, to the clerk who sells them. A truly expansive analysis of the developmental context would also include the food production, packing, and distribution systems required to make available even one box of frozen peas as well as the artists, designers, paper producers, and advertisers who package the peas and induce us to buy them.

The User Context

Refrigeration has affected our lives in such a myriad of ways that elaborating on them all would require another paper in itself. Refrigeration has important commercial uses as well as medical ones, and it would not be overstating the case to assert that there is no aspect of modern life that has not been affected by refrigeration. Nonetheless, a more limited analysis of refrigeration as it has affected domestic and family life in the United States is both revealing and instructive.

To the self-sufficient farm family of the early twentieth century, refrigeration meant release from the food production and preservation chores that dominated much of men's and women's lives: canning garden produce to get the family through the winter; butchering, smoking, and drying meat from farm-raised hogs and cattle; milking cows daily and churning butter. The advantages of owning a refrigerator in such a situation were immediate and dramatic: food could be preserved for longer periods of time so there was less spoilage; food could be cooked ahead of serving time allowing women to spend less time in meal preparation; freezing produce and meat was a faster, easier, and more sanitary process than canning or smoking, again saving women time and improving the family's health. The refrigerator thus generated positive changes for women, freeing them from hard, hot work and improving their absolute status. However, the second and third level effects of refrigeration technology were not as benign for women as the primary effects.

Since refrigeration kept food fresh for long periods of time, fresh produce could be shipped across country, thus improving nutrition nationwide. Food processing and preservation moved out of the home, and new industries and services paid workers to perform the duties that had once been almost solely women's domestic responsibility. Within the home, the nature of women's work changed from responsibility for managing food production to responsibility for managing food consumption. Also, farmers stopped growing food for family subsistence and local markets and started growing cash crops for sale on national and international markets. Opportunities for employment shifted from farm labor to industrial labor, and families moved from rural areas to cities and suburbs. Thus, the use of refrigeration changed the work roles of individual women and men and, through them, the economy, the content of work, and the nature of culture and agriculture.

The Environmental Context

An analysis of the environmental context of refrigeration technology would examine the effects of the developmental and user contexts on the environment by asking such questions as: Since refrigeration affects agriculture, what are the ecological effects of cash crop monoculture on, say, soil erosion or the use of pesticides? Since refrigeration retards the growth of bacteria and preserves blood and pharmaceuticals, what are the consequences for disease control? What are the effects of increased transportation of food on energy supplics and air pollution?

The Cultural Context

Finally, an examination of the sex role impact of refrigeration technology would reveal a disparate effect on men and women. In the United States, men have been largely responsible for food production, women for food preservation and preparation. Refrigerators were a valenced technology that affected women's lives by, generally, removing food preservation from their domestic duties and relocating it in the market economy. Women now buy what they once canned. Women's traditional roles have been eroded, as their lives have been made easier. On the other hand, men, who originally had very little to do with food preservation, canning or cooking, now control the processes by which food is manufactured and sold. Men's roles and responsibilites have been loaded and their opportunities increased, although their work has not necessarily been made easier. Refrigeration has, thus, been adopted and diffused throughout a sexist society; we should not be surprised to learn that its effects have been dissimilar and disequitable.

THE GREAT CHAIN OF CAUSATION

Of course, not one of us thinks about the effects of refrigeration on soil erosion or women's status when we open the fridge to get a glass of milk.

We are gadget-rich and assessment-poor in this society, yet each private act connects us to each other in a great chain of causation. Unfortunately, to think about the consequences of one's actions is to risk becoming immobilized; so the culture teaches us to double think rather than think, and lulls us into believing that individual solutions can work for the collective good.

Of course, we can continue to double think such things only so long as we can foist negative effects and disadvantages off onto someone else: onto women if we are men, onto blacks if we are white, onto youth if we are old, onto the aged if we are young. Equity for others need not concern us as long as *we* are immediately advantaged.

Feminists above all, must give the lie to this rationale, to unthink it; for if the women's movement teaches anything, it is that there can be no individual solutions to collective problems. A feminist transformation of technological thought must include unthinking the old myths of technology as threat or triumph and rethinking the attendant rhetoric. A feminist unthinking of technology should strive for a holistic understanding of the contexts in which it operates and should present an unflinching analysis of its advantages and disadvantages. Above all, a feminist assessment of technology must recognize technology as an equity issue. The challenge to feminists is to transform society in order to make technology equitable and to transform technology in order to make society equitable. A feminist technology should, indeed, be something else again.

NOTES

1. I am indebted for this insight to Betsy Brown and the other students in my seminar "The Future of the Female Principle," University of Idaho, Spring 1982.
2. In *Technological Change: Its Impact on Man and Society* (1970), Emmanuel Mesthene identifies "three unhelpful views about technology: technology as blessing, technology as curse, and technology as unworthy of notice." He does not mention the "technology as neutral tool argument," perhaps because he is one of its leading proponents.
3. Obviously, oral history is the only way that scholars can accumulate this data. Oral historians should ask respondents questions about their acquisition of and adaptation to household appliances. Such questions might include: "When did you get electricity?"; "What was the first appliance you bought?"; "What was your first washing machine like?"; "How long did it take you to learn how to use it?"; "What was your next machine like?"; "When did you get running water?"; "Are you usually given appliances for presents or do you buy them yourself?", etc.
4. This situation is slowly changing thanks to much good work by Elise Boulding (1976), Patricia Draper (1975), Nancy Tanner and Adrienne Zihlman (1976), and Autumn Stanley (1984, and this volume).

REFERENCES

Armitage, Susan. 1982. Wash on Monday: The housework of farm women in transition. *Plainswoman* VI, 2:3–6.

Boulding, Elise. 1976. *The underside of history: A view of women through time*. Boulder, Colo.: Westview Press.

Brownmiller, Susan. 1974. *Against our will: Men, women and rape*. New York: Simon and Schuster.

Burke, James. 1980. *Connections*. Boston: Little, Brown.

Bush, Corlann Gee. 1982. The barn is his; the house is mine: Agricultural technology and sex roles. *Energy and transport*. Eds. George Daniels and Mark Rose. Beverly Hills, Calif.: Sage Publications, 235–59.

Carson, Rachel. 1955. *The edge of the sea*. Boston: Houghton Mifflin.

Carson, Rachel. 1961. *The sea around us*. New York: Oxford University Press.

Carson, Rachel. 1962. *Silent spring*. Boston: Houghton Mifflin.

Cooper, James Fenimore. 1832. *The pioneer*. Philadelphia: Carey & Lea.

Daly, Mary. 1968. *The church and the second sex*. New York: Harper & Row.

Daly, Mary. 1973. *Beyond God the father: Toward a philosophy of women's liberation*. Boston: Beacon Press.

de Crevecoeur, Michel Guillaume St. Jean. 1968. *Letters from an American farmer: Reprint of 1782 edition*. Magnolia, Mass.: Peter Smith.

Draper, Patricia. 1975. !Kung women: Contrasts in sexual egalitarianism in foraging and sedentary contexts. *Toward an anthropology of women*, Ed. Rayna Reiter. New York: Monthly Review Press:77–109.

Dworkin, Andrea. 1974. *Woman hating*. New York: E. P. Dutton.

Ellul, Jacques. 1964. *The technological society*. New York: Knopf.

Fuller, R. Buckminster. 1969. *Utopia or oblivion: The prospects for humanity*. New York: Bantam Books.

Griffin, Susan. 1979. *Rape: The power of consciousness*. New York: Harper & Row.

Hannay, N. Bruce; and McGinn, Robert. 1980. The anatomy of modern technology: Prolegomenon to an improved public policy for the social managment of technology. *Daedalus* 109, 1:25–53.

Lasch, Christopher. 1977. *Haven in a heartless world: The family besieged*. New York: Basic Books.

Liberty, Margot. 1982. Hell came with horses: Plains Indian women in the equestrian era. *Montana: The Magazine of Western History* 32, 3:10–19.

McDermott, John. 1969. Technology: The opiate of the intellectuals. *New York Review of Books* XVI, 2 (July):25–35.

McKee, Alice. 1982. The feminization of poverty. *Graduate Woman* 76, 4:34–36.

Mesthene, Emmanuel G. 1970. *Technological change: Its impact on man and society*. Cambridge, Mass.: Harvard University Press.

Rich, Adrienne. 1975. *Poems: Selected and new 1950–1974*. New York: W. W. Norton.

Rich, Adrienne. 1979. Disloyal to civilization. *On lies, secrets and silence: Selected prose*. New York: W. W. Norton.

Roe, Frank Gilbert. 1955. *The Indian and the horse*. Norman, Okla.: University of Oklahoma Press.

Ryan, Mary P. 1979. *Womanhood in America: From colonial times to the present*. 2nd ed. New York: Franklin Watts.

Smedley, Agnes. 1973. *Daughter of earth*. Old Westbury, N.Y.: The Feminist Press.

Smith, Judy. 1978. *Something old, something new, something borrowed, something due: Women and appropriate technology*. Butte, Mont.: National Center for Appropriate Technology.

Smith, Judy. 1981. Women and technology: What is at stake? *Graduate Woman* 75, 1:33–35.

Stanley, Autumn. 1984. *Mothers of invention: Women inventors and innovators through the ages*. Metuchen, N.J.: Scarecrow Press.

Taking hold of technology: Topic guide for 1981–83. 1981. Washington, D.C.: American

Association of University Women.
Tanner, Nancy; and Zihlman, Adrienne. 1976. Women in evolution: Part I: Innovation and selection in human origins. *Signs* 1 (Spring):585–608.
Usher, Abbott Payson. 1954. *A history of mechanical inventions*. Cambridge: Harvard University Press.
Vanek, Joann. 1974. Time spent in housework. *Scientific American* 231 (November): 116–20.
Weinberg, Alvin M. 1966. Can technology replace social engineering? *University of Chicago Magazine* 59:6–10.
Winner, Langdon. 1977. *Autonomous technology: Technics-out-of-control as a theme in political thought*. Cambridge: MIT Press.
Winner, Langdon. 1979. The political philosophy of alternative technology. *Technology in Society* 1:75–86.
Zimmerman, Jan. 1981. Introduction. *Future, technology and woman: Proceedings of the conference*. San Diego, Calif.: Women's Studies Department, San Diego State University.

10

An End to Technology: A Modest Proposal*

Sally M. Gearhart

We must see technology as a continuum: the mentality that creates the digging stick or the short-handled hoe also creates computers and rockets. For present purposes of discussion and dialogue, I suggest that a definition of technology also defines homo sapiens: *Technology is the conscious and systematic manipulation of one's environment for the purpose of reducing one's dependence on environmental factors for survival.* Technology, in other words, is the enterprise produced by human animals, and human animals are those which produce technology. To be sure, we know of other animals who do, for instance, use tools—some sea otters crack abalone shells with rocks—and we are appropriately impressed by the architectural complexity of beavers' and some birds' houses which clearly suggest more than simple adaptation to the environment. However, these uses and these structures seem to be imitative in execution with no inclination toward more sophisticated or incrementally changed tool use or structure building, i.e., the otters have not begun to make more tools for eating; the birds and beavers have not tried to build bigger nests or connected systems of dams.

Other animals, when climatic changes are too severe or when food is short or predators too threatening, migrate or adapt. In contrast, homo sapiens uses its intelligence, to conquer the environment. In the beginning, we acquired weapons and turned on our predators; we began agriculture and stored surplus food beyond our yearly consumption of it; we skinned other animals and wove cloth for our body's protection. Today, we change the landscape, the weather, and the planet itself to suit our needs. We have been called the most "adaptable" species. But the word is a misnomer. Transforming one's environment goes beyond simple adaptation to that environment. It implies a motive more intense and a desire more aggressive than the altering of our selves for survival. *We* are not the adaptable species; we are the species that makes all else adapt to us.

* I am grateful to all the women, particularly Jane Gurko and Dorothy Haecker, who have struggled with me about these ideas.

By way of preventing misunderstanding, I acknowledge here that, although human history has not catalogued a very admirable record of sensitivity, compassion, or even rationality in regard to the environment, our intelligence per se does not deserve the blame for our devastation of the planet; rather, our *use* of intelligence needs evaluation. However simplistic it may seem, I make here for purposes of analysis a distinction between "intelligence" and "consciousness." By the latter term I mean that faculty which is aware of itself, which judges and makes choices about action. With intelligence, we learn how to split the atom; with our consciousness, we decide that we will build a bomb to protect ourselves from our enemies. Or, conversely, with our consciousness we decide not to use that knowledge because the risk to us all is too great.

I do not attempt to discover which of our innumerable psychological drives is the one or ones which impel us to make *ir*rational or destructive use of our intelligence. All of us experience loneliness, fear of death, desire for aggrandizement. Nor can all "drives" be labeled negative. What does seem clear is that our consciousness—that important filter, translator, safety valve, mediator between our deepest drives and our other faculties—is not foolproof. It allows us to seek quick, short-sighted, individualized solutions. It often falters and, turning to cheap justifications, becomes the ally rather than the adversary of any human weaknesses.

It is this consciousness which I am labeling as distinctly human, and which I indict as the cause of our human history of violence and exploitation. The "intelligence" which we possess as a faculty is as neutral as our senses and cannot itself be cast as the villain of the human epic. Another animal of our intelligence might have developed the benefits of technology without developing technology itself. Recent work with dolphins, for instance, reveals in them an intellect probably equal to our own and, as well, patterns of communication, education, community, and even art which challenge our traditional assumption that homo sapiens is unique as an intelligent species (Fichtelius & Sjolander 1972, Lilly 1975, McIntyre 1974). On the basis of the developing research on cetaceans, we could assume that they work, play, and relate in ways that humans might find fulfilling, yet without the pollution and exploitation that characteristically accompany human efforts at self- or species-fulfillment.

Moreover, although human abuse of the biosphere and the planet has taken us to the brink of annihilation, our fate may or may not be to continue worshipping the presumptions that have molded our past, i.e., the presumptions that underlie modern Western science. We should challenge those presumptions and, in the process, we can acknowledge the only alternative to technology, to the human enterprise as we know it. In the following pages I want first, to indict technology on the basis of its inherent values and epistemology and, then, to develop the credibility of the alternative.

Why, in our history of failed consciousness and misdirected intellect, has technology emerged as the culprit? Undoubtedly, some answers lie in the complex interweaving of the forces of mercantile capitalism and sixteenth and seventeeth century science. Did, for instance, the ideology of modern science arise to rationalize the new capitalism as Marxist theory would affirm? Or did the ingenuity that characterized applied science (the invention of such tools as the printing press, the sextant, the chimney, the moldboard) stir the profit motive into an expansive zeal? I leave the exploration of those relationships to others and concentrate for the present upon one aspect alone of those historical forces: the attempt of Western science to discover rationality in nature, to make from natural laws formulae and methodologies for the comprehension—and, therefore, for the predictability and controlability—of nature itself. This attempt to reduce nature to a machine—best articulated by Descartes—lent for all future time the justification for the mistreatment of nature; after all, we cannot damage a machine and, even if we can, then we can always repair or replace it.

From the perspective of the environmentalist, modern Western science has failed to use even the minimal level of consciousness in order to foresee the consequences of the search for reason in nature; *or*, even worse, though it has seen the consequences, it has searched anyway. Whatever failure has allowed Western science its destructive path, the entire scientific/technological enterprise indicts itself in two important ways: in its epistemology—incomplete and ego-centered; and in its value system which presumes the planet's unlimited resources and the human species' unlimited population.

Western technology stands at the extreme end of a continuum that begins with the hand tools developed by early and geographically isolated cultures and expands dramatically with the discoveries of modern science into the present high technology arena. A limited and self-serving epistemology constricts both technology and Western science. The limitations rest on almost exclusive use of the logico-deductive function of the human mind and upon the virtues of empirical data gathering, both to the exclusion of the intuitive and/or emotional functions of the human animal.

That limitation should not surprise us, given the presence at the heart of modern science of absolutist rationality, i.e., the insistence upon the discovery and use of reason in nature. Sixteenth and seventeenth century Europeans believed—apparently genuinely—that their transformation of nature into calculable methods and entities actually freed the human spirit from a totalitarian reality; in that case, from the iron hand of the church. That their efforts have resulted in a totalitarian reality equally and perhaps far more devastating constitutes one of the great ironies of human history. Our species, our planet, and even science itself have suffered incalculable harm at the hands of totalitarian reason, at the inability or the unwillingness of science to affirm either the full spectrum of human knowledge or the avenues to its acquisition.

In their loyalty to "objectivity," science and applied science restrict knowledge to verifiable sense data and to the conclusions that our reason can reach on the basis of those data. Despite recent challenges within the scientific community itself to even the most controlled experiments and to the idea that "objectivity" exists in such experiments, the message pervades all the teachings of science: objective human reason constitutes the only truly human passageway to knowledge; all "a-rational," "subjective," "intuitive," or "occult" attempts at knowing cast the knower back into the "primitive" methods of "lower" animals and do not admit of scientific proof. Clothed in such attitudes, science answers the eternal epistemological questions: "What can I know? What do I know? How can I know?" and "How do I know?" If it cannot replicate and judge objectively the information, or if it cannot verify the information's source or manner of presentation, then it simply denies the information altogether. When science or technology does admit the participation of the intuitive function (although never of the emotional one), as in the uninvited "Aha!" that sparks the formulation of an hypothesis (Koestler 1966), it still acknowledges it only as a personal belief, unacceptable until it is proven by experiment and replicated by others; after that, it may become part of an "objective" body of knowledge.

We can understand cautious scientists' desire to avoid the pitfalls of building civilizations on faith and revelation, and we can appreciate any skepticism about efforts to base all of human behavior on arbitrarily chosen symbols or accidental/coincidental occurrences. But a-rational sources and functions do reveal information; to excise from the store of acquired knowledge the substance of dreams, fantasies, or hunches because they have no probative force, i.e., do not admit of proof, not only limits the epistemology but casts suspicion on the motives of scientists themselves.

"To prove," in fact, seems to replace "to know" in Western science, thus altering the task of *discovery* to one of *justification*, and thus revealing as well a self-serving component of the epistemology. "How do I know?" or "What do I know?" has become "How/what can I prove to others?" for in the service of objectivity only others can replicate and assess. The vast and proliferating desire of scientists to show knowledge to others obscures whatever noble motive—curiosity, the love of learning—might have inspired them early in the annals of science or in their personal history. Around that kernel of scientific justification clusters the host of embarrassing profiteering associations that attach themselves to scientific research and scholarship in a competitive capitalist system: the quantity of research that scientists have published, the number of times they have "proven" their notion, becomes the yardstick for hiring and promoting; in a society given over almost entirely to the worship of reason and justification, the sheer quantity of "proof" becomes the means of lining professional pockets with few questions asked. The cycle becomes increasingly pronounced: "prove" in order to convince others and by convincing them acquire more prestige for the business (science) that has proof as its badge of legitimacy. The self-aggrandizement inherent in the drive of science to "prove" seems a far cry from even the traditionally highly touted function of science: to discover the laws of nature.

The consequences of such a limited and self-serving epistemology weave themselves into the fabric of our lives until we accept without question the prescription of the reasoned scientist above that of the counterculture healer, until we stand mystified and immobilized in the face of vast volumes of scientific justification. We accept for ourselves the status of lesser beings, those mere consumers of the benefits of scientific exploration who keep alive the presuppositions of both science and technology.

As the study of brain hemispheres and human personality development expands (Bogen 1972, Galin 1974, Jaynes 1976, Molloy 1973, Ornstein 1972, Samples 1976), it suggests that human knowledge derives from sources other than the rational and the material. Until we accept such avenues of knowing as equal to reason and scientific method, we cannot hope to enjoy the full possibilities of human knowledge; until we forsake justification and affirm discovery, we miss the point of learning.

The value system that underlies modern science and technology constitutes a greater danger even than their limited and self-serving epistemology. That value system rests upon two faulty assumptions and operates on four axioms that legislate against human and planetary survival.

First of all, the value system reflects the assumptions that we have unlimited resources and that we can support unlimited human population. Our expanding human race has concerned scholars and social commentators at least since Malthus. Yet, only within the last 20 years (Hardin 1969, Lappe and Collins 1979, Murdoch 1981, Schumacher 1975) has the concern reached a proportion that sparks controversy or touches the consciousness of the world's people. Similarly, the technological enterprise, tied inextricably to the proliferation required by a capitalist system, has developed with little or no consideration until recently of the ultimate availability of the earth's resources. Again, we can make no hard and fast connections between population growth and capitalist technological development that does not admit of the fluctuating relationship between the two, i.e., that a modern economy alternately welcomes and rejects population growth depending upon its need for workers. We can, however, understand that a capitalist system fired by a developing technology can, in the short run, support more consumers and, thus, can easily rationalize a need for more people.

It seems consistent that the animal that invents technology is also the animal that refuses to control its own species size. Technology must not fail to produce goods from natural resources in order to fill the needs of a consumer market that is doubling every thirty years. And, swept ever more inevitably into the field of such expanding surplus goods, nations must not fail to reproduce their own peoples in order to provide consumers for their constantly growing technology—for the devices, gimmicks, novelties, the proliferation of more models, the planned obsolescence of more products.

Again, the ironies prevail: that we speak these days of how technology is going to relieve us of the ills caused by technology itself; that we say that technology, which depends for its existence upon the depletion of our resources, is going to help us solve the problem of depleting resources. In the same blasé spirit, we insist that more people (6 billion of us by the year 2000) are somehow going to solve the problem of too many people. I am among those who believe that, even if the carrying capacity of the earth were great enough to support our population growth—and even popular sources now acknowledge that as a serious question (Willey & Cook 1980) —we would, nevertheless, be 5 billion too many. Even if we could find enough oxygen and arable land, even if we ceased to poison our soil, our air, and our water, still there is slim chance that we could redistribute the wealth, and any adequate personal space for a decent quality of life would be the luxury of only the well-to-do. Our interpersonal relations, not quite sterling even in the present, would grow considerably more strained and all the horrors of overcrowding suspected by social scientists (Ehrlich & Freedman 1971) would become reality. The death of all wilderness lands and of virtually all animals except our own tightly-packed species would guarantee for us a sterile and probably very loud and public existence.

Descriptions of four axioms of science and technology follow. They suggest good reasons for such recent crises as the energy shortage, the threat of nuclear holocaust, and the growing reality of environmental destruction.

The Bigger or More Widespread the Scientific or Technological Enterprise, the Better

In the service of this axiom we urge 6 percent of the world's population (the United States) to waste what the other 94 percent starves in order to produce. In service to the same axiom, we suppress the inventions that might last many years (the electric car, the long light bulb) and embrace less efficient devices that must be regularly replaced. Our commitment to bigness—how much we can produce and sell, how much territory we can conquer, how many (often useless) commodities we possess, how much money or power we have—has its temporal parallel in speed: how fast we can go, how quickly we can communicate, how rapidly we can produce (or reproduce) the new and the plentiful. We have even begun to articulate rationalizations for this speeding up of our profligate generation of bigger and faster commodities and services: the depletion of our resources is all right because by that time Jesus will be here to redeem it all (Watt 1981);

or science will surely figure out something by the time we reach that state of affairs; or we'll simply open up a frontier in space and discover *truly* limitless resources.

We have failed to see the absurdity in the race for size, failed to remember that other qualities besides speed and bigness figure in the ecological equation. Just because one teaspoon of salt may be good for the beans, ten may not be better; one woman's capacity to have a baby in nine months does not guarantee the capacity of nine women to have a baby in one month.

If It's Possible, It Must Be Done, Whatever the Consequences

This axiom, best explored by Jacques Ellul (1967), can be alternatively stated, "Any knowledge is virtuous and any step in its acquisition is thus wholly justified." "Morally neutral" science and technology only discover and develop; society must make the ethical judgments, hence, thicker ivory towers; the deification of the intellect; caged and tortured laboratory animals; germ warfare, pesticides, and pollution.

With the worship of knowledge and know-how, technology takes on a life of its own and something almost manic can happen to people who are pulled into its orbit. As one social commentator observed, technology has outstripped our capacity to control it; we are like a train with no engineer going downhill at top speed with no brakes and with the workers frantically trying to lay the track only a few feet in front of us (Pearce 1973 p. 89).

An example of the lure of knowledge occurred in the development of the atomic bomb at Los Alamos. A large team of reasonable, responsible scientists came together in a patriotic effort to beat Germany in a race to the Biggest Bomb. Absorbed in the challenge to overcome all obstacles to nuclear fission, they acknowledged but refused to defer to their growing fear that a nuclear blast might actually destroy the earth's atmosphere. When, after V-E Day, they learned that Germany had not even been close to the nuclear bomb, the raison d'être for their dangerous mission vanished. In the film, *The Day After Trinity* (Pyramid Films 1980), a few scientists (including Robert Oppenheimer's brother Frank) attempt to explain why they continued their project, suppressing criticism of it and actually doubling their efforts to develop and detonate the bomb. In paraphrase and direct quotation from that film: "The bureaucratic and scientific structures were primed and ready. The president would have had to have an iron will to stop it. . . . It is irresistible if you are a scientist." It gives you "the illusion of ultimate and illimitable power, like being God. . . . Fulfillment. Now it has been done. Our shock and horror came later." We could not resist "the attraction of doing physics on a grand scale . . . in a Faustian bargain. . . . We could not stop." Even those who considered stopping were convinced finally that it was important for the world to know what was possible, to give force to the United Nations.

Although the first atomic blast did not destroy our atmosphere, the development of nuclear fission has, nonetheless, led us to the brink that the Los Alamos group feared (but did not shun). Their feelings and actions perfectly demonstrate our human craving to *know* at all costs. But other species, equally intelligent, might face the challenge of the unknown with different values. They might decide that if to know risks unredeemable consequences, then it is better not to know. Just because we *can* do it does not mean we *must*.

If It Benefits Mankind It Must Be Done

In the service of this axiom we alienate ourselves from the thousands of other species who also inhabit the globe, arguing that Man is the Crown of Creation, the top of the food chain, the species greater than which there is no other.

Such arrogance makes an illusory separation between us and the rest of creation. We see our needs, rights, and destinies as different from that of plants and other animals without understanding our dependence on them for our very lives and without the slightest acknowledgment that they might have worth equal to our own. Human chauvinists that we are, we have chosen to enslave and exploit other living things for our own short-run convenience or profit. Thus, while they are the first victims, we suffer as well, having poisoned our water with industrial wastes, our soil with pesticides, our air with fumes. We have made even our own imprisoned livestock uneatable, our produce unnourishing. In this choice to separate ourselves morally from different species, to draw an arbitrary line between the "human" and the "non-human," we plant the seed of internal strife among our own "kind." The same impulse which seeks to justify exploitation can rationalize separation from anything which is different, especially physically different. Thus, race, sex, size, age, strength (or weakness) all become grounds for man's exploitation of his fellow man. The true ecologist understands the connection between strip mining and pornography, laboratory animals and slavery, clear-cutting and genocide—all of it earthrape. Science can no longer argue the justification of the wholesale destruction of other species on the grounds that "it benefits mankind." Without a genuine identification with the planet and *all* its creatures, we will destroy ourselves in the bargain, if not physically then certainly morally.

Might Makes Right, or, "Knowledge/Know-how Makes Right"

Another expression of this axiom: "God or the evolutionary pattern must have meant for us to do what we are doing or He/it would not have given us the capacity to do it." This axiom bears a close connection to the last two above. Here, science rests its justification on the practice of all natural predators who feed off those weaker than themselves (with, of course, the important difference that, in using and eating those weaker than ourselves, we take more than our need and romanticize even our needs far beyond proportion). Thus, if laboratory animals cannot effectively resist our use of them for experiments, then certainly we are meant to use them.

Technology's might is in know-how as well as in size and strength. If, for instance, the United States alone has the technology to get to the magnesium that lies under the ocean, then surely that magnesium must belong to the United States. If British and U.S. meat interests have the know-how and the political acumen to secure and clear-cut the Brazilian jungle for the raising of cattle, then surely the task must be theirs to do, a sort of manifest destiny, even though environmentalists warn that in losing the jungle, the earth loses 50 percent of its oxygen supply. And, if advanced medical technology can convince and coerce Puerto Rican women to test dangerous birth control methods on their own bodies, then surely such testing is justifiable (Spragus-Zones 1982). If some divine destiny had not intended the white man to conquer the North American continent, then the white man would not possess the power to conquer it. At the heart of man's dominance of the earth and at the heart of all cultural invasion lies the precept, "might makes right."

Conditioned as we have become to the epistemology and the values of Western science and technology, we grow more and more *dependent* upon those enterprises. With its tendency to speed and size, technology increases the dangers of that dependency by leaving greater and greater quantities of people helpless when the technology fails. The nuclear meltdown at Three Mile Island and the blackouts/brownouts of large metropolitan areas stand as prime examples of such helplessness. Further, computer or airline breakdowns frequently leave hosts of irate consumers stranded; the Nestlé Corporation consciously weans African babies from traditional nutrition only to see them die when their own commercial formula proves fatal (*AFSC Women's Newsletter* 1982). As technology proliferates and population increases, we may discover that we have cut off even our escapes from the growing dependency.

Not only do we cultivate a dangerous dependency on technology; as well, Western science would have us all stand in an adversarial relationship to our environment. If we are to study and control nature, then we must distinguish it from ourselves, *alienate* ourselves from it. The limited epistemology and the questionable values of science allow us to make that separation. As a consequence, we can "do to" other entities what we would never think of doing to ourselves. If we perceive an "other" to be a part of ourselves, then we deprive ourselves of the luxuries we have become so dependent upon.

One question follows on this condition: if technology is not neutral, if each time we pick up a tool we alienate ourselves by the capacity of the tool from the material or the task we are addressing ourselves to, then can we justify the use of any tool? I presently contend that we cannot, not if a human being is the user of the tool. The culprit is our human consciousness which has shown a tendency to misuse the information supplied to it by our intelligence. It is this consciousness which has acceded to the Faustian temptations of "knowledge" and has made us into the technological animal, the animal that consciously and systematically manipulates its environment. Thus, by picking up a tool, any tool, we commit ourselves to the precepts of Western science or some painfully like them; complete with the dependency and alienation that accrue to them. While I would like to hope that we can undo Western science, I seriously doubt that that can happen. The train rushes downhill too fast.

The gift of intelligence deserves a more responsible and sensitive deployment than human beings have given it. We might have asked of the use of tools, "Whom does it help, whom does it hurt?" We might have had the bigger picture, the longer view. We might have observed that personal, class, or ethnic loyalties are far too limited; so are national loyalties or even loyalties to this or that multinational corporation. We might have observed, out of the gift of our intelligence, that the deepest loyalty of any species must ultimately be to its environment, its home, the original source of its life, and in the cycle of matter—the place to which it will eventually return.

To be sure, some groups of human beings have related well to the earth, have developed a consciousness worthy of our intellectual gifts. But, precisely because they refused technology, they became vulnerable to those who didn't. Technology leads to power, domination, control. Our failed consciousness in our relationship to the planet will inevitably, alas, prevail. The one rotten apple spoils the barrel. Until the worst of us is reformed, the whole species seems doomed; our nature seems to be to destroy whole portions of our self.

We have used our consciousness not to harmonize with nature but to change and conquer it. The earth seems now to be giving unmistakable signals that it can no longer bear the weight, either of our numbers or of our arrogance. Nor, apparently, can we change our consciousness or stop the pell-mell rush to planetary destruction. Only one alternative remains.

An extraterrestrial observing our polluted and diseased planet would have to conclude that homo sapiens, the inventor of technology, was an evolutionary blunder and should now silently fold its tents and steal away. I agree with that cosmic observer. From the point of view of our fellow species and the earth itself, the best that can happen is that human beings never conceive another child, that the child being conceived at this very moment be the last human being ever to exist.

Granted, the intervention of some outside force whose magic wand sterilizes the entire race does not gather many bets. Even slimmer is the likelihood that human beings will develop the consciousness necessary for a voluntary cessation of reproduction. Those odds, however, in no way reduce the integrity or the good sense of the proposal. The idea suggests absolutely no bloodshed, no destruction of property or reputation. There will simply be no more of us. Ever. To those who cry "That flies in the face of our drive to preserve the species," I answer that recent history does not document even the slightest inclination on our part toward species preservation, but, rather, records our determination to poison and asphyxiate ourselves. The greater virtue of my solution rests in the fact that when we go we will have the decency not to take the rest of the planet with us.

What would we lose by ceasing to be as a species? What would we lose personally? One possibility, of course, if we knew we were to have no more of us, takes the form of a trigger-happy and hysterical species that pushes all the nuclear buttons right away just to be sure we don't die alone. More optimistically, we might change character pretty quickly if we knew we were the last of our kind. We might stop killing each other; human life might take on some of the dignity that all life should have; we might appreciate our children more and begin to see what we could have been, how with a different set of values and epistemological assumptions we might have managed it all differently. The last days of homo sapiens might, after all, reveal some hidden life-loving capacity, quickened only by the hope that the earth can now restore itself from its long and difficult relationship with the human race.

This alternative affirms a far-sighted and humble participation in environmental affairs. Although it condemns the species, it need in no way diminish our regard for some remarkable individuals—perhaps including ourselves—who are a part of the species. I find in this solution of our species suicide an integrity of the calibre that humanists have long claimed is possible for the human race, though such a solution may not seem at first glance to be expressive of such integrity. If some still ask "Why?" I suggest that the burden of proof has shifted, that in terms of our biosphere the question is, "Why not?"

REFERENCES

American Friends Service Committee Women's Newsletter. 1982. 3 (1 and 2):82.

Bogen, J. 1972. The other side of the brain. *Bulletin of the Los Angeles Neurological Society* 4:1–3.

Ellul, Jacques. 1967. *The technological society*. New York: Random House.
Ehrlich, Paul; and Freedman, Jonathan. 1971. Population, crowding and human behaviour. *New Scientist and Science Journal* 50 (April 1):10–14.
Fichtelius, Karl-Erik; and Sjolander, Sverre. 1972. *Smarter than man*. New York: Ballantine.
Galin, David. 1974. Implications for psychiatry of hemispheric specialization. *Archives of General Psychiatry* 71:572–83.
Hardin, Garrett, ed. 1969. *Population, evolution and birth control*, 2nd ed. San Francisco: W. H. Freeman.
Jaynes, Julian. 1976. *The origin of consciousness in the breakdown of the bicameral mind*. Boston: Houghton Mifflin.
Koestler, Arthur. 1966. The three domains of creativity. *Challenges of humanistic psychology*, ed. James F. T. Bugental. New York: McGraw-Hill.
Lappe, Frances M.; and Collins, Joseph. 1979. *Food first*. New York: Ballantine.
Lilly, John C. 1975. *Lilly on dolphins: Humans of the sea*. Garden City, N.Y.: Anchor Books.
McIntyre, John, ed. 1974. *Mind in the waters*. New York: Charles Scribner's Sons.
Molloy, Alice. 1973. *In other words*. Oakland, Calif.: The Women's Press Collective.
Murdoch, William W. 1981. *The poverty of nations: The political economy of hunger and population*. Baltimore: Johns Hopkins University Press.
Ornstein, Robert E. 1972. *The psychology of consciousness*. San Francisco: W. H. Freeman.
Pearce, Joseph. 1973. *Crack in the cosmic egg*. London: Lyrebird Press.
Pyramid Films and Video, distributers. 1980. *The day after Trinity: J. Robert Oppenheimer and the atomic bomb*. P.O. Box 1048, Santa Monica, Calif., 10406.
Samples, Bob. 1976. *The metaphoric mind*. Reading, Mass.: Addison-Wesley.
Schumacher, E. F. 1975. *Small is beautiful: Economics as if people mattered*. New York: Harper & Row.
Spragus-Zones, Jane. 1982–1983. Depo-provera, an issue that will not be dumped. *Second opinion: Coalition for the medical rights of women*. San Francisco. December-January.
Watt, James. 1981. Congressional testimony recorded in *Not man apart*. Spring issue. (San Francisco publication of Friends of the Earth.)
Willey, Fay; and Cook, William J. 1980. A grim year 2000. *Newsweek* (August 4):38.

11

Reproductive Technology: The Future for Women?

Jalna Hanmer

We are in the midst of major developments in the technology of human reproduction. An inclusive definition from the *Journal of the American Medical Association* is quoted in the first U.S. Government report on molecular biology and techniques affecting reproduction in humans:

> Anything to do with the manipulation of the gametes [eggs or sperm] or the fetus, for whatever purpose, from conception other than by sexual union, to treatment of disease in utero, to the ultimate manufacture of a human being to exact specifications. . . . Thus the earliest procedure . . . is artificial insemination; next . . . artificial fertilization . . . next artificial implantation . . . in the future total extra corporeal gestation . . . and finally, what is popularly meant by [reproductive] engineering, the production—or better, the biological manufacture—of a human being to desired specification (U.S. Congress, House 1972, p. 2).

This definition includes a range of techniques, some of which are routinely used in animal husbandry, and less frequently in human reproduction, with reasonable success rates. Others are still experimental in that success is infrequent or yet to be achieved. I will begin with the most established, artificial insemination, and move on to a discussion of in vitro fertilization and embryo transfer. Next, I will look at techniques and research in sex determination and predetermination and, lastly, the more futuristic technologies involved in cloning, parthenogenesis, and the artifical placenta.

But before I do so, we must consider these developments in a social sense, as science does not exist independently of society. The evolution of questions for study, the resources that are made available for their exploration, including financial and other support by the state, and the involvement of commercial enterprises in the marketing of products are not inevitable processes. In a capitalist society, research developments are related to issues of profitability. Research developments in reproduction also interlock with another system of social relations: that between the two sexes. Not only are most researchers male and the subjects of the research female, but these technologies have far-reaching implications for the future relations between men and women. The social meaning and implications of these research developments consistently parallel the discussion of the technologies themselves.

ARTIFICIAL INSEMINATION

Artificial insemination is the introduction of sperm into the vagina by means other than sexual intercourse. Although the function of the egg, sperm, ovaries, tubes, womb, and hormones were not understood until comparatively recently, animals were artificially inseminated from time to time during the last two millennia. The first recorded knowledge of artificial insemination is in the Talmud (AD 200–250) (see Corea 1984). The first human insemination is attributed to the Scottish anatomist and surgeon John Hunter at the end of the eighteenth century. During the seventeenth and eighteenth centuries, it was discovered that animals reproduce with eggs which travel from the ovaries to the womb through the fallopian tubes, and that seminal fluid contains sperm. The entry of sperm into an egg was not witnessed until 1854, a discovery made with frogs who have larger eggs than humans and many other species.

Artificial insemination began to be used among farm animals around the turn of this century. The first technical problem, how to obtain sperm, was solved at the time of World War I by the use of an artificial vagina for ejaculation. Methods of stimulating the horse, bull, or ram improved greatly with the development of the electro-ejaculator just after World War II. Farmers' cooperatives and companies selling cattle sperm were rapidly established and, with the advent of frozen sperm in the mid-1960s, artificial insemination became widespread. In the United States, 60 percent of dairy cows and 2 to 4 percent of beef cattle were artificially inseminated in 1980 (Corea 1984). A similar growth of artificial insemination has occurred in other developed countries. Farmers inseminate their cows and other animals in this way because it is financially profitable to do so. The sperm of prize animals is used in order to achieve genetic improvement in the stock.

While one eminent geneticist (Muller 1961) has argued that artificial insemination should be used to improve the human genetic quality, this is an unpopular view with its eugenic message of selective breeding and disregard for marriage, monogamy, and biological parenthood. Sperm banks, however, include one in California known as the Nobel sperm bank as it has sought the sperm of Nobel prize winners in order to improve the human race (Repository for Germinal Choice, Escondido, California). Among humans, artificial insemination is justified as a means of overcoming infertility and, relative to the growth of the practice in relation to commercial domestic animals, its use is highly restricted.

Artificial insemination is a simple procedure which requires neither a clinical setting nor a doctor. Self-insemination groups have been established among women who wish a child without either heterosexual intercourse or a known father or both (Anonymous 1979). The technique employed involves establishing the likely time of ovulation by daily recording of temperature and observing cervical mucus changes as with the rhythm method of contraception. At the time of ovulation, sperm is introduced into the vagina through a needleless syringe. Women who have borne babies through this method of conception continue to maintain relationships with each other, establishing kinship type relationships even though they may not live together. This activity and way of life flies in the face of conventional wisdom and dominant cultural values regarding the importance of male biological rights.

Because it is a low technology technique which any women can use, she need not relinquish control over her body to a male-dominated medical profession or control over herself and her child to the biological father. For these reasons, persistent attempts have been made to control artificial insemination by limiting its use to women deemed deserving. The basis for the cultural resistance is indicated by the two terms used to describe the technology: AIH (Artificial Insemination by Husband) and AID (Artificial Insemination by Donor). By and large, AIH meets with little medical and/or social resistance. Concern is reserved for AID: in particular, that single and lesbian women may use the technique, over the illegitimate status of such children born to married women, and over a presumed need for children to know their biological fathers or parentage. AID must be conducted with secrecy, as men obtain rights over women and children through their biological contribution.

In English common law, legitimacy is conferred on the children of married women only through biological paternity, i.e., the woman must be married to the biological father. This central tenet of patriarchal tradition is beginning to be restructured. In a minority of states in the United States, marriage itself confers legitimacy, so that a child conceived by AID is deemed the legitimate child of the woman's husband. In conjunction with this trend, the developing legal practice in the U.S. courts is to extend paternal rights to sperm donors when the woman is unmarried and to refuse to recognize these when she is (Kritchevsky 1981). In the same vein, British legislation has been proposed which will give unmarried men the same rights over women and children, i.e., to access, custody, and guardianship, now exercised by married men (Hanmer 1981). The restructuring of male rights over children, and thus male rights over women, is best understood as a response to the opportunity artificial insemination offers women to gain control over their bodies. This is greater with artificial insemination than for any of the remaining technologies to be dealt with in this chapter. With in vitro fertilization, to be discussed next, control passes firmly into the male-controlled medical profession.

IN VITRO FERTILIZATION

In vitro fertilization is the entry of the male sperm into a woman's egg cell outside her body. *In vitro* means literally "in glass." The term derives from the small glass circular dish known as a petri dish in which the fertilization takes place in the laboratory. The first external fertilization occurred in 1879 using a rabbit, but it was not until 1968 that human eggs were fertilized in this way. The technical breakthrough is attributed to the collaboration between the reproductive physiologist Bob Edwards and the gynecologist Patrick Steptoe (Edwards & Steptoe 1980).

After external fertilization, the next step toward implantation into a woman's womb was for the fertilized egg to begin cell division. In the woman's body, the egg, once released from the ovary, makes its way down the fallopian tube to the uterus where it implants itself in the lining around the fifth day after fertilization. By this time, the egg has reached the blastocyst stage. From 1968, Steptoe's patients who had come to him with infertility problems were used in the research. Women were given hormones to control the menstrual cycle, the so-called fertility drugs, and, at the right moment in the cycle, ripened eggs were removed from the woman by laparoscopy. This involves an abdominal incision near the navel and the introduction of a laparoscope that enables the inside of the woman's uterus, tubes, and ovaries to be seen (Harrison 1982). The egg is then removed and fertilized in the petri dish. It was not until a decade later that successful reimplantation occurred that resulted in a live birth, Louise Brown. Preparing the woman's uterus to receive the embryo involves hormone treatment and careful timing. Only a few babies have been born in the United States, Australia and Israel, as well as in Britain, in view of the numbers of women submitting themselves to these procedures.

Steptoe and Edward's research received support from the Ford Foundation, but its experimental nature led to a refusal of funding by the British Medical Research Council on the grounds that they had

> serious doubts about ethical aspects of the proposed investigations in humans, especially those relating to the implantation in women of oocytes fertilised *in vitro*, which were considered premature in view of the lack of preliminary studies on primates and the present deficiency of detailed knowledge of the possible hazards involved. Reservations were also expressed about the justifiability of employing the procedure of laparoscopy for purely experimental purposes (Edwards & Steptoe 1980, p. 106).

Financial support continued, however, from sources which Edwards and Steptoe describe as private and mainly American. Once Louise Brown was born, opposition to in vitro programs melted. In Britain, National Health Service hospitals began experimenting with the technique and women were not required to pay for taking part in the research. Fees at the Steptoe and Edward's clinic were in excess of 2,000 pounds sterling, payable whether or not the experiment was successful.

As these programs have spread to most, if not all, developed countries, the arguments over their desirability have now changed. In Britain, the government set up a committee in July 1982 to inquire into recent and potential developments in medicine and science related to human fertilization and embryology and to consider what policies and safeguards should be applied, including the social, ethical, and legal implications of these developments. We may anticipate that other countries will follow suit, although this should not be taken as a solution to the problem of the lack of control the subject, the woman, has over her body. Edwards reports that after the Medical Research Council's refusal and attacks during a major professional meeting,

> I would not wish the reader to imagine we were over-vulnerable. I had been a member of a small committee for some years now that had been formed to clarify ethical issues arising from advances in biology. Its Chairman was Walter Bodmer, Professor of Genetics at Oxford University. It included a theologian, Gordon Dunstan, John Maddox, who was editor of *Nature*, and two politicians, Shirley Williams, a future Cabinet Minister, and David Owen, a future Foreign Secretary (Edwards & Steptoe 1980, p. 115).

Through this committee, Edwards was able to gain considerable powerful support for his and Steptoe's in vitro experiments. This is a common pattern; the experimenter is also the ethicist who defines the terms of the debate and offers the solution. Ordinary women, including the experimented upon, are denied a voice. The potential for embryo transfer makes the need to end this exclusion more urgent.

EMBRYO TRANSFER

Embryo transfer involves placing the fertilized egg of one female into the uterus of another female. Advances in animal husbandry offer parallels for the future use of this technique in humans. Embryos of prize animals are beginning to be inserted into less valuable cows for maturation. In this way, the milk production of prize animals continues and more than one calf per year is obtained. While most highly developed for dairy cows, other domestic commercial animals are bred in this way. Even endangered species through programs in zoos are using frozen embryos.

With the perfection of freezing techniques, frozen embryos could be stored for use at a later time. Without licensing and other regulation, they could be sold, or other women (surrogate mothers) could be used to carry the embryo to a full-term baby. Surrogate mothers have already hit the headlines as men have paid women to give birth to children conceived with their sperm on the understanding that their mother would hand the baby over at birth. A recent British case involved a fifteen year old who turned to the court to claim her infant. Her baby was returned. But with embryo transfer in which the surrogate carries the fertilized egg of another woman and her husband, the legal position regarding guardianship, custody, and access becomes obscure. Surrogate motherhood is reminiscent of wet nursing when poor working class women were used to provide breast milk for the babies of well-to-do middle and upper class women, often at the expense of the lives of their own babies. Put somewhat vulgarly, "rent-a-tit gives way to rent-a-belly" (Rose & Hanmer 1976).

Mary O'Brien (1981) offers an explanation of what this means for women in terms of their reproductive experience. She explains that reproductive consciousness is different for men and women. For a man, genetic continuity is largely an idea, as reproduction begins with the alienation of the male sperm from his body. It is not until nine months later that he is able to reintervene in the reproductive process, this time as a social father. O'Brien argues that the male appropriation of the child, i.e., only fathers can confer legitimacy, mediates the opposition between this exclusion from the experience of genetic continuity and social recognition as a father. This opposition necessitates cooperative action between men to achieve "rights" to a child, a social, legal and political process. The reproductive consciousness of a woman is of a different order as she directly experiences genetic continuity through the growth of the child within her and her active laboring process of giving birth. As an ex-midwife of 25 years' experience, O'Brien knows that natural childbirth is a laboring process, using this phrase in a Marxist sense of work.

Developments in reproductive technology are progressively providing women with the same discontinuous experience men now have. The struggle over natural versus high technology childbirth is one illustration that women value the reproductive consciousness that normal childbirth gives (Corea 1979). In vitro fertilization followed by the inevitable Caesarian section grossly reduces the experience of reproductive consciousness of the woman. Embryo transplants will do so further. The future development of techniques could include genetic manipulation of embryos in various ways including their sexing. This is now possible with domestic commercial animals through examination of embryo tissue, and could become one technique for sex selection among humans.

SEX DETERMINATION AND PREDETERMINATION

In humans, the sex of an individual is controlled by special chromosomes known as sex chromosomes, of which there are two types called X and Y. There are two sex chromosomes in every cell. In a woman these are both X chromosomes while in a man there is one X and a smaller Y chromosome. Every egg has one X chromosome, and a sperm can have either an X or a Y. If an X-carrying sperm fertilizes the X-carrying egg, the baby will be a girl, while fertilization by a Y-carrying sperm produces a boy.

If the sex of the fetus could be known before the twelfth week of pregnancy, and if selective abortion on grounds of sex were acceptable, then pregnancy could be terminated by the aspiration method which is safer for the woman and less traumatic than those methods inducing normal labor contractions and birth. The only country reporting a test of this type is China and, as should be expected, the results of the few cases (100) show that many more female fetuses were aborted than male (of the 53 males predicted, one was aborted; and of the 46 females, 29 were aborted). The Chinese claim a 94 percent accuracy with the test which involves an examination of cells along the uterine wall for sex chromatin (Tietung Hospital of Anshan Iron and Steel Company, 1975). We have no further reports about this test, however.

The method used in the West has several major drawbacks (Ju et al. 1976). While almost completely reliable, it cannot take place before the sixteenth week of pregnancy. It involves some risks to the fetus, a minimum of three weeks' anxious waiting for the results, and it is expensive to carry out. A needle is inserted into the abdomen of the woman and a very small amount of amniotic fluid surrounding the fetus is withdrawn for analysis for sex chromatin. The risks, while small, are serious, including puncture of blood vessels or the fetus, the introduction of infection into the amniotic fluid, or premature labor. The use of amniocentesis is justified on the grounds that fetal abnormalities or sex-linked genetic diseases may be discovered. When these are, abortion becomes a possibility. From time to time, there are newspaper accounts of amniocentesis being used for selective abortion solely on the ground that the fetus is the wrong sex, almost always a girl. While this occurs in developed countries, the most recent report comes from India where the desire to get rid of unwanted girls is deeply rooted in the dowry system (*Guardian* 1982, p. 5).

There is a large and growing literature, mainly focused on the United States and the Third World with a little European work, on the attitudes and practices of adults of both sexes, with and without children, toward sex selection (Williamson 1976, 1978). The rationale for research on sex preferences is to explore its relation to fertility and thereby its potential contribution to population control. One study describes total family planning as regulating the size, spacing, sex, and birth order of children, arguing that family planning is moving from a negative, contraceptive phase to a positive, proceptive one (Adelman & Rosenzweig 1978). While cautious supporting statements such as "deserving some consideration" may be found in the literature (Cederqvist & Fuchs 1970), sex selection as a form of family planning is not discussed as a serious possibility by scientists in the West. Once a safe, reliable, early detection method is developed, however, we cannot assume that the Western position will remain the same given the continued preference for male children in our societies. If a technique were developed that did not involve abortion, then the use of the method is likely to be even greater.

Sex predetermination enabling women to be destroyed before being born has been described by Janice Raymond (1981) as moving us into the realm of previctimization. Desire to influence which sex is conceived and to predict the sex of the fetus afterwards are of ancient origin, to our knowledge over 4000 years old. But it was not until the last decade of the nineteenth century that the role of sex chromosomes in human reproduction was understood. Imminent success of sex predetermination has been predicted for some years now, indicating that the problem is more difficult than originally thought.

Those methods involving conception by artificial insemination experiment with a variety of processes. Early research involved electrophoresis, the separation of X and Y spermatozoa on the basis of differences in electrical charge. The Soviet biochemist, V. N. Schroder, found that rabbit spermatozoa placed in a container with a positive electrode at one end and a negative at the other migrated so that the sperm next to the positive produced female offspring and the negative produced males (Nentwig 1981). Subsequent researchers were not so successful with this technique. Another method, centrifugation, or spinning, is based on the belief that as the X and Y chromosomes differ in size, the Y being smaller, the sperm bearing the two types could be separated on the basis of different weights. This process damaged the X-carrying spermatozoa more than the Y, but reduced fertility overall, so it was abandoned as a technique by commercial livestock breeders who conducted the trial runs. Selective agglutination, the introduction of substances that encourage the filtering of X and Y spermatozoa after centrifugation, is a method currently being tested on humans. R. J. Ericsson has patented his technique and through his company, Gametrics in Sausalito, California, women may try for male children as his method separates out Y-bearing sperm only.

Methods involving intercourse concentrate on timing in relation to the menstrual cycle and altering the alkalinity or acidity of the vagina. One method involves the timing of intercourse, douching, coital position, and the desirability of female orgasm (Rorvik & Shettles 1977). The most reliable indicator that the egg has been, or is about to be, released from the ovary is the shift in body temperature that takes place on about the fourteenth day of the menstrual cycle. To conceive a girl, intercourse should take place two or more days before the shift and for a boy on the day or the day before. This advice has been challenged, as it is based on statistics of artificial insemination (Guerrero 1974, 1975). Guerrero argues that, with intercourse, female conceptions are more likely on the day of the shift and male conceptions the days before, while the reverse is true for artificial insemination. Williamson (1978) reports that Guerrero's timing schedule is being tested without publicity. It is unclear who is conducting this research and where. For example, in Britain, the Marie Stopes Clinic, a well-established private facility in London, is being used as a postal address (p. 24). To produce boys, Shettles recommends, in addition to timing, an alkaline douche, entry from the rear, and female orgasm to increase alkalinity of the vagina. To produce girls, he recommends a vinegar douche, the missionary position, and no female orgasm. Two attempts have been made to test Shettle's method, one in Singapore and another in West Germany (Williamson 1978). Both were inconclusive.

The final method involves research into the antigen-antibody reactions. A technique involving immunizing the woman against the unwanted sex has been patented by Gustaaf van den Bovencamp in the United States but no details are available about its effectiveness. Immunization research arises out of the belief that the primary sex ratio, the number of males to females conceived, is greater than the secondary sex ratio, the number of males to females born.

The outstanding impression created by the literature on sex predetermination in the Western world is a lack of questioning about ethics and morality. It is dominated by an assumption that methods of determining sex before conception will be used as soon as they are introduced, although some account is taken of the large number of respondents who express no interest in determining the sex of their children. The questions of social scientists imply that sex predetermination is an accepted and acceptable idea. It is just a matter of finding out which method is preferred and when and how many children are desired. Why people want to determine the sex of their children or why males are thought more desirable by both men and women are not explored in any depth. The disparity between the percentages of men and women who prefer males, however, has not been systematically explored, although this is a major consistent finding. In short, the area is treated as unproblematic.[1]

Findings are that sex predetermination may influence three important population variables: first-child patterns, family size, and the sex ratio (Markle & Nam 1971). Studies consistently show a preference for a boy for the first child by both men and women. It is believed that family size might be reduced if the frequent desire among those who express strong sex preferences for one child of each sex could be met with the first two children. The first sex choice study in the United States occurred 50 years ago and there has been little change in attitudes since then (Winston 1932). While it is difficult to compare studies as questions differ and attitudes vary depending on the situation under consideration, ratios can be as high as 165 boys to 100 girls (165:100). From 66 to 92 percent of men have been found to want an only child to be a boy (Clare & Kiser 1951, Dinitz et al. 1954), and from 62 to 80 percent of men prefer a first child to be a boy (Markle & Nam 1971). No study has focused on understanding these major findings. The choice of a girl for a first child is as low as 4 percent (Dinitz et al. 1954, Peterson & Peterson 1973) and for an only child as low as 15 percent (Clare & Kiser 1951). Among women who want two or four children, the resulting sex ratio is close to the actual (105/6:100); while for women wanting three, the preference is more often for two boys and one girl (Adelman & Rosenzweig 1976, Westoff & Rindfuss 1974). Women not only prefer a male first born but also express more satisfaction with male births generally (Oakley 1978).

What is universal on the societal level is preference; and, if boys and girls are wanted, it is for different reasons. For many people, the physical reproductive organs (sex) and socially acquired characteristics (gender) are one and the same thing. Cultural unisex, with the same gender identity and roles for both sexes and equal evaluation of boys and girls, is more approved of by women than men, although a minority position for both. It is imperative to study these sex-linked differences along with the factors that limit son preference and encourage daughter and no preference. Daughter-preferring societies are very rare, being limited to small, preindustrial societies.[2] However, as son preference varies in degree between countries, groups within them, and between men and women, a basis exists for serious policy-oriented research.

In deciding to use any of the reproductive techniques discussed so far, women do not act without reference to others even if, as in a self-insemination group, the action is in opposition to the dominant value system. The views of the husband and the general social proscriptions on what a woman should be and do are influential and usually decisive. Women are expected to have children. It does not seem unreasonable that women should go to any lengths, no matter how unproven the technology, to attempt to conceive. With sex selection, however, the social consensus is not quite so strong. The control of men, individually through the family and collectively through the medical profession, over women is more exposed. We must ask ourselves, why do men pursue this development more than women? And to what lengths are men prepared to go to implement it?

The last technologies and scientific areas of work to be discussed involve more futuristic developments. The successes with the techniques already discussed lay the basis for delving into the heart of human creation.

CLONING, PARTHENOGENESIS, AND THE ARTIFICIAL PLACENTA

Cloning is asexual reproduction achieved by taking single cells from an individual and inducing cell division in order eventually to produce adult organisms genetically identical to the parent. Cloning has been visualized as the basis for a new social order, as in Aldous Huxley's *Brave New World* (1960), and as a means of fulfilling individual ambitions, as in David Rorvik's, *In His Image* (1978). Science fiction writers use cloning to colonize new planets; the astronaut incubates a few skin cells from his arm, for example.

Reproduction from any cell can be accomplished with plants; for example, a carrot can be grown from a single carrot cell. In animals, it is much more difficult and it is likely that the female egg cell will always be needed. In the early 1960s the nuclei, the cell part containing virtually all the genetic information, of unfertilized toad eggs were replaced with the nuclei taken from the gut lining of tadpoles. About 1 percent of the treated eggs developed into normal adult toads. The remainder died at various stages of development or failed to start dividing at all (Gurdon 1962). While other workers had different results, research continued on nuclear transplantation in amphibians (frogs, toads, newts). Subsequently, a number of experiments have succeeded with mice, including true cloning. The nucleus taken from the cell of an embryo mouse was inserted into the fertilized egg of another and the original nuclear material in that egg was then extracted, leaving only the inserted nucleus. The egg was then introduced into the womb of another mouse where it grew to full term (Illmensee & Hoppe 1981).

Parthenogenesis is the production of an embryo from an egg without fertilization by a sperm (Kelly 1977). The embryo may or may not develop into an adult. A recent survey estimates that about one thousand animal species reproduce exclusively by parthenogenesis, and still more may use both parthenogenesis and fertilization at different times. Familiar examples are bees and aphids; but even among vertebrates as highly evolved as lizards, species have been found to consist entirely of females reproducing parthenogenetically. Among warm-blooded animals, parthenogenesis occurs in several species of birds, and early embryos can occur naturally in several species such as mice, rats, ferrets, horses, and rabbits. Mammalian parthenogenetic offspring will all be female as the mother has no Y chromosome to transmit.

For a mammalian egg to develop into an embryo, it must have the full number of chromosomes found in every body cell. In humans, this number is 46. The egg is a cell containing 46 chromosomes but, before it matures, 23 chromosomes are lost through cell division. The sperm provides the other 23 chromosomes; the fertilized egg now has a full set and development can take place. If the egg is to develop without a genetic contribution from a sperm, it must double its chromosomes at some stage. An early achievement with mice involved removing an egg cell from a female mouse immediately after fertilization but before the sperm nucleus had merged with that of the egg nucleus. One of the two nuclei was then sucked out manually with a pipette, leaving either the male or female nucleus behind. The nucleus then split to produce the double set of chromosomes necessary. Each resulting mouse had one parent's genetic material. All offspring were female as the doubling of the male Y sex chromosome is not biologically viable. The female genetic contribution could be eliminated but only the male X bearing sex cell could be reproduced (*New York Times* 1981, p. 40).

In 1955, a woman scientist gave a lecture describing her research with guppies (a type of fish) suggesting that parthenogenetic births also occurred in humans (Mittwoch 1978). A Sunday newspaper invited women who thought they had parthenogenetic daughters to have their claims tested. The mothers and daughters should have been very similar. Out of the 19 volunteer pairs, only one passed all the tests for blood and saliva similarities and eye color factors, but the probability of the claim was reduced when a skin graft from daughter to mother was rejected after four weeks. Problems involved in chromosome doubling possibly cause natural parthenogenetic conceptions in mammals to die before implantation.

Unlike parthenogenesis, cloning depends on in vitro fertilization, but both may involve embryo transplantation. These processes are necessary for experimental work on the "biological manufacture of a human being to desired specification." Recombinant DNA research lays the basis for experimental work in adding or subtracting specific genes that control particular human qualities. A woman's womb, or an artificial placenta once developed, then could be used to bring the embryo to full term.

The artificial placenta is likely to be the last of all the technical processes discussed here to be achieved. As Edwards (1974) reports.

> The first six days of embryonic development to the blastocyst stage can occur in vitro . . . mid-term abortuses have been maintained in culture for a few hours or days . . . and premature human babies can be incubated from 24 weeks of gestation. . . . Almost one-half of pregnancy is thus replaceable ex vivo [outside the womb] (p. 7).

Replacing the other half of pregnancy, given the complex and exacting requirements of the fetus, is not a simple technical issue. The placenta allows for the passage of nutrients into the embryo/fetus and the passage out of waste products, as well as providing an intricate feedback system of hormone balance. Some experimentation with premature lambs using various solutions has occurred, but basic knowledge about the workings of the placenta is yet to be established.

While genetic manipulation of the embryo could alter, and cloning fully eliminate, the woman's genetic contribution to the fetus, the artificial placenta could totally eliminate women from the reproductive process. Ancient and medieval theory held that the sperm contained the fully developed infant in miniature which then grew to term in the womb. Through modern science, women could truly become the vessel, the passive carrier of patriarchal scientific understanding from Aristotle to Thomas Aquinas.

To return to Mary O'Brien's thesis, with the artificial placenta the male and female change places in the reproductive process. Reproductive consciousness for the woman becomes synonymous with that of the male today: from providing a sex cell to social motherhood with nothing in between. Having fertilized the egg, the male in the white coat tends, or supervises the tenders of, the metal and glass machines that take the embryo to full term, "birthing" the baby at the right moment. Finally, the male becomes the creator with a continuous experience of reproductive consciousness.

Of course, not all men will have this experience. For many, the contradiction Mary O'Brien describes between alienation of the sperm and social fatherhood would continue. I am describing a hierarchically organized society with state support for the dominant interests of the medical profession. How representatives of the state intertwine with scientists has many variations, but the ability to assume all the positions, as described earlier by Edwards— of experimenter and ethicist—is the expression of class power. As new forms of technology are introduced into human reproduction, we should expect these primarily male class interests to become more dominant at the expense of women.

This, however, is not inevitable. As Hilary Rose and I wrote almost a decade ago, technology could play a positive role in creating a truly human culture (Rose & Hanmer 1976). Technology is not separate from humanity. As expressed by Marx, "Technology discloses man's mode of dealing with nature, the process of production by which he sustains his life, and thereby also lays bare the mode of formation of his social relations and of the mental conceptions that flow from them" (1887, p. 406, n. 2). In demanding control over their own bodies, through many local and national campaigns, for example around contraception, abortion, sterilization, home versus hospital births, women are making a demand for a less alienating use of reproductive technologies. Self-help attempts at providing health care, from pregnancy testing to abortion services to self-insemination groups, are examples of women taking control of these technologies. Whether women will remain the researched upon, the "nature" to be controlled, will depend upon the success of these and future challenges to the dominant social interests that lie behind the mobilization of research, funding, state and public support for the developments described in this chapter. The struggle over who shall control female biological reproductive processes involves major social restructuring that has profound implications for women, as a class, whether or not they personally use these technologies.

NOTES

1. The exception is the work of Nancy Williamson (1976, 1978).
2. The Mundugumor of New Guinea, the Tiwi of North Australia, the Garo of Assam, the Iscobakebu of Peru, and the Tolowa Indians (Williamson 1978).

REFERENCES

Adelman, Stuart; and Rosenzweig, Saul. 1978. Parental predetermination of the sex of offspring: II. The attitudes of young married couples with high school and college education. *Journal of Biosocial Science* 10:235–47.

Anonymous, Sarah and Mary. 1979. *Woman controlled conception*. Womanshare Books, 3929 24th Street, San Francisco, Calif. 94114.

Cederqvist, Lars; and Fuchs, Fritz. 1970. Antenatal sex determination: A historical review. *Clinical Obstetrics and Gynaecology* 13:159–77.

Clare, Jeanne; and Kiser, Clyde. 1951. Social and psychological factors affecting fertility. *Millbank Memorial Fund Quarterly* 29(1):440–92.

Corea, Gena. 1979. Childbirth 2000. *Omni* (April):48, 50, 104–07.

Corea, Gena. 1984. *The mother machine*. New York: Viking.

Dinitz, Simon; Dynes, Russell; and Clarke, Alfred. 1954. Preferences for male or female children: Traditional or affectional? *Marriage and Family Living* 16:128–30.

Edwards, R. G. 1974. Fertilization of human eggs in vitro: Morals, ethics, and the law. *The Quarterly Review of Biology* 49(March):3–26.

Edwards, Robert; and Steptoe, Patrick. 1980. *A matter of life*. London: Hutchinson.

Guardian. 1982. Alarm at girl foetus scandal. (July 19):5.

Guerrero, Rodrigo. 1974. Association of the type and time of insemination within the menstrual cycle and the human sex ratio at birth. *The New England Journal of Medicine* 291(20):1056–59.

Guerrero, Rodrigo. 1975. Type and time of insemination within the menstrual cycle and the human sex ratio at birth. *Studies in Family Planning* 6(10):367–71.

Gurdon, John B. 1962. The developmental capacity of nuclei taken from intestinal epithelium cells of feeding tadpoles. *Journal of Embryology and Experimental Morphology* 10:622–40.

Hanmer, Jalna. 1981. Sex predetermination, artificial insemination and the maintenance of male-dominated culture. *Women, health and reproduction*, ed. Helen Roberts. London: Routledge and Kegan Paul: 163–90.

Hanmer, Jalna; and Allen, Pat. 1980. Reproductive engineering: The final solution? *Alice through the microscope*, ed. The Brighton Women and Science Group. London: Virago: 208–27.

Harrison, Michelle. 1982. *A woman in residence*. New York: Random House.

Holmes, Helen B.; Hoskins, Betty B.; and Gross, Michael. 1981. *The custom-made child? Women-centered perspectives*. Clifton, N.J.: Humana Press.

Huxley, Aldous. 1960 (1932). *Brave New World*. New York: Bantam.

Illmensee, Karl; and Hoppe, Peter. 1981. Nuclear transplantation in mus musculus: Developmental potential of nuclei from preimplantation embryos. *Cell* 23(1) (January):9–18.

Ju, Kap Soon; Park, I. James; Jones, Howard W.; and Winn, Kevin J. 1976. Prenatal sex determination by observation of the X-Chromatin and the Y-Chromatin of exfoliated amniotic fluid cells. *Obstetrics and Gynaecology* 47(3):287–90.

Kelly, Janis. 1977. Parthenogenesis. *Off Our Backs* 7(1) (February):2–3, 11.

Kritchevsky, Barbara. 1981. The unmarried woman's right to artificial insemination: A call for an expanded definition of family. *Harvard Women's Law Journal* 4:1–42.

Markle, Gerald; and Nam, Charles. 1971. Sex predetermination: Its impact on fertility. *Social Biology* 18(1):73–83.

Marx, Karl. 1887. *Capital*. Vol. 1. New York: Modern Library.

Mittwoch, Ursula. 1978. Virgin birth. *New Scientist* 78(1107) (June 15):750–52.

Muller, Herman J. 1961. Human evolution by voluntary choice of germ plasm. *Science* 134(3480):643–49.

Nentwig, M. Ruth. 1981. Technical aspects of sex preselection. *The custom-made child*? eds. Helen B. Holmes, Betty B. Hoskins, and Michael Gross. Clifton, N.J.: Humana Press: 181–86.

The New York Times. 1981 (January 4):1, 40.

Oakley, Ann. 1978. What makes girls differ from boys? *New Society* (December 21):xii–xiv.

O'Brien, Mary. 1981. *The politics of reproduction*. Boston: Routledge and Kegan Paul.

Peterson, Candida; and Peterson, James. 1973. Preference for sex of off-spring as a measure of change in sex attitudes. *Psychology* 10:3–5.

Raymond, Janice. 1981. Introduction. *The custom-made child*? eds. Helen B. Holmes, Betty B. Hoskins, and Michael Gross. Clifton, N.J.: Humana Press: 177–79.

Rorvik, David. 1978. *In his image*. London: Hamish Hamilton.

Rorvik, David; and Shettles, Landrum. 1977. *Choose your baby's sex*. New York: Dodd, Mead.

Rose, Hilary; and Hanmer, Jalna. 1976. Women's liberation, reproduction and the technological fix. *Sexual divisions and society: Process and change*, ed. Diana Leonard Barker and Sheila Allen. London: Tavistock: 199–223.

Tietung Hospital of Anshan Iron and Steel Company, Anshan. 1975. Foetal sex prediction by sex chromatin of chorionic villi cells during early pregnancy. *Chinese Medical Journal* 1(2):117–26.

U.S. Congress, House. 1972. Report to the subcommittee on science, research and development of the Committee on science and astronautics. 92nd Congress, 2nd session: 26. Quoted from: Genetic engineering: Reprise. 1972. *Journal of the American Medical Association* 220(10):1356.

Westoff, Charles; and Rindfuss, Ronald. 1974. Sex preselection in the United States: Some implications. *Science* 184(4137):633–36.

Williamson, Nancy. 1976. *Sons or daughters? A cross-cultural survey of parental preferences*. Beverley Hills, Calif.: Sage Publications.

Williamson, Nancy. 1978. Boys or girls? Parents' preferences and sex control. *Population Bulletin* 33(1).

Winston, Sanford. 1932. Birth control and the sex-ratio at birth. *American Journal of Sociology* 38(2):225–31.

12

What If . . . Science and Technology in Feminist Utopias

Patrocinio Schweickart

THE QUEST FOR UTOPIA

Human beings have always dreamed of a beautiful nowhere land where suffering, injustice, war, disease, evil, and even death are eliminated or at least mitigated; where desires find their fulfillment; where happiness is the salient fact of life. Heaven, the Isles of the Blest, the Elysian Fields, the Garden of Eden, Plato's Republic, More's Utopia, Campanella's City of the Sun, Bacon's New Atlantis, Morris' Nowhere, Skinner's Walden II—the archetype of utopia is a persistent counterpoint to the image of the actual world as a vale of tears.

However, since Campanella's *City of the Sun* (1602)and Bacon's *New Atlantis* (1624), utopia has become wedded to a new idea—the idea of progress. Gradually, the image of a beautiful but unattainable ideal lost ground to futuristic utopias. As Oscar Wilde put it:

> A map of the world that does not include utopia is not even worth glancing at, for it leaves out the one country at which Humanity is always landing. And when Humanity lands there, it looks out, and, seeing a better country, sets sail. Progress is the realization of Utopias (Wilde 1909, p. 148).

The idea of progress was born with modern science and technology, and since the seventeenth century, utopian speculation has been linked with scientific and technological projections. Unlike its archaic forms, the modern utopia derives much of its appeal from its feasibility. The work of modern utopists testifies not only to their longing for comfort and happiness, but also, and perhaps more so, to their confidence in reason and in our power—guaranteed by the fabulous accomplishments of science and technology—to mold nature according to our wishes.

Early in the twentieth century, utopian optimism began to be disrupted with increasing frequency by tragic premonitions. There developed a growing sense that utopian life—stripped of suffering, strife, risks, and mystery—would be a bore. But more than this. In the works of Huxley and Orwell, the rage for rationalization spills over from the realm of the natural sciences to that of human affairs. Scientific and technological progress is linked to terrifying bureaucratic and authoritarian structures efficiently designed for the total administration of life. Today, a more awesome prospect—namely, that of nuclear or ecological catastrophe—undermines our confidence further, and the image of science and technology as a runaway monster has gained a foothold beside its still potent image as a useful instrument for the improvement of life.

But here we must pause. This story suffers from a crucial omission. The perspectives, experiences, intuitions, aspirations, and fantasies of women—of 51 percent of the population—have not figured in the calculations except as they have been interpreted by men. The entry of feminists into the conversation reorients the ground of discourse.

I will discuss four recent feminist utopian novels: *The Kin of Ata Are Waiting for You* by Dorothy Bryant (1971), *The Wanderground* by Sally Gearhart (1979), *Woman on theEdge of Time* by Marge Piercy (1976), and *The Dispossessed* by Ursula Le Guin (1974). These four novels present different conceptions of the place of science and technology in a feminist utopia. However, all share the following characteristics. Utopia is counterposed to a dystopia which is not a demonic inversion of utopia, but a reproduction of our own world. All four novels imply that we are living in dystopia. The ultimate dystopian nightmare is seen to be precisely the twin horrors which overshadow all our visions of the future—namely, the all too real threat of violence and war, and of ecological depletion and pollution. These impending catastrophes are traced not only to science and technology or to the misguided overconfidence in reason but, ultimately, to the domination of women in patriarchal society. Against this critique of our own world, utopia is offered as a possible alternative; not something that is bound to happen, but something attainable only by dint of conscious and prodigious effort. Utopia is necessary, not because it is logically or historically necessary, but because we need it.

ATA AND THE WANDERGROUND: THERE IS NO PLACE FOR SCIENCE AND TECHNOLOGY IN A FEMINIST UTOPIA

Dorothy Bryant's (1971) *The Kin of Ata Are Waiting for You* opens with a scene that draws much of its emotional power from the fusion of love and hate, of sexuality and violence.

> "Bastard! You son of a bitch! Bastard!"
>
> I was almost bored. She stood in front of me like a woman out of one of my books. . . . long legs, small waist, full breasts covered by tossed blond hair. I must have smiled because she swung at me again. . . .
>
> I sat on the edge of the bed and watched her. Her breasts were full, but they hung loose like bags over a torso on which I could count every rib. Her pubic hair told the true color of her bleached head: mousy brown. Her skin, breaking through the smeared make-up, was blotchy.
>
> "I exist!" She was screaming. "I'm a person!"
>
> I yawned and looked at the clock. Four a.m. "No," I told her. "I invented you, or you invented yourself, right out of my latest book" (p. 1).

The fight escalates, and eventually, the narrator (a famous writer) strangles the woman. As he flees from his apartment in panic, he wrecks his car. When he revives, he is in Ata.

Ata has three important features: it is resolutely pacifist; it is completely egalitarian; and the kin organize their entire world—their songs, dances, and rituals, as well as the plan of their village and the planting of their crops—according to their dreams. The ideals of Ata are embodied in Augustine, a black woman who is impressive for her serene dignity, courage, and self-possession. During his sojourn in Ata, the narrator learns to forego violence, and with the help of Augustine, he gradually extricates love and sexual passion from its associations with rape. Significantly, he also recognizes his gift for dreaming. In the end, he returns to his own world to accept responsibility for his crime and to tell the story of his conversion.

In Sally Gearhart's (1979) *The Wanderground*, the utopian no man's land of the hillwomen (the Wanderground of the title) is set against a dystopian City characterized by sharp sexual polarity, virulent misogyny, homophobia, and violence especially against women and children. The present inhabitants of the Wanderground are the descendants of women who had fled the violence and misogyny of the City.

As in Bryant's novel, Gearhart's utopia is distinguished from dystopia by its resolute rejection of violence, and by the absence of social, economic, and political structures that lead to unequal distribution of wealth and power. The hillwomen also rely primarily on psychic powers that appear occult and irrational from our perspective within an advanced technological society. They can enter into each other's thoughts, so that they can communicate—or, more precisely, commune—with each other without the benefit of overt speech, and across vast distances without the aid of telephones or radios. In addition, they can communicate with animals and trees, as well as fly and swim under water through extraordinarily long distances without the aid of machines.

Ata and the Wanderground are marked by the absence of anything resembling science and technology as we know them today, and this absence amounts to a repudiation—quite explicit in *The Wanderground*—of the link between utopia and technological progress. Both novels imply that science and technology are part of the problem. We must not pin our hopes on them; instead, we must recover powers and faculties which have atrophied as a result of the hegemony of scientific reason.

It is easy to fault this wholesale rejection of science and technology. How can Ata or the Wanderground work as a viable model for a world with close to three billion people? Besides, there is no convincing evidence that warrants our confidence that we can cultivate the psychic powers which in both societies fill the role vacated by science and technology. However, in spite of these obvious objections, both Ata and the Wanderground remain appealing to many feminists. In order to appreciate the source of this appeal, we need to examine the motivation for the apparently unreasonable claim that science and technology have no place in a feminist utopia.

SCIENCE AND TECHNOLOGY AND THE TRAGEDY OF THE BEDROOM

According to the still prevalent opinion, science and technology are gender-neutral. The scientific method is devoted to the attainment of objective knowledge, preserved as far as possible from the vicissitudes of subjective judgment—or, in Bacon's phrase, from the "aberrations of the human understanding" (1955, p. 474). In the language of modern positivism, the scientific method is designed to maintain the fact/value distinction—what is objectively there against what the observer wants to see. To the extent that the scientific method is an effective barrier against the scientist's personality, it is also an effective barrier against his masculinity and the values this entails.

The fact remains, however, that scientists and engineers have been predominantly male, and science and technology exude a masculine aura—an intellectual *machismo* for men who are brainy rather than brawny. One can argue that the kind of research projects which are undertaken and supported, the problems which are considered important, the way research is conducted, the techniques and devices produced, and the way these are used reflect the perspectives and values of the men who control the scientific and technological establishments. Even if the scientific method is itself gender-neutral, its applications reflect an androcentric mentality.

The repudiation of science and technology implicit in the novels of Bryant and Gearhart is based on a stronger claim: that the masculinist psychology of the men who control science also informs its logic. The scientific method itself—not just its applications—is implicated in the domination of women in patriarchal society.

This argument is based on the recognition that science and technology represent a certain relationship between human beings and nature, and that concretely, in our world, the paradigm for this relationship is that between man and nature. The classic account of this relationship is given by Simone de Beauvoir (1968).

> Man seeks in woman the Other as Nature and as his fellow-being. But we know what ambivalent feelings Nature inspires in man. He exploits her, but she crushes him, he is born of her and dies in her; she is the source of his being and the realm that he subjugates to his will; Nature is a vein of gross material in which the soul is imprisoned, and she is the supreme reality; she is contingence and Idea, the finite and the whole; she is what opposes the Spirit, and the Spirit itself. Now ally, now enemy, she appears as the dark chaos from whence life wells up, as this life itself, and as the over-yonder toward which life tends. Woman sums up Nature as Mother, Wife, and Idea; these forms now mingle and now conflict, and each of them wears a double visage (p. 144).

In periods of "vitalist romanticism," man exalts nature; he "dreams of losing himself in the maternal shadows that he may find there again the source of his being."

> But more often, man is in revolt against his carnal state; he sees himself as a fallen god . . . fallen from a bright and ordered heaven into the chaotic shadows of his mother's womb. . . . he would fain deny his animal ties; through the fact of his birth, murderous Nature has a hold upon him (pp. 145–46).

If nature appears to man in the image of woman, the converse is equally true. Man believes that

> woman was given to [him] so that he might possess her and fertilize her as he owns and fertilizes the soil; and through her he makes all nature his realm. It is not only a subjective fleeting pleasure that man seeks in the sexual act. He wishes to conquer, to take, to possess; . . . he penetrates into her as the plowshare into the furrow; he makes her his even as he makes his the land he works. . . . Woman is her husband's prey, his possession (p. 153).

Man's attitude toward nature is colored by his attitude toward woman, his attitude toward woman by his attitude toward nature. Both function as the *Other* against which he endeavors to establish his *Self*—conscious, free, essential, transcendent. Man the scientist/engineer is no exception to this rule.

At first glance, scientific detachment seems to be a model of self-effacement. Man loses himself in his role as "servant and interpreter of nature" (Bacon 1955, p. 451). However, Bacon's insight that "Nature to be commanded must be obeyed" (p. 462) lends itself easily to a shift in emphasis from obeying to commanding. Nature is to be obeyed precisely because it is to be commanded. The scientific method allows man to "penetrate into the inner soul and further recesses of nature" (p. 464). By "art and the hand of man she is [to be] forced out of her natural state, and squeezed and moulded" (p. 447), induced to yield "the many secrets of excellent use" laid up in her womb (p. 527). Knowledge of nature translates into power over her, scientific objectivity into the triumph of mind over matter.

In the masculine tradition, the dystopian premonitions take the form of the Frankenstein story: the scientist, flushed with his discovery of the astonishing powers of reason, over-reaches himself, and is betrayed by his own cleverness.[1] The tragic flaw is traced to man's illegitimate desire for omniscience and omnipotence, and to his pride in the power of reason. In the feminist tradition, nature, the Other, becomes prominent in the calculation. The issue of human pride is eclipsed by the problem of the relationship between man and nature. The dystopian plot takes the form not of the Frankenstein story, but of what Leo Tolstoy once called "the tragedy of the bedroom." The master/slave dialectic between the self and the Other breeds alienation and reciprocal hostility until the conflict escalates to a catastrophic climax of mutual destruction. Feminist utopists are keenly aware that science and technology have brought us to the verge of ecological disaster. Hounded, vexed, abused, bullied, and manipulated into submission, nature is nevertheless poised to take her revenge. One is reminded of the warring couples of Tolstoy's *The Kreutzer Sonata*, and of course, of Count and Countess Tolstoy themselves. One also recalls *Othello*, where the rage for possession ends in murder and suicide.

It is significant that *The Kin of Ata Are Waiting for You* begins with the climactic scene of the tragedy of the bedroom: the narrator murders his lover. He tells us that this scene has captivated his imagination. It has shaped his novels as well as his nightmares. His sojourn in Ata allows him to write a different story. But in order to do so, he had to learn to dream and to adapt to the logic of dreams. Specifically, he had to overcome one of the hallmarks of scientific reason—the law of noncontradiction: there are many dreams, and contradictory versions of the same dream. "There is no correct version. All are correct, all are changing" (p. 164). Reason and common sense are indispensable, "But they follow the dream" (p. 161).

Gearhart makes the association between science and technology and misogynistic violence quite explicit. Science and technology are represented primarily by the weapons and machines men use in their "cunt hunts." But:

> Once upon a time, there was one rape too many. . . . The earth finally said "no." There was no storm, no earthquake, no tidal wave or volcanic eruption, no specific moment to mark its happening. It only became apparent that it had happened and it had happened everywhere (p. 158).

Everywhere outside the City, machines and weapons failed to function and animals refused to cooperate with men. This event—remembered in Wanderground lore as "The Revolt of the Mother"—marks the beginning of the utopian society. Since then, the security of the hillwomen has been assured by this natural shield.

In these two novels, the repudiation of science and technology and the ensuing primitivism and irrationalism are qualitatively different from the more familiar version exemplified by Huxley's *Brave New World* (1960). Huxley implicitly argues that scientific reason may provide us with a comfortable, predictable, and well-managed world; but, at the same time, it will rob us of everything that makes life interesting—creativity, spontaneity, art, mystery, adventure, the possibility of romance, and the possibility of tragedy. In the novels of Bryant and Gearhart, scientific reason is rejected for a different reason: because it is seen to be in complicity with misogynistic violence and with the domination of women in patriarchy. The relationship between the self and the Other implicit in science and technology is seen to be homologous to that between man and woman in the tragedy of the bedroom. Both are informed by the dialectic of love and rape. Thus, the domination of nature is of a piece with the domination of woman, the liberation of nature with the liberation of woman.

MATTAPOISETT, MASSACHUSETTS, IN THE YEAR 2137: A GYNOCENTRIC REVISION OF SCIENCE AND TECHNOLOGY

In spite of their appeal, Ata and the Wanderground remain implausible. However, once we understand that their appeal is grounded on a radical critique of the masculinist logic of science and technology, we can speculate on utopian redefinitions that incorporate this critique. The crux of the problem, as we have seen, is the association of the scientific method with the patriarchal mentality that sets up woman and nature as the irreducible Other against which man must realize his transcendence. Can the scientific method be dissociated from this impulse to dominate the Other?

Marge Piercy's *Woman on the Edge of Time* (1976) follows the pattern we have observed in the first two novels. Utopia is counterposed against a dystopian world that is a disconcerting copy of our own. The heroine, Connie Ramos, a poor Chicana, travels back and forth between her "home"—the slums, suburbs, and insane asylums of contemporary New York and Mattapoisett, Massachusetts, in the year 2137. Mattapoisett is resolutely egalitarian. Goods and services are produced and distributed according to the communistic principle: from each according to ability, and to each according to need. It is also anarchistic: it relies on the principle of mutual aid and individual responsibility, and is structured so as to prevent hierarchical relations.

However, unlike Ata and the Wanderground, Mattapoisett is an advanced technological society. The reader encounters the sort of gadgets and technological jargon which have become the staples of science fiction: "kenners" (combination "knowledge computers" and "locator-speakers" worn on the wrist), "jizers" and "floaters" (sophisticated flying machines), "biologicals" (self-mending structures made of domesticated one-celled organisms), etc. Furthermore, the utopian character of Mattapoisett depends on certain technological innovations. All tedious, disagreeable, or dangerous tasks—e.g., mining, manufacturing, and dishwashing—are fully automated. Mattapoisettians have also succeeded in eliminating the basis for the sexual division of labor. They practice perfectly efficacious contraception, all children are born extra-utero in "brooders," and males as well as females are capable of nursing the young. In short, they have eliminated fatherhood, and made motherhood accessible to everyone.

However, Piercy's utopia combines delight in gadgets with strong conservationist tendencies. As Luciente, the principal utopian character explains to Connie:

> We have limited resources. We plan cooperatively. We can afford to waste . . . nothing. You might say our—you'd say religion?—ideas make us see ourselves as partners with water, air, birds, fish, trees (p. 125).

The people of Mattapoisett are capable of controlling the weather, but they are reluctant to do so. By our standards, their medical practices are conservative and old fashioned. They shun drugs, and they prefer treatments that are as natural and as noninvasive as possible. Their healers knit bones and ease pain, but they are concerned primarily with helping people to stay healthy and, when they are ill, to heal themselves.

Mattapoisett incorporates archaic features reminiscent of Ata and the Wanderground.

> We learned a lot from societies that people used to call primitive. Primitive technically. But socially sophisticated. . . . We tried to learn from cultures that dealt well with handling conflict, promoting cooperation, coming of age, growing a sense of community, getting sick, aging, going mad, dying (p. 125).

They distinguish two modes of knowing: "outknowing" and "inknowing." *Outknowing* is roughly what we think of as the scientific method, the quest for objective knowledge from a perspective external to and detached from the object to be known. *Inknowing* is the pursuit of subjective knowledge—knowledge of subjective processes from a perspective within subjectivity. It mobilizes mental qualities which have been traditionally associated with women: emotional susceptibility, empathy, intuition, imagination, as well as the psychic powers we encountered in the Atans and the hillwomen of the Wanderground—the ability to commune with nature and with other people, and the capacity to be in touch with oneself, to harmonize one's psychic and physical being.

Mattapoisettians recognize that their technological capabilities give them power over nature. They modify nature—sometimes quite radically—to satisfy their needs. Nevertheless, they are extremely circumspect in exercising this power. They spend considerable energy drawing the line between legitimate use and exploitative abuse of natural resources. They abhor waste, but they are not obssessed with efficiency. Their idea of order has more in common with good housewifery than with Taylor's scientific management.

One can trace the Mattapoisett attitude toward nature to a female paradigm. For woman, nature is not irreducibly Other. Her attitude toward nature is not characterized by the vacillation between ecstatic adulation and revulsion that, according to de Beauvoir (1968), marks the attitude of man to nature. Her biology (the fact that she gives birth and she nurtures the young) as well as her history (her status as Other in patriarchy) has led her to develop an intuitive kinship with nature. She is keenly aware that nature is in her as well as outside her; that she is, for all her humanity, a natural being (Griffin 1978).

In Piercy's utopia, science and technology are not informed by a master/slave relationship with nature. Nature is not an Other which must be obeyed to be commanded, but a partner in existence. More than this, the people of Mattapoisett have a healthy respect for immanence which is best illustrated by their calm acceptance of the fact of mortality: "Everybody gives back," says Luciente. "We all carry our death at the core—if you don't inknow that, your life is hollow, no?" (p. 156). Death reminds them that: "We're part of the web of nature. Don't you find that beautiful?" (p. 278).

ANARRES: THE UTOPIAN AS THE RECOVERY OF THE IDEAL

In Ursula Le Guin's (1974) *The Dispossessed*, dystopia is represented by A-Io, an advanced capitalist country in the planet Urras, in the solar system Tau Ceti. Utopia is located on Anarres, the moon of Urras. Some 160 years before the novel opens, Anarres was settled by emigrants from Urras, the disciples of Odo, a female revolutionary philosopher and activist.

Le Guin's novel raises rather complex questions. Abstractly, we are told that Anarres is completely egalitarian. There are no normative sex roles. And yet, concretely, what is portrayed is a male-centered world. The hero of the novel is Shevek, a *male* theoretical physicist who undertakes a journey to Urras in the hope of reconciling the two worlds. The strongest female character is Rulag, Shevek's mother. However, she is quite disagreeable. A cool, intelligent woman, a gifted engineer, she unfeelingly cut herself off from her infant son. Later, she becomes his most formidable opponent. Takver, Shevek's wife, is also a scientist—a marine biologist; but we see her only in her role as faithful wife and mother. Odo, the philosophical founder of Anarresti society, would certainly have been a remarkable woman. However, the story opens seven generations after her death. We encounter her only through the impact of her life and works on Anarresti society, in particular, on Shevek. All the women in the novel are defined in terms of their relationship to a man—Shevek. One can even go so far as to point out that they fall into stereotypical roles: Rulag, the bad mother and castrating bitch; Takver, the good wife and mother; Odo, the feminine symbol of the ideal, the Jungian *anima*.

Of course, one can also point out that the androcentricity of Le Guin's utopia is a function largely of her decision to anchor the utopian perspective on a male character. But in this case, isn't it self-defeating to choose a man as the representative of a feminist utopia? How feminist is Le Guin's utopia, finally?

One can also raise questions about Le Guin's vision of utopian science, as represented by Shevek's work. He is preoccupied with time. As a young man, he wrote a revolutionary treatise on the principles of simultaneity which proposed a convincing alternative to the prevailing model of time as a sequence of moments. However, Shevek's goal is more ambitious. He wants a unified theory of time, one that would reconcile the idea of simultaneity—time consists of the juxtaposition and interaction of moments—with the idea of sequence—time as the succession of moments. The Urrastis immediately recognize the significance of Shevek's work. They realize that it would give them the key to "transilience"—faster than light travel. Shevek goes to Urras hoping his theory (which is still in progress) will become the means for the reconciliation of Anarres with its parent planet.

On the face of it, there appears to be no essential difference between Shevek's physics and that of the Urrastis. In fact, physics seems to be the one thing they share in common. During his first weeks in Urras, Shevek is elated to discover "for the first time, the conversation of his equals" (p. 58). Furthermore, readers will find Shevek to be a believable scientist for he manifests the traits which we have learned to associate with scientists: intellectual curiosity and a penchant for abstract thought, a fascination with the unknown and the problematical, a questioning mind, a love of free intellectual play, and a zest for knowledge for its own sake. Above all, he is eminently rational; he is not given to occult or irrational mental processes. Now, we must ask: where is the utopian difference? In what way does he represent a utopian image of science?

As we read the novel, we see that, for the Urrastis, science is a means for self-aggrandizement ("egoizing" in the Anarresti idiom), and for dominating others. They are interested in Shevek's theory because it will allow them to dominate space. Once they have mastered transilience, the interstellar drive of the Hainish (people of another solar system) "won't amount to a hill of beans" (p. 116).

As Shevek learns more about Urras, he realizes that to be a physicist there is "to serve not society, not mankind, not the truth, but the state" (p. 219).

> To do physics. To assert, by his talent, the rights of any citizen in any society: the right to work, to be maintained while working, and to share the product with all who wanted it. The rights of an Odonian and of any human being.
>
> His benevolent and protective hosts let him work, and maintained him while working, all right. The problem came on the third limb (p. 222).

For Shevek, science has nothing to do with domination, either of fellow humans or of nature. Le Guin's description of Shevek's discovery of the key to a unified theory of time is a remarkable rendition of the thrill of scientific discovery.

> It was simplicity; and contained in it all complexity, all promise.
>
> It was revelation. It was the way clear, the way home, the light. . . .
>
> And yet in his utter ease and happiness he shook with fear; his hands trembled, and his eyes filled with tears, as if he had been looking into the sun. After all, the flesh is not transparent. And it is strange, exceedingly strange, to know that one's life has been fulfilled (pp. 225–26).

The scene is ecstatic but not triumphant. The emphasis is on a sense of wholeness, of being at home in the universe, of the end of alienation. "There were no more abysses, no more walls. There was no more exile. He had seen the foundations of the universe, and they were solid" (p. 226).

The utopian difference extends to the scientific method Shevek employs, for it is far from the "one-dimensional thought" which has dominated contemporary science (Marcuse 1964). It is difficult to make sense of the paradox of simultaneity and sequence in the context of conventional physics. However, the motivation and the significance of Shevek's problem becomes clearer when we realize that he has in mind a paradigm of time derived from a different discipline—namely, history or biography where, in one sense, the past, present, and future succeed each other: childhood is succeeded by adulthood, and then by old age; and, in another sense, each moment is an interplay of past, present, and future: both the experiences of childhood and the prospects of old age shape adult behavior. In other words, Shevek's temporal physics is informed by a dialectical conception of time. Of course,

Le Guin has to remain vague about the details of Shevek's solution to the problem. However, she strongly suggests that it involves getting around the law of noncontradiction.

Shevek is also free of another principle of contemporary science—the fact/value distinction. He makes no effort to separate his moral and philosophical concerns from his scientific interests. His meditations on the principles of Odonian philosophy—that is to say, on what it means to be human—are of a piece with his inquiry into the nature of time. He deploys the same mode of thought, the same intellectual ardor, the same sustained rational inquiry in both cases, and his moral and philosophical concerns inform his scientific research, and vice versa.

Now, let us return to the question raised at the beginning of this section. By anchoring the utopian perspective on a male character, doesn't Le Guin play into the customary conception of man as the paradigmatic human being and woman as the Other? This question cannot be fully answered here. Let me suggest, however, that the risk of reinforcing androcentricity is diminished if we see the novel in the context of other feminist utopias, in particular, the novels discussed in this chapter.

In this context, *The Dispossessed* performs a very important function. It portrays a man who has no need to dominate women; whose identity is no longer dependent on the relegation of women to the role of the Other. In Bryant's, Gearhart's, and Piercy's utopias, sexual polarity is eliminated—in the Wanderground by the exclusion of men, in Ata and Mattapoisett by the elimination of masculinity. Le Guin, however, preserves sexual polarity, the sexual tension between male and female. By so doing, she suggests that difference need not imply reciprocal alienation. For Shevek, women are fellow-beings, bound to him by relations of *identity in difference*. Moreover, he has internalized his female mentors. In particular, his personality has been formed by his reading of Odo's life and works. Thus, Shevek not only values the female perspective; he cultivates it in himself.

Finally, like other feminist utopias, Le Guin's novels can be read as an attempt to rewrite the tragedy of the bedroom. Much of the emotional appeal of the novel comes from the love between Takver and Shevek. Through this relationship, Le Guin gives us a memorable image of heterosexual love where polarity—between male and female, self and other—results not in reciprocal alienation, but in mutual realization through the play of difference. As we read the novel, we come to identify with Shevek. We are drawn into his feelings for Takver, and we learn to value and desire his love for her. Through him, we experience a love which is not based on domination or possession but on enduring and freely chosen partnership.

Earlier we noted that Shevek is a believable scientist. Similarly, Le Guin gives us believable manliness and heterosexuality. Here, the familiarity of the utopian vision is important. First of all, it suggests that utopia is more accessible than we think. It reminds us of what we are capable of, and of what we owe ourselves. At the same time, as we compare Shevek to what science, manhood, and heterosexual love have become in our own world, we realize how far we have departed from our own ideals. The familiarity of Le Guin's vision suggests that utopia is not alien to human nature but only the expression of the best in us, the authentic realization of our nature: "true journey is return."

LIBERATING VISIONS

Le Guin, Piercy, Gearhart, and Bryant enter into the ongoing conversation concerning science, technology, and utopia with a plurality of voices. But, in spite of this plurality, all represent a feminist perspective. Collectively, they reorient the ground of discourse to take account of the experience, the intuitions, and the needs of women. As we have seen, a key feature of the feminist perspective is the realization that, in patriarchy, science and technology are governed by the same principle that governs the relationship between the sexes—the master/slave dialectic between self and Other. The domination of women and the domination of nature serve as models for each other. Thus, science and technology have a place in a feminist utopia only if they can be redefined apart from the logic of domination. Bryant and Gearhart suggest that this is impossible; Piercy and Le Guin, employing different strategies, attempt to show the contrary.

Feminist utopias offer fascinating suggestions, but their value does not lie primarily in offering blueprints for the future. They perform the twin functions of exploring alternative worlds organized around feminist values, and of deepening our critical perspective on our own world. Above all, they offer us a liberating experience. They allow us to live in utopia, to escape the confines of our own world, to stretch our sense of what is possible and what is natural, to see what we could be in a better world.

NOTES

1. Of course, the original novel was written by a woman—Mary Shelley. What I am referring to, however, is the popular myth that has grown around Shelley's novel. Anyone who reads the original will be struck by its difference from the popular myth. Recently, feminist critics have argued persuasively that Shelley's novel is really a female birth myth, a horror story of sexuality, maternity, and motherlessness (Gilbert & Gubar 1979, Moers 1977), cast in a traditional "cover story"—namely, the masculine myth of Prometheus. The numerous stage, film, and comic book adaptations of the story have preserved only the traditional cover story.

REFERENCES

Bacon, Francis. 1955. *Selected writings*. Intro. and notes by Hugh G. Dick. New York: Modern Library.

de Beauvoir, Simone. 1968. *The second sex*. New York: Modern Library.
Library.

Bryant, Dorothy. 1971. *The kin of Ata are waiting for you*. Berkeley/New York: Moon Books/ Random House.

Gearhart, Sally. 1979. *The Wanderground: The stories of the hillwomen*. Watertown, Mass.: Persephone Press.

Gilbert, Sandra; and Gubar, Susan. 1979. *The madwoman in the attic: The woman writer and the nineteenth century literary imagination*. New Haven: Yale University Press.

Griffin, Susan. 1978. *Woman and nature: The roaring inside her*. New York: Harper & Row.

Huxley, Aldous. 1960. *Brave new world*. New York: Bantam.

Le Guin, Ursula. 1974. *The dispossessed*. New York: Avon Books.

Marcuse, Herbert. 1964. *One-dimensional man*. Boston: Beacon Press.

Moers, Ellen. 1977. *Literary women: The great writers*. Garden City, N.Y.: Anchor Books.

Piercy, Marge. 1976. *Woman on the edge of time*. New York: Fawcett Crest Books.

Wilde, Oscar. 1909. The soul of man under socialism. In *The works of Oscar Wilde*, VIII. Intro. Richard Le Gallienne. New York: Lamb Publishing Co.

Afterword
Machina Ex Dea and Future Research

Joan Rothschild

The works in this volume represent a variety of feminist perspectives on technology. There has been no party line on approaches either to feminism or to technology—with one exception. All chapters share the premise that a male bias exists in most technology research and analysis, and that that bias must be confronted and changed. Whether reform, radical, socialist, anarchist, or some combination of these in their feminism, and whether pro- or antitechnology, or somewhere else on the spectrum, the authors present challenges, correctives, and/or alternatives to mainstream approaches to technology studies, and to analyses of technological society. Thus, all of the chapters either explicitly or implicitly question the content, the methodology, the epistemology, and the values of the field. In what directions does feminist research in technology point for the future? There are three major areas: historical analysis, women and work, and epistemology and values. While these areas obviously overlap, the following will separate them out according to the main thrusts of the research explored.

HISTORICAL ANALYSIS

Historical analysis has develped a number of important trends that should be pursued further. We should continue the work of what Gerda Lerner (1975) has called "contribution" and "compensatory" history, as exemplified by the Stanley and Trescott chapters. This work seeks to uncover and recover the women hidden from history who have contributed to technological development, compensating for past neglect for both the history of women and the history of technology. Stanley's book, *Mothers of Invention* (1984) on the history of women inventors, accomplishes this in many technological areas. As Stanley in this volume and Cowan (1979) have suggested, such attention brings research to bear in areas once not seriously considered as subjects for technological research because they pertained to women's activities. Research of this kind on women and technology approaches Lerner's category of "woman-identified" history in which the content itself is expressly identified with women and women's roles and activities, paving the way for a "woman-defined" history of technology as the subject matter of technology itself begins to be reclassified.

Social context must receive renewed attention. In charting women's accomplishments in scientific and technological areas, researchers must ask not only who these women were and are, but seek to discover both the social factors that contributed to their achievements and the factors that kept them in obscurity. Margaret Rossiter's (1982) history of women scientists in America does an excellent job of weaving social analysis with personal history which can serve as a model for future studies. A sociological approach is useful here, as that of Sally Hacker (this volume), who grounds her analysis of the historic hierarchical gender segregation in engineering education in stratification theory.

Social history needs to take up the issue of the gender division of labor as it might relate to patterns of technological invention and use. For example, what further documentation is there for Mumford's (1966) contention that certain technologies have been almost exclusively associated with the female? If this is so, specifically which technologies? Are such patterns universal or not? What might such patterns tell us about technological and productive development and about social and power structures in any given society? For example, have women used technology as a power resource as have men (see Sacks 1974)? Two very different kinds of approaches to historical research are necessary. On the one hand, we need research centered on particular times and places for careful, in-depth analysis of technological factors in a given period and locale. But, on the other hand, borrowing approaches and methods from anthropology and sociology, we need studies that focus on cultural contexts and that can range systematically across time and culture.

The aim of such research is to relate findings, such as gender-based patterns of technological invention and use, to wider technological and social developments. Although Etienne and Leacock (1980) have cautioned against focusing on technology as the means to gain insights on sexual hierarchy, relations of production, and social organization in nonindustrial cultures, technological factors cannot be ignored and can be extremely useful. Focus on technology provides a way to get at resource use and development, which is necessary to understanding productive, social and power hierarchies in any society. The role of technology has played a part in recent research that has challenged the accepted male-dominated model of social organization among primates and early hominids (Dahlberg 1981, Tanner 1981).

WOMEN AND WORK

The productive area—women, work, and technology—has received the most attention from scholars. What has been the focus and in what directions do we need to move?

Most of the world's women still perform some kind of agriculturally-related labor, largely in the developing world. Not surprisingly, therefore, what little research exists on women, technology, and agricultural labor is focused mainly on the Third World (see Dauber & Cain 1981). There are a few exceptions, notably the work by Hacker (1977) and Bush (1982) on the effects of technological change on farm women and the family farm in the United States. The pattern found was that women's economic contribution to the family farm—albeit through traditional female activities—was eroded by farm mechanization, women losing their sense of usefulness as well. These patterns need to be studied further. Similarly, Jensen's (1982) work on a specific technology, butter-churns, as it affected women's labor and its relationship to a changing economy from 1750 to 1850, is also the kind of research approach that should be replicated for other specific technologies, kinds of work, regions, and time periods.

The literature on women and development in the Third World that deals with technology is generally grounded theoretically in Boserup's well-known 1970 study which found that modernization was displacing women's once important economic role, a role maintained through control of agricultural activity, including often market and trade. As demonstrated in the work of Chaney and Schmink (1976), Tinker (1976), and the articles in the Dauber and Cain collection (1981), we need country and region-specific analyses of the effects of technological change on women's work that take into account cultural history and practices as well as geographic factors. As we look at specific technologies in particular locales, important questions arise. For example, how do we measure gains or losses for women? If the introduction of a mechanized rice-huller in Indonesia greatly increases rice production but eliminates jobs and incomes for an estimated 7.7 million women (Cain 1981), is this technological change a gain, and for whom? Bush (in this volume) has offered an equity analysis model for technology assessment that can prove useful here, especially as research focuses necessarily on policy formulation and implementation.

As government-sponsored research becomes part of an intricate web of political, economic, social, and technological factors that bear on modernization policies formulated by both First and Third World leaders, policy-oriented research is of key concern. Funding sources for research in the developing world, in particular, have become a controversial issue for feminist research, both for possible limitations and restrictions placed on inquiry and the uses to which such research may be put. More empirical data are needed here to create models for comparative analysis that will incorporate factors of public and private power.

The major portion of the research on women, work, and technology has focused on industrialized society, especially the United States. As McGaw (1982) has pointed out, for women's paid employment, research is heaviest for the period prior to 1940. But more contemporary studies are emerging on women and work in rapidly computerizing fields, as clerical work (see *Race Against Time* 1980, and Feldberg & Glenn this volume) and printing (Hochwald 1982), or in new industries, as electronics (Enloe 1983). One of the consistent patterns found has been denial to women of access to and training to use technology, and then displacement of their low-skilled jobs by technology (see especially Hacker 1979, 1980). But there have been benefits as well, as McGaw (1979) found in the Berkshire paper industry in the last century, or through general expansion of jobs in part brought about by technological change. As Feldberg and Glenn show in this volume, the computerized office presents a mixed picture of job opportunities and working conditions for women. Another pattern, less explored than those of work degradation and displacement or of benefits vs. losses for women, is the Luddite, or less drastic, rejection of technology as a female response to technological innovation (see Cowan 1979). In her studies of the nineteenth century New England shoe industry, Mary Blewett (forthcoming) found that, even though mechanics tried to train women home workers to use the new sewing machines that were being introduced in the factory at mid-century, the women, because of their unfamiliarity with machines, resisted the training and were unable to make the transition from hand to machine work. Not until sewing machines were made for home use and a new generation of young women came along was the training successful, the women then displacing the men in the factories as sewing-machine operators.

A further growing research area concerns health hazards to women on the job as a result of new technologies. For example, studies show increasing levels of stress among clerical workers who work at video display terminals and whose pace of work is intensified through use of data-processing equipment (see *Race Against Time* 1980, ch. 8, and cited studies). Research is also focusing on women in nontraditional jobs, especially those in which the technologies are associated with male use, such as jobs involving heavy and/or dangerous machinery. Often viewed as an extremely contemporary development, we need only point to the women defense workers of World War II (Baxandall, Gordon, & Reverby 1976) and women printers in the Colonial Era (Hudak 1978) to realize the patterns are otherwise. Further attention to historical practice will not only clarify the record but place research on today's developments in proper perspective.

One focus generally missing in most of this work so far is attitudinal research. What are the subjective aspects? How do women feel about technological change and their work? Letters, diaries, oral histories, reminiscences, and photographs are important sources, used successfully by the Washington Women's Heritage Project (1980–82) to explore women's attitudes about work and caring in a historical focus. To explore women's contemporary attitudes, we can draw on a number of attitudinal research models, especially from social psychology and sociology.

Since women workers had often been ignored in the literature, the prototype being male, much of feminist analysis on technology and paid employment has concentrated specifically on women. But it is important now to develop comparisons with effects of technology on men and their work. If we control for factors such as class, race, age, ethnic origin, etc., what difference does the female variable make for the effects of technological change on her or his job? For one thing, we are usually looking at different segments of the labor force in a sex-segregated labor market. As Baxandall, Ewen, and Gordon (1976) and Glenn and Feldberg (1979, and this volume) have clearly shown, it is not enough just to add women to an analysis of technology and the work process and expect the results to be the same as for a predominantly male labor force. But the question remains as to whether any differences for technology and women's work are attributable to the different kinds of work performed, the technologies involved, to status factors, or other variables. Research must speak to the issue of how technology and the gender division of labor interact so that we can create a broader and better balanced picture of the relationship between technology and work in industrialized society.

Class and race variables often have special application to gender analysis of technology and work. This is particularly apparent in the high technology field. Whether in Silicon Valley, California (Nash 1983) or in the electronics industries of Malaysia and Singapore (Lim 1981), ill-paid assembly work of the most tedious kind is performed mainly by women, usually nonwhite and/or recent immigrants, and of the poorest classes. Although differing circumstances, depending on the area, can make comparisons difficult, feminist crosscultural analysis can usefully link the First and Third Worlds, as has recently been done for the textile industry (Chapkis & Enloe 1983). Not only can we thereby enlarge our understanding of the effects of technology on women's work as modern technology proliferates globally, but we can also learn more about the relationship between technology and econo-political structures in an increasingly internationalized economic and political order.

One focus that can link First and Third World research is women and appropriate technology. As the work of groups such as the Women's Resource Center of Missoula, Montana, has shown (e.g., *Women and Technology* 1979, Smith 1980), women's needs have often been neglected by those researching and experimenting with alternative technologies. For example, Carr (1981) reports that reflective solar cookers have made little headway in the Third World countries where they were introduced because they could not support a pot large enough to cook for a large family, and women cooked in the evening (after their other work was done) and/or traditionally indoors; researchers had simply failed to observe women's work habits or ask women what their needs were. Since the character of much appropriate technology is not only energy-saving, but small-scale, often geared to home-based activities in rural or less built-up areas, questions about the effects of this technology on women and women's work and about women's roles in developing and using such technologies need to be built into all such research (see, for example, *Taking Hold of Technology* 1981).

Another work and technology area neglected until recently is technology and women's unpaid labor in the home. As in the case for women's paid employment, this research has grown rapidly and concentrates on the American experience. Bringing together a decade of research, two full-length histories of housework and its technologies appear in the 1980s: Strasser's popularized work published in 1982, and Cowan's in 1983. The patterns may be summed up in the titles of Cowan's and Strasser's books, respectively: *More Work for Mother*, and *Never Done*, and as analyzed in Rothschild in this volume. Although technological change for the home eventually brought less work of the dirty and back-breaking kind, industrial capitalism, consumerism, patriarchal values, and technology combined to insure that housework did not disappear. It changed and proliferated, bringing more work for mother: woman's work was never done. The literature on the domestic science movement (see, for example, Ehrenreich & English 1979, and Nyhart 1982) develops these patterns as well, as does the economic analysis such as Hartmann's (1974) on technological change for the home in the first three decades of the twentieth century.

With these studies providing frameworks, historical analysis can further concentrate on specific kinds of technological developments, particularly on design for the home itself. Hayden's work on Catherine Beecher (1977; see also Sklar 1974) as well as on designs for communal household alternatives are important steps in this direction (Hayden 1981). Recent work on twentieth century home design seeks to show why some designs were readily accepted and others were not (see, for example, Horrigan 1982). We need additional research to explore the effects of home designs on women, families, and households generally, and to discover attitudes toward household design. Linking academic study to hands-on approaches, we need to examine and encourage efforts to involve women in creating their own built-environments (see Rothschild this volume, and Sprague).

While there is some attitudinal research about women and housework (see, for example, Oakley 1974, 1975) and there are some studies about the uses of household technology (for example, Bose 1979, Thrall 1982, Vanek 1974), there is little on women's attitudes and opinions about that technology. Since consumers presumably vote with their pocketbooks, we might assume they want the refrigerators, dishwashers, freezers, and microwave ovens they buy. But beyond manufacturers' marketing surveys, geared to selling more products and limited to manufacturers' options, we do not know very much about consumer preferences concerning household technologies or the reasons for acceptance or rejection when technologies are introduced. Oral history can be a useful tool here, as well as attitudinal surveys of household technology users, who are still mainly women.

Attitudinal research can help to test the hypothesis advanced by Rothschild in this volume that household technology can provide a precondition for women's liberation. What is the actual level of ease and comfort that women perceive they have through technology? To what extent do women feel themselves in control or controlled by household technology? What are the links, if any, between a sense of technological control or lack of it and a raised feminist political consciousness? The class assumptions—that is, the links between technology, privilege, and liberation—in the Rothschild analysis also need to be tested out.

Future research on household technology and the gender division of labor in the home has a solid base to work from. Such research becomes especially important in two respects as we enter a computerized and more technologized age. One, advanced by Rothschild in this volume, is that projections for home computer use suggest an even more privatized and isolated nuclear household than now exists, with present gender roles continuing and even reinforced. The second respect is that with more women coming into the labor force, especially married women and other women with family responsibilities, we may be entering an era in which the relationship between home and work will be undergoing as dramatic a change as it experienced during the Industrial Revolution. Feminist analysis has shown that, because women are still responsible for housework, women in paid employment perform more work, even though household chores are cut back and are somewhat eased by technology. Technology does not change gender roles, and may even help reinforce them. What effects will technology have in the future if these labor force and computer use trends continue? Feminist analysis has developed important theoretical frameworks for understanding the relationship between home and work (see, for example, Sokoloff 1980), which can serve as points of departure for further research. But technology is playing an even greater role today, or at least one equal to its role in nineteenth and twentieth century industrial development, in shaping changes in the nature and structure of work. Therefore, research on changing relationships between home and work must carefully build technological analyses into new theoretical frameworks.

In no field are the technological changes likely to be far greater than in one basic to women's work: biological reproduction. Because control over reproduction is a fundamental condition for women's freedom, reproductive control is a recurrent theme of feminist research on reproductive technology. Feminist analysis of the history of contraception (Stanley 1984) has revealed women's knowledge and practices of contraceptive methods and reproductive techniques throughout much of history and across many cultures. In the West, with the development of a male-controlled medical profession, not only were women's healing arts and techniques lost, but womens' control over their reproductive processes, such as childbirth, was eroded as well. Linda Gordon's history of birth control in America (1977) finds that political and social forces have been the major factors threatening women's control of their bodies. Since, as McGaw (1982) points out, this excellent study does not focus on technology specifically, we need further historical analysis to discover how social and political institutions, as well as ideology, have shaped women's technological options. Rothschild (1981) has suggested that, just as the point is reached when advances in contraceptive technology promise women greater reproductive control (see also Mitchell 1966), health hazards surface, the birth process becomes more technologized, and new technologies develop that threaten to reduce or even eliminate women's role in reproduction (Holmes et al. 1980, 1981; Hanmer this volume). Clearly, we are approaching a watershed in human reproductive technology. Although invasive, reproductive technology up to this point has been seen as helping nature. It did not and could not substantially alter it. But, as Hanmer shows in this volume and elsewhere in her writings (see, for example, Rose & Hanmer 1976), from in vitro fertilization and sex predetermination, to embryo transplants and genetic manipulation of the fetus, to cloning and real test-tube babies, we are moving into a realm where women could be expendable and reproduction controlled by the state in a Brave New World scenario. Hanmer's work raises important social, legal, political, and moral issues that feminist research on reproductive technology needs to pursue (see also *Women's Rights Law Reporter* 1982, Holmes et al. 1981). The moral and philosophical issues become overriding as we gain the power to become gods and goddesses over nature, over creation itself.

EPISTEMOLOGY AND VALUES

Issues raised by reproductive technology research brings us to the third area for feminist research in technology: values and epistemology. Feminist analysis, ranging from philosophy of science, psychoanalytic theory, radical and ecofeminism, to religion, has focused on nature and technology in a way that forces us to rethink and question technological values. While approaches vary, a feminist orientation here agrees that a man-machine-nature discussion that ignores the female element is incomplete. Such treatment ignores nature's identification with woman as well as female-male dualism and its relationship to other cultural dualisms.

A central theme of feminist research here is the connection between the domination of nature and the domination of woman as an underlying value of Western science and technology. Research should build on Merchant's work (this volume, and 1980) on the transformation of the concept of nature during the Scientific Revolution to try to show more explicitly the links between the domination of woman and of nature as expressed in changing attitudes and practices of science and technology. The ecological dimensions are important to explore not only historically but crossculturally. As Merchant and Gearhart (this volume), for example, suggest, other cultures exist that do not necessarily share the exploitative views of nature that underpin science and technology in the West. What are the views of women and what is women's status in such societies; what are the levels of technological development and the ways technological control are exercised?

The psychological dimensions of the woman-man-nature-science relationship developed by Keller (this volume, 1978, forthcoming) also need to be explored further. For example, do other schools of psychoanalytic theory that have been subjected to feminist revisionism bear out Keller's thesis that personality development along gender lines holds an important key to gender ideology in the practice of our science? Another perspective to be further explored is the religious one in which both domination of nature and of woman are set in a Judeo-Christian framework (see Gray 1981, Reuther 1975). How does this interpretation of the dualism fit with Merchant's and Keller's approaches? Are the twin and interconnected domination themes limited to Western religions? We find male-female dualisms in other cultures and religions, but how or in what ways might such dualism be connected to views of nature and to religious beliefs (see, for example, al-Hibri 1981)?

Feminist analysis has also linked female-male dualism to nature-culture dualism (see de Beauvoir 1953, Ortner 1974) with a view to transcending nature, women becoming a part of culture. Firestone's (1970) is the most radical expression of that position, as she seeks to separate women from their biological nature entirely, through technology. Dividing culture into female (aesthetic) and male (technological) modes, she proposes a synthesis to restore the aesthetic ideal to technology in order to realize the ideal in the actual and merge art and reality. For others, the separation of woman and humanity from nature returns us to the problem of domination (see Schweickart this volume) and threatened technological and ecological disaster. If we opt for culture, is nature destroyed—and woman as well? One direction for feminist research is to search for a nature-culture and female-male synthesis that will not destroy nature on the one hand, nor lead to the impasse envisioned by Gearhart (this volume). King (in this volume) suggests a possible ecological model. Feminist research needs to create and explore a variety of alternatives for redefining the relationship between nature and culture.

In these ways, feminist analysis develops questions about the values that underlie Western science and technology, challenging the climate of thought and understanding, and seeking to fashion a new epistemology. The stakes are high. Fundamental to the ways we think about technology are the actual development and use of that science and technology. Feminists make no claim to moral superiority: others have raised questions about the directions of our technology, including the fundamental one about "the fate of the earth" (Schell 1982). But feminists do claim an approach to research and scholarship that widens human perspectives in special ways. Bringing the female back into the technological picture—from which she had long been excluded—not only restores a necessary balance to scholarly inquiry. Feminist perspectives also bring an experiential and holistic approach that can transform such inquiry to be greater than the sum of its female and male parts.

REFERENCES

Baxandall, Rosalyn; Ewen, Elizabeth; and Gordon, Linda. 1976. The working class has two sexes. *Monthly Review* 28 (July-August):1–9.

Baxandall, Rosalyn; Gordon, Linda; Reverby, Susan, comp. and eds. 1976. *America's working women*. New York: Vintage Books.

de Beauvoir, Simone. 1953. *The second sex*. Trans. and ed. H. M. Parshley. New York: Alfred A. Knopf.

Blewett, Mary H. *Men, women and work: A study in class, gender and protest in the New England shoe industry*. Philadelphia: Temple University Press (forthcoming).

Bose, Christine. 1979. Technology and changes in the division of labor in the American home. *Women's Studies International Quarterly* 2:295–304.

Boserup, Ester. 1970. *Woman's role in economic development*. New York: St. Martin's Press.

Bush, Corlann G. 1982. The barn is his, the house is mine: Agricultural technology and sex roles. *Energy and transport*, ed. George Daniels and Mark Rose. Beverly Hills, Calif.: Sage Publications: 235–59.

Cain, Melinda L. 1981. Java, Indonesia: The introduction of rice processing technology. *Women and technological change in developing countries*, ed. Roslyn Dauber and Melinda Cain. Boulder, Colo.: Westview Press: 127–37.

Carr, Marilyn. 1981. Technologies appropriate for women: Theory, practice and policy. *Women and technological change in developing countries*, ed. Roslyn Dauber and Melinda Cain. Boulder, Colo.: Westview Press: 193–203.

Chaney, Elsa M.; and Schmink, Marianne. 1976. Women and modernization: Access to tools. *Sex and class in Latin America*, eds. June Nash and Helen I. Safa. New York: Praeger.

Chapkis, Wendy; and Enloe, Cynthia H. 1983. *Women textile workers in the international economy*. Amsterdam: Transnational Institute: Washington, D.C.: Institute for Policy Studies; London: Pluto Press.

Cowan, Ruth Schwartz. 1979. From Virginia Dare to Virginia Slims: Women and technology in American life. *Technology and Culture* 20 (January):51–63.

Cowan, Ruth Schwartz. 1983. *More work for mother: The ironies of household technology from the open hearth to the microwave*. New York: Basic Books.

Dahlberg, Frances, ed. 1981. *Woman the gatherer*. New Haven, CT: Yale University Press.

Dauber, Roslyn; and Cain, Melinda, eds. 1981. *Women and technological change in developing countries*. Boulder, Colo.: Westview Press.

Ehrenreich, Barbara; and English, Deirdre. 1979. *For her own good: 150 years of the experts' advice to women*. Garden City, N.Y.: Anchor Press/Doubleday.

Enloe, Cynthia H. 1983. *Does khaki become you? The militarization of women's lives*. Boston: South End Press; London: Pluto Press.

Etienne, Mona; and Leacock, Eleanor, eds. 1980. *Women and colonization*. New York: Praeger.

Firestone, Shulamith. 1970. *The dialectic of sex: The case for feminist revolution*. New York: William Morrow.

Glenn, Evelyn Nakano; and Feldberg, Roslyn L. 1979. Proletarianizing clerical work: Technology and organizational control in the office. *Case studies in the labor process*, ed. Andrew Zimbalist. New York: Monthly Review Press: 51–72.

Gordon, Linda. 1977. *Woman's body, woman's right: A social history of birth control in America*. New York: Penguin Books.

Gray, Elizabeth Dodson. 1981. *Green paradise lost*. Wellesley, Mass.: Roundtable Press.

Hacker, Sally. 1977. Farming out the home: Women and agribusiness. *The Second Wave* 5 (Spring/Summer):38–49.

Hacker, Sally. 1979. Sex stratification, technology and organizational change: A longitudinal case study of AT&T. *Social Problems* 26 (June):539–57.

Hacker, Sally L. 1980. The automated and the automaters: Human and social costs of automation. Presented at annual meeting of the International Federation of Automatic Control, Rabat, Morocco.

Hartmann, Heidi. 1974. Capitalism and women's work in the home. 1900–1930. Ph.D. thesis, Yale University.

Hayden, Dolores. 1977. Catherine Beecher and the politics of housework. *Women in American architecture: A historic and contemporary perspective*, ed. Susana Torre. New York: Whitney Library of Design: 40–49.

Hayden, Dolores. 1981. *The grand domestic revolution*. Cambridge, Mass.: MIT Press.

al-Hibri, Azizah. 1981. Capitalism is an advanced stage of patriarchy: But Marxism is not feminism. *Women and Revolution*, ed. Lydia Sargent. Boston: South End Press: 165–93.

Hochwald, Eve. 1982. Women, technology, and workplace equality in the newspaper industry. *New Political Science* 3 (1/2, Summer/Fall):137–41.

Holmes, Helen B.; Hoskins, Betty B.; and Gross, Michael, eds. 1980. *Birth control and controlling birth: Women's perspectives*. Clifton, N.J.: The Humana Press.

Holmes, Helen B.; Hoskins, Betty B.; and Gross, Michael, eds. 1981. *The custom-made child? Women's perspectives*. Clifton, N.J.: The Humana Press.

Horrigan, Brian. 1982. Future perfect: The idea of the home of tomorrow in American architecture and culture between the wars. Presented at annual meeting of the Society for the History of Technology, Philadelphia, Pa.

Hudak, Leona M. 1978. *Early American women printers and publishers 1639–1820*. Metuchen, N.J.: Scarecrow Press.

Jensen, Joan M. 1982. Churns and butter making in the mid-Atlantic farm economy, 1750–1850. *Working papers from the Regional Economic History Research Center* 5, nos. 2 & 3:60–100. Greenville/Wilmington, Del.: Eleutherian Mills-Hagley Foundation.

Keller, Evelyn Fox. 1978. Gender and science. *Psychoanalysis and Contemporary Thought* 1:409–33.

Keller, Evelyn Fox. *Reflections on gender and science*. New York: Longman. (forthcoming)

Lerner, Gerda. 1975. Placing women in history: Definitions and challenges. *Feminist Studies* 3 (Fall):5–14.

Lim, Linda Y. C. 1981. Women's work in multinational electronics factories. *Women and technological change in developing countries*, eds. Roslyn Dauber and Melinda Cain. Boulder, Colo.: Westview Press: 181–90.

McGaw, Judith A. 1979. Technological change and women's work: Mechanization in the Berkshire paper industry. *Dynamos and virgins revisited: Women and technological change in history*, ed. Martha Moore Trescott. Metuchen, N.J.: Scarecrow Press: 77–99.

McGaw, Judith A. 1982. Women and the history of American technology. *Signs: Journal of Women in Culture and Society* 7 (Summer):798–828.

Merchant, Carolyn. 1980. *The death of nature: Women, ecology, and the Scientific Revolution.* New York: Harper & Row.

Mitchell, Juliet. 1966. Women: The longest revolution. *New Left Review* 40 (Nov./Dec.).

Mumford, Lewis. 1966. *The myth of the machine*. vol. 1: *Technics and human development.* New York: Harcourt, Brace & World.

Nash, June, ed. 1983. *Women and men in the international division of labor*. Albany, N.Y.: State University of New York Press.

Nyhart, Lynn. 1982. Introducing "Scientific Management" into the home: Efficiency and the Home Economics Movement, 1900–1920. Presented at annual meeting of Society for the History of Technology, Philadelphia, Pa.

Oakley, Ann. 1974. *The sociology of housework*. New York: Pantheon Books.

Oakley, Ann. 1975. *Woman's work: The housewife, past and present.* New York: Pantheon Books.

Ortner, Sherry B. 1974. Is female to male as nature is to culture? *Woman, culture, and society*, eds. Michelle Zimbalist Rosaldo and Louise Lamphere. Stanford, Calif.: Stanford University Press: 67–87.

Race against time: Automation of the office. 1980. Cleveland, Ohio: Working Women, National Association of Office Workers (April).

Reuther, Rosemary Radford. 1975. *New woman new earth: Sexist ideologies and human liberation*. New York: Seabury Press.

Rose, Hilary; and Hanmer, Jalna. 1976. Women's liberation, reproduction, and the technological fix. *Sexual divisions and society: Process and change*, eds. Diana Leonard Barker and Sheila Allen. London: Tavistock: 199–223.

Rossiter, Margaret W. 1982. *Women scientists in America: Struggles and strategies to 1940.* Baltimore: Johns Hopkins University Press.

Rothschild, Joan. 1981. Technology, "women's work" and the social control of women. *Women, power and political systems*, ed. Margherita Rendel. London: Croom Helm: 160–83.

Sacks, Karen. 1974. Engels revisited: Women, the organization of production, and private property. *Woman, culture, and society*, eds. Michelle Zimbalist Rosaldo and Louise Lamphere. Stanford, Calif.: Stanford University Press: 207–22.

Schell, Jonathan. 1982. *The fate of the earth*. New York: Avon Books.

Sklar, Kathryn Kish. 1974. *Catherine Beecher: A study in American domesticity*. New Haven, Conn.: Yale University Press.

Smith, Judy. 1980. *Something old, something new, something borrowed, something due*. Missoula, Mont.: Women and Technology Network. (Originally published: Butte, Mont.: National Center for Appropriate Technology, 1978.)

Sokoloff, Natalie. 1980. *Between money and love: The dialectics of women's home and market work*. New York: Praeger.

Sprague, Joan Forrester, Executive Director. Women's Institute for Housing and Economic Development. Boston, MA.

Stanley, Autumn. 1984. *Mothers of invention: Women inventors and innovators through the ages*. Metuchen, N.J.: Scarecrow Press.

Strasser, Susan. 1982. *Never done: A history of American housework.* New York: Pantheon.

Taking hold of technology: Topic guide for 1981–83. 1981. Washington, DC: American Association of University Women.

Tanner, Nancy Makepeace. 1981. *On becoming human.* New York: Cambridge University Press.

Thrall, Charles A. 1982. The conservative use of modern household technology. *Technology and Culture* 23 (April):175–94.

Tinker, Irene. 1976. The adverse effects of development on women. *Women and world development*, eds. Irene Tinker and Michele Bo Bramsen. Washington, D.C.: Overseas Development Council.

Vanek, Joann. 1974. Time spent in housework. *Scientific American* 231 (November):116–20.

Washington Women's Heritage Project. 1980–82. Women's Studies Program, Washington State University, University of Puget Sound, Fairhaven College, University of Washington.

Women and technology: Deciding what's appropriate: Conference proceedings. 1979. Missoula, Mont.: Women's Resource Center.

Women's Rights Law Reporter. 1982. Symposium Issue: Reproductive Rights. 7 (3, Spring).

Index

About the Editor and Contributors

The Editor

Joan Rothschild is professor of political science and coordinator of the Women's Studies Program at the University of Lowell (Mass.), as well as a participant in the university's Technology, Society and Values Program. She holds a B.A. in English literature from Cornell University and an M.A. and Ph.D. in politics from New York University. The guest editor of a special issue of *Women's Studies International Quarterly* 4 (3: 1981), "Women, Technology and Innovation," she has also published articles and reviews in political theory, feminist theory, and women and technology in various journals and anthologies. A former research associate at the Harvard University Program on Technology and Society, Prof. Rothschild had an earlier career as a professional writer in the publishing field in New York City. She is a founding member of the National Women's Studies Association and the New England Women's Studies Association. Her continuing research interest is the impact of feminist scholarship on technology and values.

The Contributors

Corlann Gee Bush, who prefers to be called Corky, is the Assistant Dean of Students at the University of Idaho in Moscow. She has recently completed a two-year term as Chair of the Committee on Technology for the American Association of University Women. She has written the guide, *Taking Hold of Technology*, published articles, and spoken widely on the impact of technology on women's lives.

Roslyn Feldberg has taught women's studies and sociology at Boston University for the past ten years. Her many articles on women and work, with emphasis on clerical work, have been published in *Social Problems* and a number of anthologies. She is currently writing a book on clerical work and women clerical workers.

Sally M. Gearhart is a radical lesbian-feminist who chairs the Department of Speech and Communication Studies at San Francisco State University.

She is the author of *The Wanderground: Stories of the Hill Women* (Persephone 1979), *A Feminist Tarot* (Persephone 1981), and *Loving Women/Loving Men: Gay Liberation and the Church* (Glide Publications 1974), as well as of shorter articles on feminist ideology. She participated in the gay documentary, *Word Is Out*, and is active in the Animal Rights Movement. She is addicted to barbershop harmony and aikido.

Evelyn Nakano Glenn is assistant professor of sociology at Boston University. Her research and teaching interests are focused on issues of gender, race, and work. She has written extensively and coauthored a number of articles on clerical work with her colleague Roslyn Feldberg, their work appearing in journals such as *Social Problems* and several anthologies. Her own studies of Japanese- and Chinese-American women, work, and family have appeared in *Feminist Studies* and *Journal of Marriage and the Family*.

Sally L. Hacker has been a feminist activist/researcher for over 15 years, working on problems related to technology and employment. She holds a Ph.D. in sociology from the University of Chicago, and is a member of the Sociology Department faculty at Oregon State University. She is the author of numerous publications in the areas of technological displacement, the culture and ideology of engineering, agribusiness, and mental health. She continues her education with seminars and formal courses in engineering, technology, and philosophy. Currently, she is studying effects of microprocessing on displacement of engineers and technicians, and women's entry into these fields.

Jalna Hanmer was born in the United States and studied sociology at the University of California, Berkeley. Moving to England in 1959, she was a community worker in London's East End and then taught community work at the London School of Economics. She now teaches at the University of Bradford (West Yorkshire) where she coordinates the postgraduate Diploma/M.A. in Women's Studies (Applied). She writes and researches on violence to women, as well as on reproductive technology, and is active in Women's Aid (the British shelter movement). Her articles, published in Great Britain and the United States, have appeared in a number of journals and anthologies including *Alice through the Microscope* (Virago 1980) and *Women, Health and Reproduction*, ed. Helen Roberts (Routledge & Kegan Paul 1981).

Evelyn Fox Keller is professor of mathematics and humanities at Northeastern University (Boston, Mass.). She is author of *A Feeling for the Organism: The Life and Work of Barbara McClintock* (W. H. Freeman 1983) and the forthcoming *Reflections on Gender and Science* to be published by Longman.

Her publications also include numerous articles in mathematical biology, theoretical physics, and feminism and science.

Ynestra King works on the connections between feminism, ecology, and anti-militarism. Her article in this volume is drawn from a larger work in progress, *Feminism and the Reenchantment of the World*. She has taught at several colleges and universities including the University of Massachusetts, Goddard College, and Hampshire College. She is also a founder of Women and Life on Earth and the Women's Pentagon Action.

Carolyn Merchant is a member of the faculty of the Department of Conservation and Resource Studies at the University of California, Berkeley, where she teaches environmental history, philosophy, and ethics. She is the author of *The Death of Nature: Women, Ecology, and the Scientific Revolution* (Harper & Row 1980), and of articles in the history and philosophy of science. Currently, she is writing a book on the environmental history of New England.

Patrocinio Schweickart is assistant professor of English at the University of New Hampshire. She holds degrees in chemical engineering and mathematics from the University of the Philippines and the University of Virginia, and a doctorate in English from Ohio State University. Her published work has appeared in the *American Institute of Chemical Engineering Journal*, *Michigan Papers in Women's Studies*, and *Signs*. She serves on the steering committee of the New England Women's Studies Association.

Autumn Stanley has been variously a college teacher, part of a hepatitis research unit, science textbook editor and, most recently, free-lance scholar and writer in women's studies. She has published fiction and poetry and an asparagus cookbook as well as scholarly articles in English philology and the history of technology. A resident artist at the Montalvo Center for the Arts in Saratoga, California in summer 1983, she is completing a book on women inventors entitled *Mothers of Invention* (Scarecrow 1984) and starting a biography of nineteenth century reformer and gadfly Charlotte Smith.

Martha Moore Trescott holds degrees in chemistry and in the history of technology. She is the author of *The Rise of the American Electrochemicals Industry, 1880–1910: Studies in the American Technological Environment* (Greenwood 1981), and editor of *Dynamos and Virgins Revisited: Women and Technological Change in History* (Scarecrow 1979). She has published numerous articles in women's history of technology and in the history of technology generally. Currently affiliated with the College of Engineering at the University of Illinois at Urbana-Champaign, she is engaged in a study of the history of women engineers, 1850–1975.